Crossroads of Insolvency and Arbitration

Crossroads of Insolvency and Arbitration

Comparative Law Yearbook of International Business

Special Issue, 2022

PUBLISHED UNDER THE AUSPICES
OF THE CENTER FOR INTERNATIONAL LEGAL STUDIES

General Editors

Ishaan Madaan
Christian Campbell

Wolters Kluwer

Published by:
Kluwer Law International B.V.
PO Box 316
2400 AH Alphen aan den Rijn
The Netherlands
E-mail: lrs-sales@wolterskluwer.com
Website: www.wolterskluwer.com/en/solutions/kluwerlawinternational

Sold and distributed by:
Wolters Kluwer Legal & Regulatory U.S.
7201 McKinney Circle
Frederick, MD 21704
United States of America
E-mail: customer.service@wolterskluwer.com

Printed on acid-free paper.

ISBN 978-94-035-4531-8

e-Book: ISBN 978-94-035-4541-7
web-PDF: ISBN 978-94-035-4551-6

Printed in the United Kingdom.

The Center for International Legal Studies

The Center for International Legal Studies is a nonprofit research and publications institute established and operating under Austrian law, with its international headquarters in Salzburg, Austria.

The Center has operated since 1976 in Salzburg, and it has close cooperation with the faculties of law of the University of Salzburg, Boston University and Suffolk University in the United States, Lazarski University in Poland, Eötvös Loránd University in Hungary, and numerous other universities and educational institutions in Europe.

The *Comparative Law Yearbook of International Business* prints matter it deems worthy of publication. Views expressed in material appearing herein are those of the authors and do not necessarily reflect the policies or opinions of the *Comparative Law Yearbook of International Business*, its editors, or the Center for International Legal Studies.

Manuscripts proposed for publication may be sent by email to:

The Editor

Comparative Law Yearbook of International Business
christian.campbell@cils.org

Summary of Contents

Table of Contents

Editors' Note

Each year, a Special Issue of the *Comparative Law Yearbook of International Business* is published under the auspices of the Center for International Legal Studies. The 2022 Special Issue addresses the intersection of arbitration and insolvency. This junction has been made all the more topical and intense by the adverse effects of COVID-19 on a broad range of businesses' finances and supply chains, and by the still growing recourse to arbitration (and other forms of ADR) to resolve business disputes. A diverse pool of contributors gives a broad range of perspectives from Europe (Italy, Lithuania, The United Kingdom), the Middle East (Palestine, UAE), Asia (India), Africa (Malawi), North America (Canada) and public international law on several common issues posed when one or more parties to an arbitration (agreement) are faced with a financial crisis – or vice versa when an over-indebted party is expected to resolve claims that it has or faces, not in State courts but before 'private' adjudicators.

This Special Issue is aimed at bringing to fore the multitude of issues that exist at the convergences of the domains – a step towards better understanding the intricacies and the complexities that arise in different jurisdictions, and how stakeholders react. To highlight just a few of the aspects addressed:

- the law to be applied by arbitral tribunals in regard to insolvency issues;
- insolvency arbitrations and tax claims;
- how the representatives of bankrupt entities may participate in international investment claims;
- avoidance of transactions and anti-suit injunctions; and
- the uneasy but unavoidable cohabitation of insolvency and arbitration in the MENA Region.

Editors: Ishaan Madaan and Christian Campbell

Foreword

It would be a first statement to make that since the start of this century we have experienced a much greater financial volatility in a relatively short period of time: from the Asian financial crises, to Latin America to the financial crises in Europe.[1] To top these financial turbulences the COVID-19 pandemic added to the business uncertainty and with the consequence of several insolvencies with local, regional or international impact. At the same time the use of arbitration and ADR for the resolution of business disputes has been constantly increasing. Hence it comes as no surprise that arbitration tribunals encounter issues of insolvency more frequently than in the past. While the divergence of approaches is highlighted in the *Elektrim/Vivendi* cases in England[2] and Switzerland[3], the theoretical debate[4] and its practical impact is less than settled. This has prompted the International Bar Association to produce a toolkit on the issue of arbitration and insolvency.[5]

The main issue of tension is that insolvency is a fundamentally public process involving all creditors while arbitration is primarily bilateral and confidential. In addition, a public policy argument is also being made – insolvency should remain in the purview of national courts (although this argument does not fully address global or multi-jurisdictional bankruptcies). Of course, there is hardly an argument that arbitration should replace bankruptcy courts; a bankruptcy court has to distribute assets to creditors. This is not what an arbitration tribunal should aspire to do. The main issue from an arbitration prism is the fate of the arbitration agreement and the arbitration proceedings if one party becomes insolvent. Given that insolvency involves a range of situations where an insolvent party may not lose its legal personality and capacity, it may well be argued that the impact on

---

1 In this respect see the QMUL and PwC survey which considers, in part, the impact of the financial crisis on arbitration: 2013 Corporate Choices in International Arbitration: Industry Perspectives - School of International Arbitration (qmul.ac.uk).

2 *Syska and another v. Vivendi Universal SA and others*, [2009] EWCA Civ 677, [2009] Bus. L.R. 1494.

3 *Elektrim v. Vivendi*, Decision 4A_428/2008 dated 31 Mach 2009, published in ASA Bull. 1/2010, 104ff. See, however, the different approach in Decision 4A_50/2008 dated 16 October 2012 (138 III 714), published in ASA Bull. 2/2013, 35.

4 A number of authors including Stefan Kröll, Vesna Lazic, Fernando Mantilla Serano, Manuel Penadez Fons, Stefan Riegler, and Philipp Wagner, to name but few, have produced substantial work on the topic.

5 IBA Toolkit, https://www.ibanet.org/MediaHandler?id=087B4D4A-B82E-4FAC-817F-64EE50091D66.

arbitration should be limited or negligible. Even where the insolvent party is represented by an administrator under certain circumstances the arbitration may proceed. Hence, in the last 20 years we have seen that a significant number of tribunals in various arbitral seats felt confident enough to proceed with arbitrations involving a party under bankruptcy protection or represented by an administrator. It seems that issue of arbitrability of disputes with insolvent parties is being gradually albeit reluctantly addressed in favour of arbitration. Still, several procedural and jurisdictional issues remain.

Against this background this volume is a joint venture of the Center for International Legal Studies and Arbinsol and is edited by Ishaan Madaan and Christian Campbell. It is a forward-looking collection of essays on the intersection or arbitration and insolvency. It offers a number of thoughtful and insightful contributions ranging from applicable law to regional and national perspectives (including Europe, Middle East, Africa, and the Americas), insolvency administrators in investment disputes as well as the role of tax authorities in such arbitration proceedings and the impact of the COVID pandemic.

I am impressed by the diversity or contributors and topics and most importantly by the quality of the chapters. I do commend the publication and the excellent work of editors and contributors. This volume makes a substantial and original contribution to the topic and hence I extend my warmest congratulations.

April 2022
Prof Loukas Mistelis

Preface

In a world of increasingly complex commercial transactions and investments, and volatile economic growth, arbitration and insolvency act as tools for the resolution of claims. The efficacy of these resolution mechanisms depends on a plethora of factors, and at times can result in conflicting – and often frustrating – scenarios, especially when insolvency and arbitration intersect. Insolvency law is a centralized, formalistic body of law. By contrast, arbitration is decentralized, contractual and party-autonomy based.

Since primary objects of insolvency include preservation of assets and maximization of their value, a pivotal method to achieve these ends is the abatement of claim proceedings against the entity undergoing insolvency. This naturally includes arbitration proceedings as well, including those commenced by creditors that are not subject to the domestic laws of the insolvent. The implications of an insolvency on an affected arbitration are so intricate that there is an impending need to decipher the various points of intersections and examine possible outcomes – both in a theoretical and in a practical sense. The insight into issues at the crossroads of insolvency and international arbitration is still underdeveloped.

In recent years, the dialogue around these issues has gained an audience. The onset of the pandemic disrupted economic order around the world. There were strict measures taken across the world to tackle its spread, and these inevitably resulted in lockdowns and slowdowns in trade and commerce. No wonder, the abilities to perform obligations were thwarted, and force majeure suddenly became the buzz term when the pandemic made landfall. The drought in cash flow and lack of liquidity inevitably pushed countless corporate entities to seek refuge under bankruptcy laws, and some were pushed towards the corporate death-knell by creditors. Many of those entities have been parties to arbitration proceedings or arbitration agreements.

On the one hand, there is the parties' promise to commit themselves to arbitration, and on the other hand, one of the parties finds itself entangled in the web of insolvency. In most jurisdictions, insolvency means a big pause to everything 'dispute resolution'. Triggers of insolvency, one might argue, would run contrary to the same entity's promise to arbitrate. One may have to look at the local laws of the struggling entity to figure out whether or not it can be compelled to arbitrate. That may also conflict with the law of the arbitration agreement. Another question would be to see what happens to ongoing arbitration proceedings where a party is suddenly declared insolvent. The administrator of the estate finds itself confronted with a variety of issues to be addressed in terms of the law governing the insolvency process. The creditors are required to comply with the set of laws while asserting their claims, and the judicial body(ies) overseeing the insolvency process are to assist the process envisaged under the law. In a domestic scenario, it is easier to determine these issues; but in an international scenario – a conflict emerges between domestic laws and (in a majority of cases) the New York Convention. It does not just stop there. As we have seen in recent years, like in the *Herzig v. Turkmenistan* case (ICSID), insolvency of the investor opens doors to an array of issues in investment arbitration as well. The pandemic has necessitated a revision of the basic issues that arise in different jurisdictions, the implications thereof, and the consequences of these actions at various stages, including concerning those of temporal primacy.

The authors in the Special Issue were invited to address areas of commercial and business law at the crossroads of insolvency and international arbitration from an international comparative perspective. The chapters in this edition touch upon not just the basics of the 'crossroads' but dive deep into regional and international issues that arise at the junctures; and for various stakeholders. All this, while also sharing at length how these issues are handled domestically in national systems in Europe, the Middle East, Asia, Africa, and the Americas. Though conceptually, the issues still remain and are similar across these jurisdictions, there has been more than a single sighting of jurisprudential evolution with a flavour – at times – of a pro-arbitration response.

The worldwide readership may not only find answers to certain domestic issues at the 'crossroads' in some jurisdictions but also a jurisprudential understanding of a multitude of issues along the way. This includes, broadly, questions on applicable law, treatment of claims by revenue authorities, binding and non-binding nature of arbitration agreements, scope of avoidance powers of the insolvency administrator, as well as the handling of investment treaty arbitration instituted by an impecunious claimant.

The purpose of this book is not to provide a solution to the conflicts that exist at the convergences of the domains, but it is a step towards better understanding the intricacies and the complexities that arise in different jurisdictions and steps that stakeholders take or may take. This book is both a substantive as well as a comparative study of the variety of issues that come to the fore and the juxtapositions that stakeholders find themselves in. We expect to periodically publish a revision of this understanding, with growing contributions from current and new authors.

Ishaan Madaan
March 2022, New York

Acknowledgements

We express our gratitude to each of the authors for their invaluable contributions, their support with the editorial process, and in converting this discussion into a publishable edition.

It is important to recap the journey leading to the conception of this edition. During my days as Professor Jan Paulsson's student, I wrote a paper on 'The Conflict Between International Arbitration and Domestic Insolvency' under his cherished guidance. The arbitration and insolvency conundrum, and the COVID-19 pandemic, lead to the founding of Arbinsol – a platform advancing research, dialogue and thought leadership on the interplay of International Arbitration and Insolvency. Arbinsol could not have been conceptualized without the meticulous academic support of my dear friend Professor P. Chauhan – Associate Professor at Jindal Global Law School and a contributor to the present edition.

It was the Center for International Legal Studies, Austria (CILS) – more specifically my co-editor Christian Campbell, and my mentor Professor John Rooney, who were the wind beneath Arbinsol's wings. Our collective efforts to expand dialogue on Arbitration and Insolvency was thoroughly supported by celebrated academics and arbitrators including Professor Loukas Mistelis, Prof. Dr Patricia Shaughnessy, Dr Francisco Reyes Villamizar, Kiran N. Gore, and Dr Kabir A.N. Duggal.

The onset of the pandemic – through early 2021 – saw several panel discussions and debates co-organized by CILS and Arbinsol on several aspects falling on the 'crossroads' of insolvency and arbitration. The growing importance of the contiguous issues weighed in on the importance of the present edition, to commence publication of research on the 'crossroads'. The editorial process was graciously assisted by the authors across a long-drawn and pandemic stricken process. The discussions regarding the contributions were had at many places and mustered critical analysis with the most generous support from my significant other.

It is with deep gratitude to family, friends in our ever-expanding yet well-knit community, and last but most, Christian Campbell, that I share our editorial work in what we believe will be an important step in commencing a structured and thorough dialogue on the 'crossroads'.

Ishaan Madaan

Cross-Border Insolvency Issues in Arbitral Proceedings and the Question of Applicable Law

Yağmur Hortoğlu

The National University of Ireland, Maynooth
Mariavilla
W23 F2K8 Maynooth
Co. Kildare
Ireland
Phone number: 00353(0)894837648
Email addresses: yagmur.hortoglu@mu.ie; yh3868@nyu.edu

The Treatment of Claims by Revenue Authorities in Insolvency Arbitrations: Some Salient Private International Law Considerations

Richard Mike Mlambe

Malawi University of Business and Applied Sciences
Private Bag 303
Chichiri
Blantyre 3
Malawi
Phone number: +265 994 81 76 80
Email addresses: mlamberichard3@gmail.com; rmlambe@mubas.ac.mw

Standing of Insolvency Administrators in Investment Treaty Arbitration

Nikola Kurková Klímová

Faculty of Law, Charles University
Department of International Law, Faculty of Law,
Charles University,
nám. Curieových 7,
116 40 Prague
Czech Republic
Email address: klimovni@prf.cuni.cz

On (Non) Binding Nature of Pre-insolvency Arbitration Agreements When Avoiding an Underlying Transaction, Executory Contracts, and Anti-suit Injunctions in Support of Arbitration Against Foreign Insolvency Debtors: News from England and Canada

Vesna Lazic

Utrecht University T.M.C. Asser Institute

R.J. Schimmelpennincklaan 20-22
2517 JN The Hague
The Netherlands
Phone number: +31 6 21258794
Email address: vlazic@uu.nl
and

P. Chauhan

Jindal Global Law School, O.P. Jindal Global University
Sonipat-Narela Road
Sonipat 131001
Haryana
India
Email address: chauhan.prakhar@gmail.com

The "Wonderland" of Insolvency and Arbitration: "Re-cohabitation" of the Duo as an Inevitable Destiny (Pre-award Phase)

Mahmoud M. Moghrabi

KILAW (Kuwait International Law School)
n. 208 bldg, abdallah bin Masoud st, bloc 2
20002 Salmiya
Kuwait
Phone number: +965 69300479
Email address: m.moghrabi@kilaw.edu.kw

Nadim M. Al Jisr

Mohammad & Abbad Al Jisr Law Office
Dubai Media City – Thomson Reuters Building No. 1- 1st Floor
33714 Dubai
United Arab Emirates
Phone number: 00971 56 417 9235
Email address: nadjisr@gmail.com

Crossroads of Insolvency and Arbitration in Italy

Roberto Oliva

Pavia e Ansaldo law firm
7, via del Lauro
20121 Milan

Italy
Phone number: +39-02-85581
Email address: roberto.oliva@pavia-ansaldo.it

Arbitration and Insolvency: A Conflict of Near Polar Extremes: Contrary Perspective

Bishwajit Dubey, Radhika Bishwajit Dubey & Mr Prafful Goyal

Level 1 & 2, Maw Towers, C-001/A, Sector 16B
Noida – 201 301
Uttar Pradesh,
India
Phone numbers: +91 9910224345; +91 8448391294
Email addresses: bishwajit.dubey@cyrilshroff.com; radhika.dubey@cyril shroff.com; prafful.goyal@cyrilshroff.com

Effectiveness of Corporate Insolvency Proceedings and Commercial Arbitration

Vigintas Višinskis, Remigijus Jokubauskas & Mykolas Kirkutis

Zirmunu str. 98-31
09122 Vilnius
Lithuania
Phone number: +37 068625179
Email address: remigijus@jokubauskas.org

COVID-19 and Arbitrability of Insolvency: Cross-Country Comparative Analysis in MENA Region

Amir Khalil, Nawal Hend & Mohammed Alqaisi

Birzeit University
PO Box 14
627 Birzeit, West Bank
Palastine
Phone number: +970 2 2982951
Email address: amkhalil@birzeit.edu; nawalhend@gmail.com; MQaisi@birzeit.edu

Cross-Border Insolvency Issues in Arbitral Proceedings and the Question of Applicable Law

Yağmur Hortoğlu
Assistant Professor in Law National University of Ireland Maynooth

Introduction

With the increasing recourse to arbitration today, arbitrators are expected to address complex issues. In this regard, the corporate insolvency of a party to arbitration is a hypothesis that might be encountered during an arbitration procedure.

Insolvency law and arbitration law are two legal fields that are almost opposites, hence are not a priori expected to cross paths: the first one is a public policy matter[1] while the second one is permeated by the principle of party autonomy. The legal policies adopted in both legal fields are, as a matter of fact, contrasting or even conflicting:[2] insolvency policy advocates a formalistic centralized approach while arbitration law prioritizes a decentralized one.[3] Yet, it should be acknowledged that there is, in reality, no inconsistency between the autonomy in arbitration and the necessity to tackle the question of financial distress. Despite of this, while the use of mediation by the state courts in most countries is relatively common in insolvency proceedings, the recourse to arbitration remains new in the field.[4]

1 On this point and regarding the relation of mandatory character of insolvency legislations with the United Nations Convention on the Recognition and Enforcement of Foreign Arbitral Awards of 1958, *see* Ishaan Madaan, *Insolvency and International Arbitration: An Alternate Perspective*, Kluwer Arbitration Blog, June 15, 2020, available at: http://arbitrationblog.kluwerarbitration.com/2020/06/15/insolvency-and-international-arbitration-an-alternate-perspective/ (last accessed July 5, 2021).

2 *See* Larsen Oil and Gas Pte Ltd *v.* Petroprod Ltd [2011] 3 SLR 414. This observation had already been made in previous cases. *See for example*, In re United States Lines, 197 F 3d 631 (640) (2d Civ 1999); Societé Nationale Algérienne (Sonatrach) *v.* Distrigas Corp. 80BR 606, 610 (D. Mass. 1987); MBNA America Bank v. Hill, 436. F.3d 104, 111 (2d Cir. 2006).

3 For more detail, see *infra*.

4 Stephan Madaus, *The (Underdeveloped) Use of Arbitration in International Insolvency Proceedings*, 37 Journal of International Arbitration 4, 449, 451 (2020).

The number of insolvencies escalates and will probably continue increasing considerably all around the world as due to the restrictive measures taken in the framework of the sanitary crisis, many businesses face uncertainties.[5] This caused a significant economic disruption and the world economy entered into a period of an important financial instability; hence a deep global recession was inevitable. The importance of the dynamic between insolvency law and arbitration certainly surfaces and evolves with the rise of insolvencies and commercial disputes resulting from the COVID-19 pandemic. The current conjuncture also brings an increase in the number of commercial disputes and insolvencies that involve more than one country, meanly cross-border insolvencies. To adapt their legislation to exceptional conditions created by the pandemic, some states already brought some modifications, such as the interruption of time limits or the suspension of insolvency filing duties, to their insolvency and restructuring laws.

In the above-described context, more and more arbitration proceedings will encounter the problem that one of the parties becomes subject to insolvency proceedings. Because of the conflicting objectives that arbitration and insolvency law try to achieve, some issues are expected to arise whenever their policies interact. Indeed, the ubiquity of arbitration agreements, especially in commercial contracts, makes the intersection between arbitration and insolvency law more likely, even irrespective of the current economic context. In arbitral practice, the interaction of insolvency law with arbitration law becomes usually relevant where a party to an arbitration agreement, proceeding, or award becomes subject to insolvency triggers.[6] However, legislators usually tend to restrict the parties' ability to arbitrate in the field of insolvency law. It is possible to observe two types of insolvency procedures in most insolvency legislations: the core issues and

5 *See* the June 2020 Global Economic Prospects, available on: https://www.worldbank.org/en/publication/global-economic-prospects (last accessed July 22, 2021). *See also*, OECD Economic Outlook, Volume 2021 Issue 1, available at: https://doi.org/10.1787/16097408 (last accessed July 5, 2021).

6 *See for instance* in this sense, Paul F. Kirgis, *Arbitration, Bankruptcy, and Public Policy: A Contractarian Analysis*, 17 Am. Bankr. Inst. L. Rev. 503 et seq. (2009); Jay Lawrence Westbrook, *International Arbitration and Multinational Insolvency*, 29 Penn State Int'l L. Rev. 635 (2011); Andrew Chan Chee Yin, Jonathan Chan Tuan San, Jo Tay Yu Xi & Alexander Lawrence Yeo Han Tiong, *Cross-Border Insolvency and Its Impact on Arbitration*, 26 SAcLJ 999 (2014); Deyan Draguiev, *The Effect of Insolvency on Pending International Arbitration: What Is and What Should Not Be*, 32 Journal of International Arbitration 5, 511 (2015); Richard Bamforth & Stephanie Woods, Insolvency and Arbitration, 29 Insolvency Intelligence 33 (2016); Stephan Madaus, *The (Underdeveloped) Use of Arbitration in International Insolvency Proceedings*, 37 Journal of International Arbitration 4, 449, 464 (2020).

the non-core issues. On the one hand, the core issues of insolvency constitute the essence of insolvency proceedings and refer usually to their administration, namely the declaration, initiation, and the termination of insolvency proceedings. Therefore, these disputes are a priori not considered as arbitrable in most countries.[7] The non-core issues of insolvency arise, on the other hand, from contractual issues between the parties, such as creditors' claims and are usually considered arbitrable.[8]

The international dimension of these insolvency procedures can be conferred particularly to the involvement of creditors or assets located in more than one country.[9] In this respect, the arbitral seat as the place of insolvency proceedings does not matter as—vis-à-vis the arbitrators—all laws can be considered *foreign*. The most important question in the aforementioned framework seems to be the one that concerns the law governing the effects of insolvency that commence in parallel with on-going arbitration procedures. The arbitrators may not necessarily hold adequate guidance to address the consequences of the rise of insolvency issues simultaneously with an on-going arbitration procedure. This lack of guidance makes the process of selecting an adequate applicable law, which could reconcile these two domains in order to achieve a logical result, even more complicated.

The analysis of different perceptions regarding the interaction of insolvency and arbitration results a priori in the lack of specific conflict rules although some principles and basic features may seem to be similar in most legal systems. There may be different hypotheses in which the insolvencies and arbitration law meet. In this regard, the question of applicable law is to be answered by the arbitral tribunal in the hypothesis where the insolvency related issues arise during an on-going arbitration.[10] The aforementioned legislative gap increases, without any doubt, the importance of addressing

7 Vesna Lazić, Insolvency Proceedings and Commercial Arbitration, Kluwer Law International, p. 154 (1998); Jelena V. Marković, *Impact of EU Insolvency Regulation on Process of Resolving Disputes Before International Commercial Arbitration*, EU and Comparative Law Issues and Challenges Series (ECLIC) 1, 127, 130–131 (2018), available at: https://doi.org/10.25234/eclic/6525 (last accessed July 5, 2021).

8 Jelena V. Marković, *Impact of EU Insolvency Regulation on Process of Resolving Disputes Before International Commercial Arbitration*, EU and Comparative Law Issues and Challenges Series (ECLIC) 1, 127, 130 (2018), available at: https://doi.org/10.25234/eclic/6525 (last accessed July 5, 2021); Stefan Kröll, *Chapter 18. Arbitration and insolvency – Selected Conflict of Laws Problems*, *in* Conflict of laws in International Commercial Arbitration 657, 658 (F. Ferrari & S. Kröll eds., 2019).

9 Deyan Draguiev, *The Effect of Insolvency on Pending International Arbitration: What Is and What Should Not Be*, 32 Journal of International Arbitration 5, 511, 517 (2015).

10 *Ibid.*, p. 511.

the question of applicable law to insolvency issues in the framework of arbitration procedures; in order to find guidelines adequate to facilitate the decision-making by arbitrators. Therefore, this chapter address the question of applicable law that could arise at the crossroads of insolvency and arbitration in this hypothesis. Finally, the accent will be put on different factors that the arbitrators should consider while selecting the method to adopt in their search for the applicable law.

In the Quest for a Common Framework of Insolvency Law

No legal instrument has been implemented yet at an international level to tackle the substantive issues on insolvency proceedings and its cross-border effects. Under the Regulation (EU) 2015/848 of the European Parliament and of the Council of 20 May 2015 on insolvency proceedings (hereinafter "Recast EU Insolvency Regulation"),[11] which applies only to procedures related to a debtor whose center of main interests is located in the European Union.[12] Insolvency procedures brought in that EU Member State are considered as the "main proceedings"[13] and are recognized in all other Member States.[14] But what about insolvencies and arbitration proceedings that are not opened in EU Member States?

From universality to territoriality, there is a range of various theories adopted by different legal systems to address the issues that arise from the

11 *See* Regulation (EU) No 2015/848 of the European Parliament and of the Council of 20 May 2015 on insolvency proceedings (recast), Official Journal of the European Union, L141/19 of June 5, 2015 replaced the earlier version of 2000, Council Regulation (EC) No 1346/2000 of May 29, 2000 on insolvency proceedings, Official Journal of the European Union, L160/1 of June 30, 2000.

12 *See* Recital (25) of the Recast EU Insolvency Regulation, which states that "This Regulation applies only to proceedings in respect of a debtor whose centre of main interests is located in the Union".

13 *See* Recital (23) of the Recast EU Insolvency Regulation, which states that "This Regulation enables the main insolvency proceedings to be opened in the Member State where the debtor has the centre of its main interests."

14 *See* Article 19.1 of the Recast EU Insolvency Regulation, which states that, "Any judgment opening insolvency proceedings handed down by a court of a Member State which has jurisdiction pursuant to Article 3 shall be recognised in all other Member States from the moment that it becomes effective in the State of the opening of proceedings. The rule laid down in the first subparagraph shall also apply where, on account of a debtor's capacity, insolvency proceedings cannot be brought against that debtor in other Member States."

effects of a cross-border insolvency. The objective of this section is not in reviewing each of these theories and the divergences among different insolvency legislations, areas that have been addressed already by many authors.[15] It could be, however, compelling to detect principles and basic features that could and should be similar throughout different countries and legal systems.[16] The importance of such a general framework of insolvency is high as it could assist the arbitrators in their reasoning.

To reconcile insolvency and arbitration, these two fields that present important differences, it is necessary to acknowledge their respective objectives and *raison d'être*. As it is impregnated by party autonomy, arbitration law can be considered as a flexible field, hence it might seem like it is not the one that will create a problem in the equation with insolvency law. However, as a dispute resolution mechanism of essentially consensual nature, arbitration is a contract-based dispute resolution process between commercial parties that results in an award that only binds on these parties to the arbitration proceedings.[17] Accordingly, it is also a private and, at times, a confidential process. It seems like the opposite observations can be made for insolvency law.

It is not surprising to encounter national differences in a domain which is as much attached to domestic systems as insolvency law.[18] However, it should also be admitted that some common features and grounds can be detected among these different legislations.[19] In this regard, it can be observed that in most legal systems, insolvency laws are destined to realize mainly economic objectives of a state. To realize these objectives, insolvency law first aims at restructuring or reorganizing the company to ensure

---

15 *See* for instance, Simon Vorburger, International Arbitration and Cross-Border Insolvency: Comparative Perspectives 11 (Kluwer 2014); S. Kröll, *Arbitration and Insolvency – Selected Conflict of Laws Problems, in* Conflict of Laws in International Commercial Arbitration 657 (Franco Ferrari & Stefan Kröll eds., 2019).

16 Not only a complete comparative study is not within the scope of this article but also such a study would have been without any practical interest.

17 Wolfgang Kuhn, *Arbitration and Insolvency*, 5 Disp. Resol. INT'L 203, 204 (2011).

18 The differences among different national legislations on insolvency law are usually and mainly detected in the importance given to economic, social and political interests that are implicated in insolvency law. For an overview on this point, *see for instance*, Bob Wessels, *Insolvency Law, in*: Elgar Encyclopedia of Comparative Law, J. M. Smits (ed.) 383 (2nd ed. 2012). *See also* Vesna Lazić, *Arbitration and Insolvency Proceedings: Claims of Ordinary Bankruptcy Creditors*, 3 Electr. J. Comp. l, 2 (1999); Stefan Kröll, *Chapter 18. Arbitration and insolvency – Selected Conflict of Laws Problems, in* Conflict of Laws in International Commercial Arbitration 657, 662 (F. Ferrari & S. Kröll eds., 2019).

19 For an overview of basic principles of insolvency laws, *see* Wolfgang Kuhn, *Arbitration and Insolvency*, 5 Disp. Resol. INT'L 203, 207 et seq. (2011).

its survival.[20] If this is not possible, it will provide for the liquidation of the debtor's assets in respect of the equal treatment of all creditors, which is a procedure that requires the centralization of the claims.[21] In other words, the company, which is subject to insolvency proceedings, may then find itself in approximately three different cases. In the worst-case scenario, the given company will be declared insolvent, and its assets will be liquidated and then distributed to its creditors. The company that suffers from financial difficulties can sometimes be reorganized which could make it recover financially. In the best-case scenario, the company that is subject to insolvency proceedings will become solvent.

Considering the aforementioned objectives and hypotheses, it is not surprising to observe that insolvency proceedings are court-regulated; hence party autonomy does not hold a place as important as it does in arbitration law.[22] Indeed, the interests that are implicated in an insolvency proceeding—such as the liquidation of a company's business, possible losses to shareholders or workforce—mostly requires, if not always, the regulation of insolvency by mandatory rules.

The lack of party autonomy and the mandatory character of the laws applicable to insolvency issues are the main features of insolvency law that are common to the majority of the legal systems. In this regard, while the first remark ensures a discretionary power to arbitrators; the second one makes the search for the applicable law even more complicated for arbitrators.[23] Therefore, it is important that arbitrators find a way to create a balance among these different policy objectives. Otherwise, the enforcement of their award can be refused. In this regard, the most important question is to know in which way these two different policy objectives can

20 Ishaan Madaan, *Insolvency and International Arbitration: An Alternate Perspective*, Kluwer Arbitration Blog, June 15, 2020, available at: http://arbitrationblog.kluwerarbitration.com/2020/06/15/insolvency-and-international-arbitration-an-alternate-perspective/ (last accessed July 5, 2021).

21 Domitille Baizeau, *Arbitration and Insolvency: Issues of Applicable Law*, *in*: C. Müller & A. Rigozzi (eds.), 1 New Developments in International Commercial Arbitration, 97, 98 (2009).

22 Deyan Draguiev, *The Effect of Insolvency on Pending International Arbitration: What Is and What Should Not Be*, 32 Journal of International Arbitration 5, 511, 516 (2015); Stefan Kröll, *Chapter 18. Arbitration and insolvency – Selected Conflict of Laws Problems*, *in*: Conflict of Laws in International Commercial Arbitration 657, 662 (F. Ferrari & S. Kröll eds., 2019); Jelena V. Marković, *Impact of EU Insolvency Regulation on Process of Resolving Disputes Before International Commercial Arbitration*, EU and Comparative Law Issues and Challenges Series (ECLIC) 1, 127, 130 (2018), available at: https://doi.org/10.25234/eclic/6525 (last accessed July 5, 2021).

23 Also, in this sense, *see* Wolfgang Kuhn, *Arbitration and Insolvency*, 5 Disp. Resol. INT'L 203, 209 (2011).

be reconciled. Suggesting a balanced method to achieve the applicable law might be a way of achieving such result.

The Law Governing the Effects of Insolvency on Arbitration

Do the insolvency proceedings affect the arbitration agreement and the arbitrability of certain claims? Should the arbitral tribunal take insolvency proceedings into consideration? To what extent would an insolvency law, that compels the arbitrators to stay or to terminate the arbitration, be binding on the arbitral tribunal? To what extent is the arbitral tribunal bound by an insolvency law at the arbitral seat or in a foreign country? Would the arbitrators risk the annulment of their award if they ignore the insolvency proceedings? Owing to the differences among various national insolvency laws and their possible effects on arbitration, the outcome of an interaction between arbitration and insolvencies depends on the law applicable to procedural and substantive law questions.

It is important to indicate that while some delays may be legitimate and be required to comply with due process requirements, the possibility of dilatory tactics should not be completely excluded. If the insolvency proceedings are filed to interrupt or to delay a given arbitration, the arbitral tribunal is expected to ignore them without risking to see its award being set aside by the courts.

Where the insolvency proceedings are filed in good faith, the commencement of an insolvency does not per se invalidate preexisting arbitration agreements in most leading arbitration seats, such as France, the United Kingdom, or Singapore. However, the involvement of insolvency definitely requires the determination of the issues that arise and especially the laws that will govern the effects thereof. In this regard, it would already help arbitrators to have a universal approach to insolvency. This way, a balance can be achieved in the method that will be applied to find the applicable law.

The importance of such a uniform approach got attention especially in the framework of the Model Law on Cross-Border Insolvency suggested by the United Nations Commission on International Trade Law

(UNCITRAL)[24] and certain case laws.[25] In this regard, a common approach to this issue is expected to be applied widely to the extent that the Model Law is ratified in different countries. The increasing value of this instrument to an important arbitral seat such as the United Kingdom due to the end of Brexit transition period gives hope for a possible implementation of such a uniform approach to insolvency.

As it raises some complex questions, it could be then a solution for arbitrators to recognize general principles of insolvency proceedings. In other words, the effects of insolvency proceedings that serve the objectives of the insolvency laws which are widely accepted could be recognized by tribunals that do not necessarily sit in the state where such proceedings are opened.[26] It is, however, important to indicate that this evolution should take place in its natural flow. In other words, it is important to acknowledge that a broad acceptance of the general principles of insolvency law should not be forced. It should be, nevertheless, possible to implement such principles that are established in arbitral practice, in an internationally renowned instrument such as the rules established by the International Bar Association—the IBA Rules on the Taking of Evidence in International Arbitration. Such implementation would serve as a guidance for arbitrators before they recognize an insolvency proceeding.

As arbitration is a consensual procedure, the parties could agree on terminating it on the basis of the insolvency of one of the parties. However, if this is not their intention, the effects of the commencement of insolvency proceedings on the arbitral tribunal depend primarily on the applicable insolvency law.[27]

There is no one sole methodology, but multiple ways to tackle the question of applicable law where laws governing arbitration and insolvency interact. However, it is important as well as challenging to seek out the method that would guarantee the most appropriate applicable law that conforms with the interests implicated in both insolvency law and arbitration law. Today, arbitration legislations tend to guarantee arbitrators a

---

24 United Nations Commission on International Commercial Law Model Law on Cross-Border Insolvency 1997.

25 *See* for instance, Cambridge Gas Transport Corporation *v.* The Official Committee of Unsecured Creditors. (of Navigator Holding PLC and others) (2006) UKPC 26 [16], 2006 WL 1546603 (judgment of Lord Hoffmann).

26 *See* in this sense also, Vesna Lazić, *Cross-Border Insolvency and Arbitration, in*: S. Kröll, L.A. Mistelis, P. Perales Viscasillas & V. Rogers (eds.), Liber Amicorum Eric Bergsten. International Arbitration and International Commercial Law: Synergy, Convergence and Evolution, 337, 362 (Kluwer Law International, 2011).

27 Stephan Madaus, *The (Underdeveloped) Use of Arbitration in International Insolvency Proceedings*, 37 Journal of International Arbitration 4, 449, 465 (2020).

degree of flexibility that state courts do not usually enjoy.[28] The recognition of general principles would already be an approach in line with this observation, hence it would be unnecessary to try and artificially maximize party autonomy.[29] Therefore, adopting such an "arbitration friendly" approach while ensuring a balance between interests of insolvency law and arbitration law might be a solution for arbitrators.[30] This would also likely encourage protagonists and legislators to consider the use of arbitration for insolvency matters.

Regarding this, some authors investigated the importance of the impact that the arbitral seat could have on the intersection between arbitration and insolvency. In other words, they examined whether the approach to arbitration adopted by the arbitral seat could have an effect on the degree to which the arbitrator will be bound by the national insolvency law.[31] It is not possible to assert that parties who chose a state that adopts a territorial approach to arbitration as arbitral seat also had the intention to be bound by the insolvency law of that state. In any case, the provisions are usually implemented in insolvency law and not in arbitration law,[32] which reduces the impact of territorial approach. What about the opposite, hence the hypothesis in which the arbitral seat accepts a transnational approach to arbitration?

Today, the territorial approach of arbitration is perceived as outdated in most legal systems that are also considered as important arbitral seats.[33] Therefore, it would have been more interesting on this point to focus on the

---

28 Wolfgang Kuhn, *Arbitration and Insolvency*, 5 Disp. Resol. INT'L 203, 210 (2011).

29 For more detail, *see infra*.

30 *Contra* Stefan Kröll, *Chapter 18. Arbitration and insolvency – Selected Conflict of Laws Problems*, *in* Conflict of Laws in International Commercial Arbitration 657, 710 (F. Ferrari & S. Kröll eds., 2019). According to this author, the principle of party autonomy should be privileged and maximized where insolvency law interacts with arbitration law. We do believe that the arbitration-friendly approach does not necessarily refer to the maximization of party autonomy. A balance between the interests of insolvency law on the one hand, and the arbitration law on the other hand would not be contrary to the idea of an arbitration-friendly process. Actually, the guarantee of the interests prevailing in insolvency law would satisfy the interests of arbitration law, such as the enforcement of the given award. For further detail in this regard, *see infra*.

31 *See* for instance, Wolfgang Kuhn, *Arbitration and Insolvency*, 5 Disp. Resol. INT'L 203, 204 (2011); Stefan Kröll, *Chapter 18. Arbitration and insolvency – Selected Conflict of Laws Problems*, *in* Conflict of Laws in International Commercial Arbitration 657, 671 et seq. (F. Ferrari & S. Kröll eds., 2019).

32 IBA Toolkit on Insolvency and Arbitration, available at: https://www.ibanet.org/LPD/Dispute_Resolution_Section/Arbitration/toolkit-arbitration-insolvency (last accessed July 5, 2021).

33 Vitek Danilowicz, *The Choice of Applicable Law in International Arbitration*, 9 Hastings Int'l & Comp. L. Rev., 235, 235 et seq. (1986).

transnational approach to arbitration and its possible impact on the way in which the implication of insolvency law will be considered. If the arbitral tribunal has its seat in a state that adopts the transnational approach to arbitration, then foreign insolvency proceedings would be considered as non-binding on the arbitral tribunal.[34] Nevertheless, following the same line of idea, the given arbitration may also be affected by any insolvency law. The arbitral tribunal should take into consideration a given insolvency law depending on its impact on the outcome of the dispute as if it is relevant for the outcome of the dispute, it could have impact on the enforcement of the given award. In any event, the recognition of an insolvency based on general principles that are widely accepted in most legislations should be valid irrespective of the arbitration theory that is adopted in the arbitral seat.

Once the foreign insolvency proceedings are recognized in principle, the question of the law governing the effects of insolvency is the second issue to be addressed. The choice of law method is the most common approach that is used to tackle the questions of applicable law in arbitration law.[35] Because of its impact on the outcome of the dispute, a thorough analysis of the conflict of laws rules is compulsory. Once the issue has been characterized or classified into a certain category, the second step is then to select the relevant choice of law rules on the basis of the classification made. The application of the choice of law rule will then lead to the applicable law that will govern the relevant question.

In this regard, the importance of the characterization of a given insolvency issue needs also to be highlighted. Indeed, divergent characterizations of the same effect of an insolvency may lead to very different conflict-of-laws rules, hence to radically different substantive results.[36]

---

34 Wolfgang Kuhn, *Arbitration and Insolvency*, 5 Disp. Resol. INT'L 203, 210 (2011).

35 Gabrielle Kaufmann-Kohler, Laurent Lévy & Sabina Sacco, *The Survival of the Arbitration Agreement and Arbitration Proceedings in Cases of Cross-Border Insolvency: An Analysis from the Swiss Perspective*, Les cahiers de l'arbitrage, 371-390, 376 et seq. (2010). For other methods that the arbitral tribunal has at its disposal, *see*, e.g., Philippe Fouchard, Emmanuel Gaillard & Berthold Goldman, International Commercial Arbitration, E. Gaillard and J. Savage (eds.), 247–248 (Kluwer Law International, 1999).

36 In this regard, the *Vivendi/Elektrim* case is a striking example. *See* Syska (Elektrim SA) *v.* Vivendi Universal SA [2009] EWCA Civ 677; Stefan Kröll, *Chapter 18. Arbitration and insolvency – Selected Conflict of Laws Problems*, *in* Conflict of Laws in International Commercial Arbitration 657, 697 (F. Ferrari & S. Kröll eds., 2019); Gabrielle Kaufmann-Kohler, Laurent Lévy & Sabina Sacco, *The Survival of the Arbitration Agreement and Arbitration Proceedings in Cases of Cross-Border Insolvency: An Analysis from the Swiss Perspective*, Les cahiers de l'arbitrage, 371–390, 377 (2010).

Therefore, it would be accurate to affirm that the effects of foreign insolvency proceedings on an arbitration procedure depend closely on the characterization of the issues involved and may sometimes lead to arbitration-friendly, or, on the contrary, to very hostile results. This has been widely illustrated by the *Elektrim* case. In this decision, Swiss Supreme Court had characterized the problem related to effects of a Polish bankruptcy proceedings on a Swiss arbitration as a problem of capacity of the insolvent. This approach made the Swiss judges apply an old provision of Polish law that invalidates the arbitration agreement.[37] The English High Court had to rule on the same issue for an LCIA arbitration in which *Elektrim* was a party and followed an opposite position by applying Council Regulation (EC) 1346/2000 on insolvency proceedings (Insolvency Regulation).

Apart from several treaties regulating only a number of international aspects of insolvencies, such as the Recast EU Insolvency Regulation and UNCITRAL Model Law on Cross-Border Insolvency, cross-border insolvencies remain mainly regulated by national laws.[38] But it is difficult to imagine that, in practice, the applicable law which will govern an insolvency will already have been selected by the parties.[39]

The conflict-of-laws rule under Article 7 of the Recast European Insolvency Regulation provides for a choice of law regime that gives

---

37 For an analysis of this case, *see*, for instance, Vesna Lazić, *Cross-Border Insolvency and Arbitration*, in: S. Kröll, L.A. Mistelis, P. Perales Viscasillas & V. Rogers (eds.), Liber Amicorum Eric Bergsten. International Arbitration and International Commercial Law: Synergy, Convergence and Evolution, 337, 361 (Kluwer Law International 2011); Gabrielle Kaufmann-Kohler, Laurent Lévy & Sabina Sacco, *The Survival of the Arbitration Agreement and Arbitration Proceedings in Cases of Cross-Border Insolvency: An Analysis from the Swiss Perspective*, Les cahiers de l'arbitrage, 371–390, 376 et seq. (2010).

38 Wolfgang Kuhn, *Arbitration and Insolvency*, 5 Disp. Resol. INT'L 203, 205 (2011).

39 Allan L. Gropper, *The Arbitration of Cross-Border Insolvencies*, 86 AM. Bankr. L.J. 201, 233–234 (2012): "Since the choice of a law to govern a dispute can be outcome determinative, it might be unrealistic to expect the insolvency administrators of the affiliates to agree on the governing law. In any event, the parties could submit the question of governing law to the arbitrators, who would then determine the applicable law. In a debt restructuring, on the other hand, the choice of a venue, a method for selecting the arbitrators, and a governing law would ideally be decided at the time arbitration is chosen as a dispute-resolution mechanism. Agreement on these issues would establish the procedures that would be used in the arbitration. A well-drafted arbitration clause could also address the scope of the arbitrators' authority and discretion, narrowing it in appropriate cases." In this regard, it is also possible to affirm that in case of parallel insolvency and arbitration proceedings, the hypothesis will be even more exceptional as the parties, or at least the one that does not become subject to insolvency, will not have already foreseen the possibility of the commencement of insolvency proceedings.

extraterritorial effect to the law of the country where the insolvency proceedings are commenced, hence the *lex concursus*. Article 7 states that the law of the EU Member State, in which insolvency proceedings were commenced, applies to the effects of insolvency proceedings "on current contracts to which the debtor is party."[40] That law applies extraterritorially to all arbitration procedures taking place in other EU Member States and that commence after the opening of the insolvency proceedings. The *lex concursus* governs all, procedural and substantive, the effects of the insolvency proceedings on the parties and their relations.[41] However, that insolvency law does not apply extraterritorially to pending arbitrations. Indeed, Article 18 of the same regulation brings an exception to this provision and indicates that the effects of the insolvency of a party on pending arbitration proceedings is governed by the law of the Member State in which the arbitral tribunal has its seat.

The Model Law suggested by the UNCITRAL served as a model for amendments of domestic insolvency laws, but it is not per se binding. Therefore, it is clear that the only binding international legal source is the Recast EU Insolvency Regulations, which apply only to EU Member States. The provisions of the Recast EU Insolvency Regulation constitute a consensus on the principles of conflict of laws. Although these rules are not binding on arbitrators, they could serve as guidance for arbitrators. The arbitrators can then exercise an important discretion in the way they choose to apply these rules. In other words, where these choice of law rules result in the application of rules that order the termination of the proceedings they can be interpreted by the arbitrators as a stay of proceedings depending on the needs of the dispute at hand.[42]

---

40 Article 7.2 of the Recast European Insolvency Regulation states that, "The law of the State of the opening of proceedings shall determine the conditions for the opening of those proceedings, their conduct and their closure. In particular, it shall determine the following: (e) the effects of insolvency proceedings on current contracts to which the debtor is party."

41 Jelena V. Marković, *Impact of EU Insolvency Regulation on Process of Resolving Disputes Before International Commercial Arbitration*, EU and Comparative Law Issues and Challenges Series (ECLIC) 1, 127, 139 (2018), available at: https://doi.org/10.25234/eclic/6525 (last accessed July 5, 2021).

42 Gabrielle Kaufmann-Kohler, Laurent Lévy & Sabina Sacco, *The Survival of the Arbitration Agreement and Arbitration Proceedings in Cases of Cross-Border Insolvency: An Analysis from the Swiss Perspective*, Les cahiers de l'arbitrage, 371, 389 (2010): "Even so, the arbitrator has ample discretion in the way he or she chooses to apply that provision. This would include, for example, ordering a stay of the proceedings even if the foreign law requires their termination."

Most legislations provide for conflict-of-laws rules on cross-border insolvency situations that govern the effects of the foreign insolvency.[43] This situation may lead to parallel proceedings with contradictory results, hence the high importance of the recognition of foreign insolvency proceedings by the arbitral tribunal. This situation results often in the lack of specific conflict rules and brings diversity in applicable laws.[44]

The Path to the Appropriate Applicable Law

The lack of specific conflict rules and the proliferation of possible applicable laws bring the need for arbitrators to conduct a deeper analysis in the search for an ideal method in the interaction between arbitration and insolvency. There exists no universal conflict-of-laws rules in this regard. It is true that this observation is in perfect line with arbitration's "tailored justice" feature. However, it also creates uncertainty—not only for the litigants but also for the arbitrators—who need guidelines to address the difficult question of applicable law. Therefore, the factors that the arbitral tribunal should consider while choosing the applicable law are discussed here.

It can be observed that in this domain, authors have the tendency to base their arguments on the analysis of the *Elektrim* case.[45] The present study has the objective to undertake the study of different factors related to arbitration law on the one hand, and to insolvency law on the other, in order to achieve an appropriate applicable law.

The arbitrators take into consideration different factors in the making of their decision. Unsurprisingly, things are not different when one of the parties to an arbitration becomes subject to an insolvency proceeding.[46] However, in this hypothesis, it is possible to observe that the number of

---

43 Deyan Draguiev, *The Effect of Insolvency on Pending International Arbitration: What Is and What Should Not Be*, 32 Journal of International Arbitration 5, 511, 517 (2015).

44 *See* IBA Toolkit on Insolvency and Arbitration, available at: https://www.ibanet.org/LPD/Dispute_Resolution_Section/Arbitration/toolkit-arbitration-insolvency (last accessed July 5, 2021).

45 This observation had also been made by another author. *See* Deyan Draguiev, *The Effect of Insolvency on Pending International Arbitration: What Is and What Should Not Be*, 32 Journal of International Arbitration 5, 511, 512 (2015).

46 Wolfgang Kuhn, *Arbitration and Insolvency*, 5 Disp. Resol. INT'L 203, 211 (2011): "It cannot be said that all is lost for arbitration if one of the parties to the arbitration agreement or proceedings becomes insolvent. However, an arbitral tribunal that is faced

factors increases and the efforts to create a balance between them becomes relatively difficult.

In private international law, state courts usually characterize an issue *lege fori*, hence according to the notions of the *lex fori*. Although arbitrators do not have their own *lex fori*, they can take the *lex arbitri* as reference. In this regard, a universal characterization of the effects of insolvency proceedings on an on-going arbitration procedure could constitute a solution for arbitrators to address the question of applicable law in a more guided way. The example of *Elektrim* case illustrates that a procedural perception of arbitration results in more arbitration-friendly outcomes.[47] Once the characterization has been made with an arbitration-friendly approach, it will certainly have an effect on the selection of the most appropriate applicable law. In this hypothesis, the arbitral tribunal's choice of law question will be addressed on the basis of *lex arbitri*. Is such a process in line with the relevant factors?

In case of an insolvency proceedings continuing during an arbitration, the arbitrators cannot omit to take such insolvency proceedings into consideration.[48] In this regard, as aforementioned, the relevant factors can be separated into two categories: insolvency related factors and arbitration related factors. The enforcement of the award is one of the "all-time concerns" of arbitrators.[49] On this point, one of the biggest risks is that the

---

with a claim in which national or international insolvency law becomes relevant is faced with a myriad of factors that will determine how, and if, the arbitral proceedings are continued."

47 Stephan Madaus, *The (Underdeveloped) Use of Arbitration in International Insolvency Proceedings*, 37 Journal of International Arbitration 4, 449, 467 (2020). According to this author, with whom we agree, the adoption of such an approach by the English courts and the European legislator may be considered as an indication in favor of a trend to a broader recourse to arbitration in the field of insolvency.

48 Deyan Draguiev, *The Effect of Insolvency on Pending International Arbitration: What Is and What Should Not Be*, 32 Journal of International Arbitration 5, 511–513 (2015): "If, in the specific circumstances of a case, the continuation of the arbitral proceedings might prejudice subsequent attempts to enforce the award, the tribunal might have to consider suspension or even termination of the international arbitration. Otherwise, there is the risk that after expensive proceedings held in a jurisdiction renowned for its pro-arbitration approach, the award creditor may have to face dissatisfactory results when trying to enforce in the insolvent party's jurisdiction."

49 In this regard, *see* Wolfgang Kuhn, *Arbitration and Insolvency*, 5 Disp. Resol. INT'L 203, 204 (2011); Pierre A. Karrer, *Must an Arbitral Tribunal Ensure that its Award is Enforceable*, *in*: G. Aksen et al. (eds.), Global Reflections on International Law, Commerce and Dispute Resolution: Liber Amicorum in honour of Robert Briner, ICC Publishing, ICC Publication 693, Nov. 2005, pp. 429–437, 433, para. 22: "Whether the award will be enforced abroad in any other of some 160 countries is difficult to say. Even in the 136 counties where the NYC is in force there is no consistency in its

result of the arbitration is affected by the insolvency of one of the parties.[50] In this regard, the issue would be that the creditor of a foreign insolvency proceeding spends time and money in obtaining an award against the debtor just to find out that it cannot be enforced on the ground of contrariety with crucial principles of insolvency law[51] or because there is simply no available asset to enforce the award against.[52]

Ensuring an enforceable award would also conform with the parties' expectations. In this sense, would the *lex arbitri*, provided by the Recast EU Insolvency Regulation, be the law expected to be applied? While the insolvent party could expect that the insolvency law of the state where insolvency proceedings are opened could apply, the other party might

---

application. Often a claimant does not know where the award will be enforced, even less so the arbitral tribunal." *See also* Matti S. Kurkela, *Criminal laws in International Arbitration – the May, the Must, the Should and the Should Not*, 26 ASA Bull. 2, pp. 280, 283 (2008): "If one is to accept the existence of a duty to render an enforceable award the enforcement of the award should in light of the above not violate public policy. Since enforcement of the award may be sought in a large number of jurisdictions and none of these jurisdictions applies necessarily the law of lex arbitri or lex causae, the duty to ensure the enforceability of the award may become overwhelmingly tedious involving a comparative analysis of a number of jurisdictions." Apart from the fact that a good quality arbitration must result in the rendering of a correct and a fair award. *See* Nadia Darwazeh, *Chapter 7: Is Efficiency and Arbitrator's Duty or Simply a Character Trait?*, in: P. Shaughnessy et S. Tung (eds.), The Powers and Duties of an Arbitrator Liber Amicorum Pierre A. Karrer, 57, 61 (Wolters Kluwer, 2017); William W. Park, *Chapter 26: Arbitration and Fine Dining: Two Faces of Efficiency*, *in*: P. Shaugnessy et S. Tung (eds.), The Powers and Duties of an Arbitrator Liber Amicorum Pierre A. Karrer, 251, 253 et seq. (Wolters Kluwer, 2017).

50 Deyan Draguiev, *The Effect of Insolvency on Pending International Arbitration: What Is and What Should Not Be*, 32 Journal of International Arbitration 5, 511, 519 (2015).

51 *See* in this sense, Gabrielle Kaufmann-Kohler, Laurent Lévy & Sabina Sacco, *The Survival of the Arbitration Agreement and Arbitration Proceedings in Cases of Cross-Border Insolvency: An Analysis from the Swiss Perspective*, Les cahiers de l'arbitrage, 371, 389–390 (2010): "Finally, arbitrators faced with such provisions should also bear in mind that an award rendered in violation of the lex concursus could potentially be denied enforcement in the State where the insolvency proceedings were opened, if such a provision is considered to be part of that State' s international public policy." *See also* Deyan Draguiev, *The Effect of Insolvency on Pending International Arbitration: What Is and What Should Not Be*, 32 Journal of International Arbitration 5, 511, 519 (2015), which states that, "[i]n insolvency cases the affected interests might be even graver than in other situations." For some examples the case law which illustrate the difficulties that can be encountered in the enforcement of awards *see* Stefan Kröll, *Chapter 18. Arbitration and insolvency – Selected Conflict of Laws Problems*, *in* Conflict of Laws in International Commercial Arbitration 657, 658, note n°6 (F. Ferrari & S. Kröll eds., 2019).

52 In this regard, an author notes that "a debtor has assets outside the jurisdiction in which the insolvency proceedings take place and which are not subject to the insolvency proceedings." *See* Wolfgang Kuhn, *Arbitration and Insolvency*, 5 Disp. Resol. INT'L, 203, 204 (2011).

revendicate the application of the law of the arbitral seat. It is, however, possible to affirm that between *lex concursus* and *lex arbitri*, the latter is the law which is the most familiar to both parties, hence its application seems like the most coherent and in line with the relevant factors.

To conform with their duty of rendering an enforceable award,[53] the arbitrators should respect the applicable insolvency law. Regarding the insolvency law related factors, it should be acknowledged that the selected governing law will establish the substantive rules of insolvency law.

In this regard, as aforementioned, the majority of insolvency laws have the objective of an equal treatment of creditors with the centralization of claims.[54] This scheme is not unfamiliar with arbitrators who already have the duty to conform with *due process* during proceedings before them. More specifically, the stage of the implicated insolvency proceedings is important to take into consideration. For example, if the insolvency proceedings are about the restructuring or reorganization of one of the parties to the arbitration, the arbitral tribunal should make sure that the plan suggested in this perspective is feasible in practice.[55]

---

53 There is, nevertheless, no consensus on this subject in the legal scholarship or in the case law. The arbitrator is usually considered as being bound by a moral duty of rendering an efficient award. In this perspective, he or she is expected to make sure the award is not annulled or refused exequatur. In other words, the arbitrator should not only make an award, but also be aware of his or her obligation to ensure that the award is enforceable. The principle of effectiveness of arbitration and the obligation of the arbitrator to make an effective award are generally used interchangeably in the doctrine. Such duty is not set out in any arbitration instrument for the moment. Nevertheless, some arbitration rules refer to it. In this regard, *see* Matti S. Kurkela, *Criminal laws in International Arbitration – the May, the Must, the Should and the Should Not*, 26 ASA Bull. 2, 280, 283 (2008); Richard Kreindler, *Aspects of Illegality in the Formation and Performance of Contracts*, 3 TDM 2, (2006), available at: https://www.transnational-disputemanagement.com/article.asp?key=742 (last accessed July 5, 2021). For an author in favor of such duty, *see for example* Jennifer Kirby, *What Is an Award, Anyway?*, 31 J. Int'l Arb. 4, 692 (2014). On the principle of effectiveness in arbitration and the importance of balancing the speed and the delivery of a correct award, *see* William W. Park, *Arbitrators and accuracy*, 1 J. Int'l Disp. Settl. 1, 25 et seq. (2010); Nadia Darwazeh, *Chapter 7: Is Efficiency and Arbitrator's Duty or Simply a Character Trait?*, in: P. Shaughnessy et S. Tung (eds.), The Powers and Duties of an Arbitrator Liber Amicorum Pierre A. Karrer, 57, 57–64 (Wolters Kluwer, 2017).

54 Indeed, the proceedings will be effective only where all parties and all of their claims are adjudicated uniformly before the same forum. *See* Wolfgang Kuhn, *Arbitration and Insolvency*, 5 Disp. Resol. INT'L 203, 204 (2011); Domitille Baizeau, *Arbitration and Insolvency: Issues of Applicable Law*, *in* C. Müller & A. Rigozzi (eds.), 1 New Developments in International Commercial Arbitration, 97, 98 (2009).

55 For an example from American law, *see* for instance, Allan L. Gropper, *The Arbitration of Cross-Border Insolvencies*, 86 AM. Bankr. L.J. 201, 235 (2012).

The factors regarding arbitration law on the one hand, and insolvency law on the other hand are, in reality, interconnected. Indeed, if the implicated rules of insolvency law are violated, the arbitrators will also have violated fair trial and *due process*. Then, is it possible to conclude that arbitrators can indirectly conform with insolvency law obligations by *only* respecting the *due process*? In other words, wouldn't it be sufficient for the arbitrators to comply with these two duties that are already included in arbitration to have been indirectly considered in line with the implicated insolvency law?

Conclusion

In light of the above, it is understood that insolvency and arbitration pursue two different policy objectives that appear difficult to reconcile, especially because of a certain clash of implicated interests. Therefore, the use of arbitration does not seem to be an obvious issue in case of an insolvency and has been considered as inappropriate in connection with insolvency matters.[56] However, with the global pandemic and its effects still looming large, the interaction of these two areas is just inevitable. Would there be sufficient advantages of the use of arbitration in case of a party at the edge of insolvency so that the possible disadvantages—such as the lack of direct judicial control—can be ignored?

Although insolvency law and arbitration law have conflicting principles, there is no solid ground that the practitioners of insolvency fear arbitration. Arbitration law remains a viable option, especially as a continuation of dispute resolution process where negotiation or mediation fail.[57] It is true that if one of the parties to a contractual relationship is on the edge of an insolvency, the recourse to arbitration can be thoroughly considered. In any event, arbitration is a consensual procedure and as long as parties think that arbitration is the best way to preserve their rights, they should have recourse to this dispute resolution method. It is important to bear in mind that state courts will in any case have control over the award and the arbitration-friendly approach that is triumphing in the field is balanced with the consideration of the factors relevant to insolvency law.

---

56 Allan L. Gropper, *The Arbitration of Cross-Border Insolvencies*, 86 AM. Bankr. L.J. 201, 241 (2012).

57 Stephan Madaus, *The (Underdeveloped) Use of Arbitration in International Insolvency Proceedings*, 37 Journal of International Arbitration 4, 449, 476 (2020).

Regarding this, a hybrid method, combining a universal recognition of certain insolvency law principles with conflict of laws method, has been considered in this chapter. This approach consists of recognizing insolvency proceedings that are in line with general principles of insolvency widely accepted in comparative law, and then characterizing the issue of effects of insolvency as a procedural issue before applying *lex arbitri* to address the issue.

In the hypothesis of a cross-border insolvency proceeding started in parallel with an arbitration proceeding, the arbitral tribunal should apply the law of the state of the arbitral seat following an arbitration-friendly and careful characterization at hand.[58] Such an approach is validated by a deep analysis based on relevant factors that should be taken into consideration. It is not only in line with the arbitrators' duty of enforcement, especially because most insolvency laws are mandatory, but also ensures the parties' legitimate expectations as the law that is known by all parties. The aforementioned method is ideal not only because it is the least risky one but also because it creates a certain balance between the interests of both fields. As long as the implicated insolvency law is not mandatory, the discretion of the arbitral tribunal to interpret it keeps the reputation of arbitration as a dispute resolution method that is adapted to the needs of the dispute at hand.

58 Jelena V. Marković, *Impact of EU Insolvency Regulation on Process of Resolving Disputes Before International Commercial Arbitration*, EU and Comparative Law Issues and Challenges Series (ECLIC) 1, 127, 140 (2018), available at: https://doi.org/10.25234/eclic/6525 (last accessed July 5, 2021).

The Treatment of Claims by Revenue Authorities in Insolvency Arbitrations: Some Salient Private International Law Considerations

Richard Mike Mlambe
LLM (University of Johannesburg); LLB (Hons) (University of Malawi) Lecturer at The Malawi University of Business and Applied Sciences (formerly University of Malawi: The Polytechnic) Head of Management Studies Department: Faculty of Commerce Member of the Malawian bar

Introduction

Insolvency proceedings have recently undergone a substantial increase in terms of both frequency and value due to several factors including the Coronavirus pandemic.[1] The growth and expansion of global investment and trade has also led to an increase in cross-border insolvency proceedings. This has prompted states to devise methods of cooperating in such transactions since the traditional territorial and parochial approach has been challenged by the transnational dimension of such transactions.[2] Both global and regional efforts have been made to harmonize the approaches to the management of international insolvency proceedings.[3] It is important to note that these efforts concerned the conduct of international insolvency proceedings primarily (if not exclusively) before national courts.

1 Antonia Menezes and Sergio Muro, '*COVID-19 Outbreak: Implications on Corporate and Individual Insolvency*', COVID-19 notes, Finance Series, World Bank Group (2010).

2 Neil Hannan 'Cross-border Insolvency: The Enactment and Interpretation of the UNCITRAL Model Law' (Springer) 2017 p. 1.

3 *See* UNCITRAL Model Law on Cross-Border Insolvency (1997); the Regulation (EU) 2015/848 of the European Parliament and of the Council of 20 May 2015 on insolvency proceedings (Recast).

When insolvency proceedings are instituted, revenue authorities are usually among the creditors of the debtor for taxes due by the time of the commencement of the proceedings.[4] This chapter intends to carry out an examination of the manner in which claims for taxes due to revenue authorities should be handled before arbitral tribunals. The focus shall be on the handling of cross-border insolvency proceedings before such tribunals which are connected with more than one country. Apart from the question of arbitrability of such claims, the chapter also examines certain private international law[5] concerns namely:

(i) Whether an arbitral tribunal seated in one country can apply the foreign revenue laws of another country
(ii) Whether the nature or classification of claims brought by revenue authorities has any bearing on their admissibility and treatment by arbitral tribunals
(iii) Whether foreign arbitral awards can/should be recognized by national courts to the extent that they include an award of taxes due to a revenue authority.

As stated above, the focus is on cross-border insolvency proceedings before arbitral tribunals because the above-mentioned private international law concerns arise more substantially in the context of such proceedings unlike in purely local arbitral proceedings.

The Fundamental Question: Are Insolvency Proceedings Arbitrable? If They Are Arbitrable, Does It Include Claims by Revenue Authorities for Tax Due?

The question of arbitrability of a cause of action is fundamental in arbitration. According to Gary Born, certain types of disputes may not be arbitrated, notwithstanding an otherwise valid arbitration agreement. The distinguished author has stated:

> The types of disputes that are non-arbitrable differ from nation to nation. In general, disputes or claims are deemed 'non-arbitrable' because of their public importance or a perceived need for judicial protections. Among other things, various nations refuse to permit arbitration of at least some disputes concerning criminal law, labour

4 *See*, for example, the case of In Re Ayers (1981) 34 A.L.R. 582.

5 'Private international law' and 'conflict of laws' are used interchangeably.

> grievances; intellectual property; real estate; bankruptcy; and domestic relations.[6]

The author includes bankruptcy matters on the list of non-arbitrable matters on the basis of their 'public importance or perceived need for judicial protection.' Further, he states that 'Disputes concerning these "core" bankruptcy functions are almost universally considered non-arbitrable, whether in domestic or international arbitrations'.[7] These sentiments are echoed by many other writers. According to Margaret Moses, 'A country's laws may provide that certain types of disputes are not arbitrable. For example, child custody disputes, criminal matters, bankruptcy, the validity of trademarks or patents, and other kinds of disputes that will have an impact on third parties or have some kind of consequences in the public domain will usually have to be decided in a court of law.'[8] Therefore, that insolvency matters are non-arbitrable appears to be the position in many jurisdictions.[9]

However, in practice, there is a distinction between 'pure' bankruptcy[10] proceedings and proceedings in relation to insolvency. Arbitrability of the former appears to be more controversial than of the latter. As stated by Tang:

> Although the insolvency law of every country differs, the common practice is that insolvency per se is inarbitrable. It is justified by two reasons. First, 'pure' insolvency proceedings do not concern commercial disputes but execution of debts. Pure bankruptcy proceedings are described by Lord Hoffmann as proceedings not to determine the existence of rights but 'to provide a mechanism of collective execution against the property of the debtor by creditors whose rights are admitted or established'. Second, insolvency proceedings affect not only private interests between immediate contractual parties but the public at large, which should be reserved for jurisdiction of courts. However, disputes that are not 'pure' insolvency matters, but in relation to insolvency proceedings, such as the

6 Gary Born 'International Arbitration'; Kluwer Law International BV, 2012, para 3.02(B).

7 *Ibid.*

8 Margaret Moses 'The Principles and Practice of International Commercial Arbitration' (Cambridge University Press) 2008 p. 216.

9 *See also Continental Airlines Inc. v. Zimmerman* 464 U.S. 1038 for a discussion of arbitrability of insolvency matters under United States law.

10 In this chapter, unless otherwise expressly stated, the terms 'bankruptcy' and 'insolvency' are used interchangeably.

existence of debt, restitution claims and post-insolvency sales, are generally arbitrable'.[11]

This distinction is important in that to the extent that certain issues do not fall within the ambit of 'pure' insolvency issues, it is possible that the non-arbitrability doctrine may not be applicable to them. In our understanding, 'pure' insolvency proceedings refer to the actual management and distribution of assets subject to the proceedings, whereas matters in relation to insolvency proceedings involve not the collection, sale, and distribution of the assets, but the determination of certain preliminary/incidental questions, such as the status of a creditor or validity of transactions.[12] This chapter agrees with this distinction between the two types of matters, and it is submitted that while 'pure' insolvency proceedings should be reserved exclusively to the courts, matters in relation to insolvency can properly be referred to arbitration without offending the values which the non-arbitrability doctrine is aimed at safeguarding.

Further support for the arbitrability of the disputes in relation to insolvency is the practice of states of entrusting the determination of such issues in other officers rather than the courts, in particular, insolvency practitioners.[13] These practitioners can act as liquidators, administrators, and receivers in relation to the assets subject to the insolvency under the general supervision of the courts. In the same vein, it is submitted that there is no harm which may be occasioned on the creditors, debtors, and the public by entrusting the determination of disputes relating to insolvency in the hands of arbitral tribunals as these are also under the supervision of the courts.[14] In addition, by referring this category of disputes to arbitration, the proceedings will benefit from the usual advantages of arbitration over litigation such as expertise and speed.[15]

---

11 Zheng Sophia Tang, 'Jurisdiction and Arbitration agreements in international commercial law International' Routledge (2014) p. 98.

12 *See* Robert B. Kovacs 'A Transnational Approach to the Arbitrability of Insolvency Proceedings in International Arbitration', International Insolvency Institute, 2012.

13 *See*, for example, s. 308 of the Malawian Insolvency Act No. 9 of 2016.

14 For present purposes, supervision of the court refers to the general supervisory powers such as the powers to stay proceedings brought before the court in breach of a valid arbitration clause.

15 Moses, 'The Principles and Practice of International Commercial Arbitration', p. 3.

The Private International Law Concerns

Can an Arbitral Tribunal Seated in One Country Apply the Revenue Laws of Another Country?

Traditionally, national courts do not apply the revenue laws of foreign jurisdictions.[16] They decline to enforce any claim founded on foreign tax laws. The main reason for the refusal to apply foreign tax laws is the public nature of such laws. The enactment and enforcement of tax laws is a sovereign act. As such, it is inappropriate for laws and acts of such nature to be interpreted and enforced through courts of foreign jurisdictions. According to Professor Briggs:

> The second broad area in which the common law of private international law applies the *lex fori* or (if this is different) ignores any provision of what might otherwise have been the *lex causae*, is in the area of penal, revenue, and other public laws: the usual formulation of the rule is that an English court has no jurisdiction to enforce a foreign penal law or a foreign revenue law, or an 'other public law', though it is widely understood that the matter is not one of jurisdiction in the strict sense.[17]

Commenting on the treatment of foreign revenue laws under American jurisprudence at common law, Symeonides has stated that:

> Although the obligation to pay taxes is not penal, the foreign tax-law exception (also known as 'the revenue rule') resembles the penal-law exception in the sense that: (1) they both function as effective defenses to the application of the otherwise-governing foreign law, and (2) both involve foreign laws enacted in jure imperii – that is, in the exercise of direct sovereign authority. The revenue rule stands for the proposition that, in the absence of a treaty, the courts of one country do not directly enforce the tax judgments or laws of another country. At a minimum, this means that American courts will not entertain a suit by a foreign government seeking to directly enforce its tax laws or judgments.[18]

---

16 *Government of India v. Taylor* (1955) A.C. 491.
17 Adrian Briggs 'Conflict of Laws' Oxford University Press (2013) p. 200.
18 Symeon C. Symeonides 'Choice of Law' Oxford University Press (2016) p. 85.

An interesting question that arises is whether the above-mentioned rule against application of foreign revenue laws ought to be followed by arbitral tribunals. This is so because national courts and arbitral tribunals are different in certain fundamental and material respects. Courts are creatures of the law of the country in which they sit. They are organs of the state and accordingly have the obligation not only to uphold the public policy of the state in which they sit, but also to refrain from determining matters that involve the exercise of sovereignty of foreign states. They also hold the nationality of the state in which they are established. On the contrary, although provision for the institution of arbitral tribunals is made by the laws, they are a creature of the contract between the parties. They are not a public institution. Accordingly, they are much less concerned about the public policy and sovereignty matters relating to the issues that fall to be determined by them than courts are.

These differences between courts and arbitral tribunals notwithstanding, the latter invariably have a legal system to which they are connected. For a purely domestic arbitral tribunal, its nationality (or perhaps domicile) is the country in which it is created. For an international arbitral tribunal, it also ought to have at least one jurisdiction to which it is most closely connected among the two or more to which it has some connections. This takes us to one of the central concepts in international arbitration law – the concept of the 'seat' of the arbitral tribunal, to which we now turn.

Born describes the seat as follows:

> The 'arbitral seat' or 'place of arbitration' is a legal construct, not a geographic location. The arbitral seat is the nation where an international arbitration has its legal domicile or juridical home. As a practical matter, in virtually all cases, the seat will be the state that the parties have specified in their arbitration agreement as the place or seat of the arbitration (or, in the absence of agreement between the parties, the place that the arbitrators or an arbitral institution has selected as the seat of the arbitration).[19]

The learned author proceeds to distinguish the 'seat' of arbitration from the geographical place where the hearings take place. He states:

> It is important to distinguish between the legal "seat" or "place" of the arbitration and the geographic location of the hearings or meetings. The arbitral seat is the legal or juridical home (or domicile) of

---

19 Gary Born, 'International Arbitration' Kluwer Law International BV, 2012, Para. 6.01.

> the arbitration, the choice of which results in a number of significant legal consequences; the arbitral seat is not necessarily the geographic location where arbitral hearings are conducted. Rather, virtually all national laws and institutional rules permit hearings and meetings to be conducted outside the arbitral seat, for reasons of convenience.[20]

The seat of arbitration is regarded as the place where the award is made, notwithstanding that the proceedings were conducted elsewhere. As stated by Bělohlávek:

> [T]he seat of arbitration also influences the place where the arbitral award is made. The reason is that the seat of arbitration is also usually considered to be the place where the award is made. Most legal systems stipulate (or at least factually assume) the presumption that the determination of the place where the arbitral award is made is not legally contingent on the place where the terms of the arbitral award were debated or where the arbitral award was signed – unless the parties agree otherwise … Consequently, the place where the arbitral award is made usually determines whether the award is a domestic or a foreign award.[21]

As stated earlier, the 'seat' of arbitration is not necessarily the same as the place where the proceedings take place. The seat is the arbitration's domicile.

Given that the country of the seat of arbitration may be different from the country where the proceedings are conducted, the two possible scenarios that may arise are that (I) an arbitral tribunal may have its seat in the jurisdiction where the hearing takes place; or (II) an arbitral tribunal may conduct its hearing outside the country where it has its seat.

Under scenario (I), there are two further possibilities: (a) the claim for taxes due may be made by a revenue authority based in the country of the seat; or (b) it may be made by an authority originating from another country. Under scenario (II), there are three possibilities: (a) the claim may be made by a tax authority from the country of the seat; or (b) it may be made by an authority from the country where the hearing is taking place

---

20 *Ibid.*, 6.01 (B).

21 Alexander J. Bělohlávek 'Seat of Arbitration and Supporting and Supervising Function of Courts' Czech (& Central European) Yearbook of Arbitration paras 2.21-2.23.

and not from the seat; or (c) it may be made by an authority from a third country.

Where the claim is made by a tax authority based in the country of the seat of the arbitration, there will be no conflict of law problems since it is a purely local scenario. The only issue that may arise is that of arbitrability of the claim, determination of which will depend on the relevant provisions of the laws of the seat.[22] Differences arise when the claims are made by a tax authority from another country than that of the seat. Under scenario (I)(b), the claim by the tax authority from the foreign country will give rise to the problem of applicability of that country's revenue laws. The tribunal must determine whether it is bound to apply the rule against non-application of such laws under private international law.

In cases where arbitral proceedings are conducted outside the seat and the claim is made by a revenue authority from the country of the seat, this is essentially a local transaction since the award will be deemed to have been made in the country of the seat which is also the country of origin of the tax authority. Accordingly, there would be very few private international law issues. Where arbitral proceedings are conducted outside the seat and the claim is made by a revenue authority from the country in which the proceedings are taking place, it is debatable whether this should be regarded as a local claim or foreign claim as the seat of the arbitration is different from the venue of the hearing. If it is a foreign claim, the usual private international law questions, in particular the non-applicability of foreign revenue laws, will arise. In cases where arbitral proceedings are conducted outside the seat and the claim is made by a revenue authority from a third country, this will certainly be a claim based on foreign revenue laws and the issue of non-applicability of foreign revenue laws will also arise.

For present purposes, the focus is on cases in which the claim is by revenue authority outside the country of the seat of arbitration and, thereby, a foreign tax authority.

In this chapter, for reasons that are discussed in detail below, it is submitted that within certain limits, arbitral tribunals should be regarded as having the competence to deal with and determine claims by foreign revenue authorities for taxes due to them, notwithstanding that national courts may not determine such claims.

22 *Ibid.*, para. 2.01.

What Role Does Characterization Play in Determining Whether Arbitral Tribunals Can Deal with Claims by Foreign Revenue Authorities in Insolvency Proceedings?

The next salient private international law issue in the treatment of claims for taxes due by foreign revenue authorities relates to the characterization of such claims. In conflict of laws, where a court or arbitral tribunal finds that it has jurisdiction to adjudicate the matter before it, the next question relates to the choice of law. This process, also referred to as the 'choice/determination of the applicable law', involves determining the system of law (among several systems to which the case is connected) that is applicable to the issue(s). Characterization arises within the choice of law analysis.

Characterization[23] is the process under which a legal issue is placed in its correct legal category.[24] For example, during international insolvency arbitral proceedings, it may be necessary to determine whether a claim sounds in contract or in tort, or whether property subject to the claim is real property or personal property. Commenting on the concept of characterization, professor Oppong states that:

> Problems of characterisation occur in private international law systems, such as those found in Africa, which are based on categories and connecting factors. It is a problem inherent in the application of multi-lateral choice of law rules. It has given rise to very engaging writings in which various approaches have been espoused.[25]

How do claims by foreign revenue authorities give rise to characterization problems? This issue arises because the types of claims that may be brought before a tribunal may take various forms. For example, a foreign revenue authority may bring a claim for breach of contract against a supplier of goods or services who is a debtor in the insolvency proceedings in question. This claim will have nothing to do with tax law. Alternatively, the claim may be based on certain equitable obligation owed by the debtor to the authority under which some money is held on the latter's behalf and payable to it by the debtor.[26] In further alternative, the claim may be for

---

23 It is also referred to as 'classification' or 'categorization'.

24 O'Brien, 'Conflict of Laws' Cavendish Publishing Ltd (1999) 2nd ed p. 93.

25 Richard Frimpong Oppong, 'Private International Law in Commonwealth Africa' Cambridge University Press (2013) p. 6.

26 Restitutionary claims, e.g., money held by the debtor as constructive trustee for the authority.

taxes due for the business activities of the debtor within the jurisdiction of that authority. This last example is precisely the claim based on revenue laws. Then the question that arises is whether it is necessary, in view of the variety of claims that may be brought by revenue authorities before arbitral tribunals, to characterize the claim. In other words, is there a need to characterize the claim and determine whether the claim is based on tax law or not? If the claim is not based on revenue law and is based on, for instance, contract law, does the fact that it is a claim by a foreign tax revenue affect its admissibility and enforceability by the tribunal?

A survey of the treatment of this issue in the insolvency laws of several jurisdictions will be relevant. As a starting point, let us consider the relevant provision of the United Nation Commission on International Trade Law (UNICITRAL) Model Law on Cross-Border Insolvency (1997).[27] The Model Law makes provision for the access of foreign creditors to a proceeding before the courts of the state in which the insolvency proceedings are taking place. It provides

> (1) Subject to paragraph (2) of this article, foreign creditors have the same rights regarding the commencement of, and participation in, a proceeding under [identify laws of the enacting State relating to insolvency] as creditors in this State.
> (2) Paragraph (1) of this article does not affect the ranking of claims in a proceeding under [identify laws of the enacting State relating to insolvency], except that the claims of foreign creditors shall not be ranked lower than [identify the class of general non-preference claims, while providing that a foreign claim is to be ranked lower than the general non-preference claims if an equivalent local claim (e.g., claim for a penalty or deferred-payment claim) has a rank lower than the general non-preference claims].[28]

This provision has been adopted in the insolvency laws of many jurisdictions. We shall carry out a survey of some of the jurisdictions and compare them below. Malawi's[29] new insolvency legislation which came into force in 2016, not only enjoins Malawian courts to make reference to the Model Law in interpreting the provisions of the said legislation relating to cross-border insolvency, but also contains a provision that reproduces and

---

27 Adopted by the United Nations General Assembly in 1998.
28 Art. 13 of the Model Law.
29 Malawi is selected due to the author's expertise in Malawian law.

localizes the provision relating to access of foreign creditors to a proceeding under the said legislation. This provision is as follows:

(1) Subject to subsection (2), foreign creditors shall have the same rights regarding the commencement of, and participation in, a proceeding under this Act as creditors in Malawi.
(2) Subsection (1) shall not affect the ranking of claims in a proceeding under this, Act, except that the claim of a foreign creditor shall not be given a lower priority than that of the general unsecured creditors solely because the holder of such a claim is a foreign creditor.
(3) A claim shall not be challenged solely on the grounds that it is a claim by a foreign tax or social security authority, but such a claim may be challenged-
  (a) on the ground that it is in whole or in part a penalty, or
  (b) on any other ground that a claim might be rejected in a proceeding under this Act.[30]

Under British law, the equivalent law reads:

1. Subject to paragraph 2 of this article, foreign creditors have the same rights regarding the commencement of, and participation in, a proceeding under British insolvency law as creditors in Great Britain.
2. Paragraph 1 of this article does not affect the ranking of claims in a proceeding under British insolvency law, except that the claim of a foreign creditor shall not be given a lower priority than that of general unsecured claims solely because the holder of such a claim is a foreign creditor.
3. A claim may not be challenged solely on the grounds that it is a claim by a foreign tax or social security authority but such a claim may be challenged –
   (a) on the ground that it is in whole or in part a penalty, or
   (b) on any other ground that a claim might be rejected in a proceeding under British insolvency law.[31]

Kenya has declared that the Model Law shall form part of the laws of the Republic.[32] The relevant provision is in the following terms:

30 Section 329 of the Malawian Insolvency Act.
31 Art. 13 of the Cross-border Insolvency Regulations 2006.
32 Section 720 of the Insolvency Act 2015.

(1) Subject to subparagraph (2), foreign creditors have the same rights regarding the commencement of, and participation in, a proceeding under this Act or any other written law relating to insolvency, as creditors in Kenya. (2) Subparagraph (1) does not affect the ranking of claims in a proceeding under this Act or the exclusion of foreign tax and social security claims from such a proceeding.[33]

The equivalent provision under Zambian law is substantially in identical terms to that of Kenya.[34]

Two important observations can be made based on the provisions cited above. First, there is a diversity of approaches to the admissibility of claims by foreign revenue authorities before national courts. On the one hand, there are jurisdictions that require or at least permit the exclusion of such claims from being entertained and determined, as a result of the exclusion of application of foreign tax laws. The position in Zambia and Kenya represents this approach. On the other hand, there are jurisdictions which, at least arguably, do not reject outright the admissibility of claims by revenue authorities. In those jurisdictions, there is possibility of enforcement of claims by revenue authorities, the only question being the extent to which the same may be done. Malawi and Great Britain are examples of jurisdictions falling in the latter category.[35]

Regarding jurisdictions that exclude claims by foreign tax authorities from being determined, there are two ways in which arbitral tribunals dealing with such claims and having their seat within those jurisdictions may determine the claims. They may either simply dismiss such claims in their entirety or, alternatively, they may admit and determine such claims to the extent that they are not 'pure' insolvency matters.

With respect to jurisdictions taking the other approach, there are several possible ways of dealing with the claims and characterization issues. It is to these that our attention is now turned below.

As stated above, the provisions of the relevant law in Malawi and Great Britain on access to local proceedings by foreign creditors are substantially identical. In both jurisdictions, the relevant provision on the treatment of claims by foreign tax authorities is in the third paragraph of the law. This

33 Para. 15 of the fifth schedule on Cross Border Insolvency under s. 720 of the Insolvency Act 2015.

34 Section 151 of the Corporate Insolvency Act 2017.

35 This chapter acknowledges that there may be other approaches to the justiciability of claims by foreign revenue authorities than the two under discussion. For present purposes, however, the two approaches suffice to deal with the questions under discussion in this chapter.

provision states that a claim may not be challenged solely on the grounds that it is a claim by a foreign tax or social security authority. It is provided further that such a claim may be challenged on the ground that it is in whole or in part a penalty or on any other ground that a claim might be rejected in a proceeding under the law.

By providing that a claim may not be challenged solely on the grounds that it is a claim by a foreign tax or social security authority, the legislator, it is submitted, intended to make certain types of claims capable of being determined by tribunals notwithstanding that they are brought by foreign tax authorities. In other words, the fact that the claim in question is brought by a foreign tax authority is not determinative as to whether the same can be dealt with by the tribunal. For the tribunal to make a determination whether it should deal with the claim brought before it, it has to characterize the claim. Based on its findings after characterization of the claim, it can decide whether the claim should or should not be entertained. As stated earlier, claims based on foreign tax laws are generally not entertained. If this rule is equally binding on arbitral tribunals, we can conclude that under this provision, tribunals must classify the claim so as to determine whether it is based on foreign tax laws or not. If it determines that the claim falls under that category, the tribunal should refuse to enforce it. If, on the other hand, it finds that the claim, although brought by a foreign tax authority, is not based on tax law, the same should be allowed. This may include, among others, claims based on the law of contract, tort, and unjust enrichment.

The law further provides, in jurisdictions such as Malawi, that a claim brought by a foreign tax authority may be challenged on the ground that it is in whole or in part a penalty or on any other ground that a claim might be rejected in a proceeding under the law. This provision is against the enforcement of penalties based on foreign laws. Therefore, where the claim is brought by foreign tax authority, the tribunal ought to classify the claim in order to determine whether the same is a penalty and if it finds that it is, it should refuse to enforce it.

The totality of these provisions leads to the conclusion that upon characterizing the claim brought by foreign tax authorities, three possible situations may arise in the result:

(I) a tribunal may find that the claim brought by a foreign tax authority is based on causes of action other than tax law (such as contract law), or

(II) a claim may be brought by a foreign tax authority and be based on tax law, or

(III) a claim may be brought by a foreign tax authority aimed at enforcing a penalty (with or without other claims as well).

For claims founded on contract law, etc., the arbitral tribunals are entitled to handle them. For claims based on penal laws, these may be challenged, and an arbitral tribunal should not entertain them. The present chapter is of the opinion that it is inappropriate to subject the enforcement of penal laws to the jurisdiction of arbitral tribunals. There are very strong public interest reasons for that position which the present chapter finds convincing. How, then, does the above-quoted law from Malawian and British insolvency legislation resolve the issue of the enforceability of claims based on foreign tax laws before arbitral tribunal? Should arbitral tribunals be able to deal with and determine such claims?

For reasons explained below, based on both authority and principle, it is submitted in this chapter that arbitral tribunals, unlike national courts, are entitled to handle claims by foreign tax authorities for taxes payable by the debtor. First, as a matter of statutory interpretation, claims by foreign tax authorities are not entitled to enforcement by arbitral tribunals only if the said claims are intended to enforce penalties. An analysis of the position in jurisdictions such as Malawi and Britain reveals that the rule against enforcement of foreign public laws in the insolvency legislation applies only to those laws that are based on penal laws.

Under this provision, the law specifies that claims intended to enforce penalties are not to be entertained. While the law expressly mentions penalties, it does not do so with regard to taxes. It is an elementary rule of statutory interpretation that the express mention of something will exclude that which is not mentioned *(expressio unius est exclusio altenus)*.[36]For present purposes, the express mention of claims that are penalties as liable to be challenged in the proceedings excludes other types of claims which are not mentioned. Such claims include, it is contended, claims based on foreign tax laws. Writing on the rational for this rule of statutory interpretation, Sullivan states:

> An implied exclusion argument lies whenever the legislature sets out some but not all members of a category or class, or mentions some things but fails to mention others that are comparable. The reasoning goes as follows: if the legislature had intended to include all possible members or things, it would have mentioned them all or described them using general terms; it would not have mentioned

36 *See Rep. v. Brown* (H.C.) (1975-1977) 8 MLR 190 for the position in Malawi.

> one or some while saying nothing of the others, for that would be irrational and disorderly. Legislation is supposed to be drafted in a coherent and orderly way. It thus follows from sound drafting practice that a partial enumeration of like things is meant to be exhaustive, and anything left off the list is by implication meant to be excluded.[37]

Accordingly, it is submitted that arbitral tribunals are not, as a matter of statutory interpretation, precluded from entertaining claims by foreign tax authorities based on foreign tax laws. In the author's view, this interpretation is also applicable in the treatment of claims by foreign tax authorities before national courts. In that case, any refusal to handle such claims on the part of the courts is not to be premised on the above provision, but on other bases such as the common law, in the case of common law jurisdictions. It may be contended that this view is limited to jurisdictions that incorporate provisions such as those in Malawi and Britain and not those taking the approach obtaining in countries such as in Kenya and Zambia. However, a critical look at the relevant provisions shows that the exclusion of revenue laws from applicability is stated in permissive and not mandatory terms, giving arbitral tribunals the option to entertain such claims without stepping outside their mandate.

The second reason in support of the arbitral tribunals' entitlement to deal with claims by foreign revenue authorities for taxes due is the need to avoid rendering assistance to debtors who are guilty of tax evasion. Both judicial and scholarly pronouncements support the enforceability of claims for foreign taxes. As has been recently stated by the English Judicial Committee of the Privy Council:

> That is not to say the principle is without limits, however. Thus, whilst a court will not entertain an action by a foreign state directly or indirectly to enforce that foreign state's exchange control legislation, a court may properly recognise a foreign revenue law where necessary to do so. So, for example, a court declined to prevent trustees of a foreign trust from remitting moneys to comply with the exchange control legislation of the foreign state whose law was the proper law of the trust, where the trustees were obliged to obey that

37 Ruth Sullivan 'Statutory Interpretation' Irwin Law Inc (2nd ed) pp. 190-91. *See also Zeitel v. Ellscheid* (1994) 2 S.C.R. 142.

> law and where their failure to do so might have serious penal consequences: In re Lord Cable, decd (1977) 1 WLR 7.[38]

Further, as professor Oppong has observed, 'The propriety of the foreign revenue rule is open to question. Indeed, the policy rationales for the rule have not been critically discussed by the courts. It is suggested that in cases of tax evasion, it would be inappropriate for courts to side with the tax evader and not assist a foreign government to recover the taxes due. To assist a taxpayer to evade his/her legal obligation is, arguably, a negation of international comity.'[39]

We submit that the above observation applies equally, if not more forcefully, in relation to the handling of the claims by foreign revenue authorities before arbitral tribunals than national courts. This chapter finds it fitting and proper that claims by foreign tax authorities for taxes owed to them by the debtor should be entertained by at least arbitral tribunals as a way of avoiding rendering assistance to the debtor in tax evasion. This is particularly appropriate where the claim for taxes is not the only or predominant claim but only one among many more substantial claims against the debtor.

The third reason in favour of enforcement of claims by foreign revenue authorities for taxes due is the private character of the arbitration process. In arbitration, the parties enjoy great autonomy in the conduct and management of the proceedings. Although the proceedings are generally subject to the general supervision of the courts of the seat, it is important to note that the choice of the seat is made by the parties themselves.[40] As it was stated by the Auckland High Court, arbitration is 'a contractual method of resolving disputes. By their contract the parties agree to entrust the differences between them to the decision of an arbitrator or panel of arbitrators, to the exclusion of the Courts, and they bind themselves to accept that decision, once made, whether or not they think it right'.[41] The parties agree to *privatize* the resolution of their disputes and as such, the enforcement of public policy by the arbitral tribunals is not expected. Similarly, sovereignty considerations are not taken into account in determining claims brought before such tribunals, particularly in international arbitrations.

38 *Webb v. Webb* (2020) UKPC 22 at para. 38.
39 Oppong, 'Private International Law in Commonwealth Africa', p. 26.
40 Unless the seat is determined by the tribunal if no choice was made by the parties.
41 *Motunui Ltd v. Methanex Spellman* (2004) 1 NZLR 95.

Bělohlávek has discussed the distinction between the roles of courts and international arbitral tribunals in a greatly illuminating manner as follows:

> "The assessment of the seat of arbitration highlights one of the typical features of arbitration, namely the great autonomy of the parties; it also demonstrates the weakening of the connection between the seat of arbitration and the arbitration process itself, in the case of international arbitration. The reason is that litigation is governed by the principle that the court always applies its own procedural rules (the principle of *lex fori*), which is a traditional and generally recognized principle that applies in most jurisdictions without any reservations. Consequently, there are no conflicts as such in the case of procedural rules applicable to court proceedings. This branch of law is controlled by the principle of territoriality, and the courts' procedural rules have a clearly territorial nature; in other words, litigation excludes the possibility of conflicts with the procedural rules of other countries. The state adopts its own procedural rules in order to regulate the procedure applied by courts, other state authorities, parties, and other participants to the proceedings conducted in the territory of the state. This activity is exclusively limited to the territory of the given state. When declaring a connection to the territory of states, i.e. especially when determining the jurisdiction (international jurisdiction) of courts, the state should take account of the connection between the situation (the factual and legal findings and circumstances of applying a particular law) and the territory of the state (personal or territorial). Assuming jurisdiction over situations which have no [special] connection to a particular territory could be perceived as interference with the internal affairs of another state, i.e. a violation of sovereignty. *However, arbitration is different, because arbitrators (arbitral tribunals) cannot be considered state authorities, despite the fact that their duties are similar to the duties of the courts and that they could frequently be defined as 'different authorities'; moreover, the parties to arbitration are principally endowed with a high degree of autonomy*"[42] (Italics by the author).

42 Alexander J. Bělohlávek 'Seat of Arbitration and Supporting and Supervising Function of Courts' paras 2.03-2.05.

In view of the autonomy accorded to arbitral tribunals, it is hereby submitted that it is open to such tribunals to enforce claims based on foreign tax laws and that the same should not be regarded as an infringement of the sovereignty of any jurisdiction to which the arbitration proceedings are connected, because arbitration is a distinct and parallel means of settlement of dispute, which is consensual and autonomous. It is not a creature of the state in the exercise of its sovereignty, but it is a creature of the will and consent of private parties to it. Such fundamental differences from litigation justify the liberty of arbitral tribunals to disregard certain rules based on considerations of sovereignty, such as the rule against application of foreign tax laws.

Conflict of Laws in the Recognition and Enforcement of Foreign Arbitral Awards

For many reasons, international arbitration awards oftentimes have to be enforced in a jurisdiction outside the country in which they were made. This is the case because it is not uncommon that the party who is successful in the award and to whom money is payable discovers that the other party has assets in a foreign jurisdiction which may be used to satisfy the award. In general, there is a strong presumption in favour of enforceability of arbitral awards. Refusal to enforce foreign awards can only be countenanced upon certain specified and limited grounds. Of relevance to private international law is the ground that the court finds that the award in question was not in respect of a matter which may lawfully be referred to arbitration under the local law, and that the enforcement thereof is contrary to the local public policy.[43]

This position enjoys international recognition and has been codified in the most important treaty on the recognition and enforcement of foreign arbitral awards – the New York Convention on the Recognition and Enforcement of Foreign Arbitral Awards (hereinafter referred to as 'the Convention').[44] The above-mentioned grounds for refusal of recognition and enforcement are recognized in this Convention.[45] From a private international law perspective, it is important to note that whether a matter is capable of settlement by arbitration or whether the recognition and enforcement of the award would be contrary to public policy, reference is

43 *See*, for example, s. 38(e) of the Malawian Arbitration Act Chapter 6:03 of the Laws of Malawi.

44 Done at New York on 10 June 1958.

45 Art. V (2) (a) and (b) of the Convention.

made to the law of the country in which recognition and enforcement is sought (the requested state). If an award is made and recognition or enforcement is sought in another state, that state may refuse to recognize or enforce it based on the ground that such recognition or enforcement violates its own public policy or that under its laws, the matter was not arbitrable.

For present purposes, this would mean that if an arbitral tribunal renders an award which includes an award for payment of taxes due to a revenue authority, and recognition and enforcement of the same is sought in a state in which the arbitration was not seated, the court of that state may refuse to recognize or enforce the said award if according to its laws, insolvency matters are not arbitrable or the enforcement of the awards will be contrary to its public policy. This also implies that while the arbitral proceedings leading to the award in question were subject to the law of the seat and to any other applicable laws on certain aspects, at the point of recognition or enforcement the award will be subjected to yet another system of law, namely, the law of the jurisdiction in which recognition and enforcement of the award is sought.

The present author is of the view that this position undermines the predictability and certainty which the Convention was intended to bring forth. This is the case because it allows the requested court not only to look at the arbitrability issue based on system of law entirely different from the one to which the arbitration was subject. When the arbitral proceedings are being conducted, it is open to the respondent to challenge the arbitrability of any issue under consideration and the supervisory powers of the courts of the seat of the arbitration may be invoked. Therefore, where an award has been rendered, it means either there were no disputes as to arbitrability of the issues or that the disputes were resolved in the claimant's favour. When the award is rendered, it means either the respondent waived the right to raise the arbitrability issue before the courts or that the same was determined against him or her and is therefore res judicata. Now, to allow the requested court to determine the arbitration of the issues again not only is an affront to the res judicata principle but also creates uncertainty in the recognition and enforcement of awards. For present purposes, it is hereby submitted that where an award has been made in insolvency matters, and the award includes a sum payable to a revenue authority for taxes due to it by the debtor, and recognition or enforcement of the same is sought in another state, it should not be open to the court to consider the arbitrability issue at that point for foreign arbitral awards.[46] In the present author's view, this is consistent with the Convention which provides that '*recognition and enforcement may be refused, at the request of the party against whom it is invoked ... [upon providing proof] that the award has not yet become binding on the parties, or has been set aside or suspended by a competent authority of the country in which, or under the law of which, that award was made*'.[47] If we are to consider this provision critically, it will be appreciated that the provision that gives the requested court the power to reconsider the arbitrability issues under Article V(2)(a) is redundant and unnecessary. How is this so?

An award can only be described as '*not yet binding on the parties or set aside or suspended*' only if it is already made. This contemplates that the party against whom the award was made invoked the courts of the state in which the award was made for it to suspend or set aside the award. Therefore, as far as the Convention is concerned, the courts of the state in which or under the law of which the award was made are the ones possessing the authority to set aside or suspend the award on various grounds including, undoubtedly, non-arbitrability of the issues dealt with in the award. The respondent has the opportunity to invoke the courts of the country in which or under the law of which the award was made for it to be set aside. It should be noted that the opportunity on the part of the party against whom the award was made is in addition to the opportunity he or she already had to challenge the arbitrability of the issues before the award was made.[48] In view of this, why should the requested court be concerned with the arbitrability issue at the recognition or enforcement stage?

It is submitted that such an approach undermines certainty and predictability in the recognition and enforcement of arbitral awards. This chapter understands that while it is for the party against whom an award was made to prove that the award was set aside or suspended, the court in the requested state may invoke non-arbitrability under Article V (2)(a) on its own motion and refuse to recognize or enforce the award on that basis. In a world where there are numerous states with different laws, it should be expected that the position from one country to another may differ as to whether any particular issue is arbitrable or not. However, for the sake of predictability and certainty, as well as security of commercial transactions,

46 The court may do so for local awards but not, it is submitted, foreign awards based on arbitral proceedings conducted in accordance with the law according to which the issues before the tribunal were properly arbitrable.

47 Art. V (1) (e).

48 That is, when the proceedings are still in progress.

it is necessary that there should be only one system of law under which arbitrability should be determined where there are disputes on that.

In the present chapter's view, it is in accordance with both common sense and convenience that the appropriate system of law on the basis of which arbitrability of issues should be determined is the system to which the parties have agreed to subject their proceedings – the seat. Once an award is rendered and the issue was arbitrable under the law of the seat or at least the applicable substantive law, a requested court should not re-open the issue and determine it in accordance with its own law. That is the only approach that is consistent with the reality that there are many jurisdictions with different laws. The author recommends a review of Article V (2) of the Convention in view of these concerns.

Conclusion

On arbitrability of insolvency matters, it is contended that within certain limits, insolvency matters can be properly referred to arbitration. Arbitral tribunals should be allowed, alongside courts, at least to handle what are referred in this chapter and in literature as *proceedings in relation to insolvency*.

Second, in relation to the exclusion of foreign revenue laws, arbitral tribunals are at liberty to apply the foreign revenue law of country under whose law a debtor incurred an obligation to pay taxes. If the debtor and the creditors agree to refer their matters to arbitration, arbitral tribunals should be able to entertain claims by foreign revenue authorities despite the courts' inability to do so. This is the case because of the private character of arbitration.

Third, during the characterization stage, arbitral tribunals should be able to handle and entertain claims by foreign revenue authorities in various causes of action, including claims for taxes due. The only type of claims that are clearly and justifiably not to be handled by the tribunals are claims based on foreign penal law.

Finally, national courts should recognize and enforce foreign arbitral awards in favour of foreign revenue authorities for taxes payable to them by the debtor, notwithstanding that insolvency and revenue matters are not arbitrable under the local law of the requested court. This is so because the arbitrability of such matters should be determined with reference only to the law of the seat of the arbitration or an otherwise applicable substantive law, and should not be open for consideration again at the recognition and enforcement stage.

Standing of Insolvency Administrators in Investment Treaty Arbitration

Nikola Kurková Klímová
(Mgr.) Charles University, (LL.M.) Cambridge University, Ph.D. Candidate, Faculty of Law, Charles University, Associate Researcher Peace Research Center Prague

Introduction

The outbreak of the COVID-19 pandemic has caused unprecedented levels of disruption across all national economies that have been left counting the costs as governments strived to tackle the spread of the virus with stringent health-related restrictions. With the regular business operations being brought to a near standstill, entrepreneurs were required to adapt to the new climate, struggling with a sharp decline in consumption,[1] supply shocks,[2] and late payments of their business partners that alone found themselves in dire financial straits. Although governments put in place robust financial aid programmes, the OECD study of November 2020 estimated firms' profits to decline by as much as 40% to 50% as a result of the COVID-19 shock, with up to 36% of firms turning unprofitable and unable to cover their interest expenses.[3] Insolvency proceedings have thus become inevitable for many.

1 Hodbod, A et al., 'The COVID-19 Consumption Game-changer: Evidence from a Large-scale Multi-country Survey' Working Paper Series No 2599, European Central Bank, Oct. 2021, available at: <https://www.ecb.europa.eu/pub/pdf/scpwps/ecb.wp2599~23adf24d3a.en.pdf>.

2 del Rio-Chanona, R. M. et al., 'Supply and Demand Shocks in the COVID-19 Pandemic: An Industry and Occupation Perspective' (2020) 36(1) Oxford Review of Economic Policy, p. 94.

3 OECD, 'Insolvency and Debt Overhang Following the Covid-19 Outbreak: The Assessment of Risks and Policy Responses' *OECD Policy Responses to Coronavirus (COVID 19)*, 27 Nov. 2020, available at: <https://www.oecd.org/coronavirus/policy-responses/insolvency-and-debt-overhang-following-the-covid-19-outbreak-assessment-of-risks-and-policy-responses-7806f078/>.

The COVID-19 crisis has impeded the economic activities not only of domestic businesses but also of foreign investors.[4] While their local counterparts have been left to seek compensation for their losses mostly through court actions, foreign investors can consider filing their damage claims also before international tribunals established under multilateral or bilateral investment treaties which embody a broad range of guarantees for the investors' undisrupted operations.[5] The capacity to pursue the legal action and take part in the arbitral proceedings can be, however, curtailed when insolvency is looming on the horizon. In this respect, the COVID-19 pandemic has re-opened the debate regarding the effect of the claimant's insolvency on investment treaty arbitration.

In practice, the imposition of an insolvency administration on the claimant investor is a frequently invoked ground for a challenge of its standing in the arbitral proceedings. During insolvency, the indebted legal entity is generally represented by an administrator who primarily supervises its activities and takes steps with a view to business rescue or, where this is not possible, sale of the estate. The scope of the administrator's powers largely depends on the type of the insolvency proceedings and differs also across individual jurisdictions. As the common goal is maximising the value of the debtor's assets, the administrators are usually empowered to grant or refuse authorisation for the debtors' legal acts and to varying degrees also dispose of the estate. For investors involved in arbitration against the host state, insolvency may bring several practical difficulties as administrators can assume the power to represent the claimant in the proceedings instead of legal counsels and their control over the investor's activities can raise doubts as to the claimant's nationality pursuant to the applicable investment agreement. Their effects further exacerbate where the claimant is an insolvent subsidiary seated in the host state. Although insolvency administrators are required to act impartially and independently in discharging their duties, one can point to the risk of the

---

4 UNCTAD, 'World Investment Report 2020: International Production Beyond the Pandemic' *UNCTAD/WIR/2020*, 2020, available at: <https://unctad.org/system/files/official-document/wir2020_en.pdf>.

5 For instance, on 19 Jan. 2021, the main shareholders of a French consortium controlling a concession for Arturo Merino Benítez international airport in Santiago notified the Chilean President of their intention to file an ICSID claim against Chile for $37 million loss as a result of emergency measures taken in response to the COVID-19 pandemic. *See* IISD, 'French consortium kicks off an ICSID claim against Chile after USD 37 million loss due to COVID-19 Pandemic' *Investment Treaty News*, 23 March 2021, available at: <https://www.iisd.org/itn/en/2021/03/23/french-consortium-kicks-off-an-icsid-claim-against-chile-after-usd-37-million-loss-due-to-covid-19-pandemic/>.

host state abusing insolvency to subvert the arbitral proceedings and compel the claimant to withdraw its claims.

This chapter aims to explore the consequences of the insolvency administration for the standing of the claimants in investment arbitration and discuss the safeguards that are available to tribunals when there is a suspicion of the host state's undue influence over the insolvency proceedings.

Standing in Investment Treaty Arbitration

The issue of standing generally refers to the legal right or interest in pursuing a claim regarding a specific subject matter. It entails an examination into whether the parties seeking a legal remedy have a sufficient connection to the suffered harm and are thus entitled to appear in the proceedings in their respective procedural positions.[6]

In investment treaty arbitration, the standing of the claimant is closely related to tribunal's jurisdiction which is delimited by state's consent to arbitrate.[7] In the absence of a direct contractual relationship between the state and the foreign investor, the consent is formed by the state's unilateral offer to arbitrate expressed in an international investment agreement (IIA) relating to the investors that are nationals of the other contracting state party and becomes perfected only upon its express or implied acceptance by the investor.[8] The mechanism was famously dubbed 'arbitration without privity',[9] pointing to the investors' right to seek independent protection against a violation of the host state's international obligations in arbitration in their own name. The investors thus do not need to rely on their home state to initiate the arbitral proceedings but can bring their claims before a tribunal directly.[10] To be arbitrable, their dispute must, however, fall within

6 Del Vecchio, A., 'International Courts and Tribunals, Standing' *Max Planck Encyclopedia of Public International Law* (2010), para. 2.

7 Yannaca-Small, K., 'Who is Entitled to Claim? Nationality Challenges' In: Yannaca-Small, K. (ed.), *Arbitration under International Investment Agreements: A Guide to the Key Issues* (2010, Oxford University Press), p. 211.

8 For the discussion on the forms of consent in international investment arbitration, *see* Schreuer, C., 'Consent to Arbitration' In: Muchlinski, P., Ortino, F. and Schreuer Ch. (eds.), *The Oxford Handbook of International Investment Law* (2008, Oxford University Press).

9 Paulsson, J., 'Arbitration Without Privity' (1995) 10(2) *ICSID Review—Foreign Investment Law Journal*, p. 233.

10 Cf. Leys, D., 'Diplomatic Protection and Individual Rights: A Complementary Approach' (2016) 57 *Harvard International Law Journal Online*, pp. 4-5.

the jurisdictional confines of the applicable treaty related to the type of protected investments (jurisdiction *ratione materiae*), nationality of the investor (jurisdiction *ratione personae*), and timing of the dispute (jurisdiction *ratione temporis*).

Nationality of Investors

The investment protection regime is based on the principle that merely investors who are nationals of a contracting state can benefit from the guarantees of investment treatment set out in the underlying IIA.[11] Nationality of investors determines their standing as claimants in the arbitral proceedings. If the claims are brought by an investor without the nationality of a state party to the treaty, the tribunal cannot decide on the dispute and must declare that it lacks jurisdiction *ratione personae*.

Procedurally, the burden of proof rests on claimants who must provide evidence that they are nationals of a contracting state to the applicable IIA.[12] Under the basic premise of international law, the inquiry is confined to the domestic laws of each state which retain the sovereign power to decide who acquires their nationality.[13] At the same time, customary international law mandates that the status of a national under the respective domestic laws does not *per se* entitle a person to claim ensuing benefits on the international plane if they do not share a genuine link to the home state.[14] Having 'effective nationality' remains the prerequisite for affording diplomatic protection to both natural and juridical persons.[15] International investment law has, however, notably departed from this traditional mechanism, providing access to arbitration to all claimants who satisfy the definition of a protected investor in the underlying treaty. These treaties thus operate as *lex specialis*.

To delimit jurisdiction *ratione personae*, IIAs have introduced different requirements for a national of a contracting state. The nationality of natural persons is normally defined with a *renvoi* to the domestic laws of the state

---

11 McLachlan, C.; Shore, L. and Weiniger, M., *International Investment Arbitration: Substantive Principles* (2017, Oxford University Press), p. 156.

12 *Perenco Ecuador Ltd. v. Republic of Ecuador and Empresa Estatal Petróleos del Ecuador (Petroecuador)*, ICSID Case No. ARB/08/6, Decision on Jurisdiction (30 June 2011), para. 98; *Emilio Agustín Maffezini v. The Kingdom of Spain*, ICSID Case No. ARB/97/7, Decision on Objections to Jurisdiction (25 Jan. 2000), paras 69-70.

13 Crawford, J., *Brownlie's Principles of Public International Law* (2019, Oxford University Press), p. 495.

14 *Nottebohm Case (second phase)*, Judgment, 6 April 1955, ICJ Reports 1955, p. 23.

15 ILC, *Draft Articles on Diplomatic Protection*, 2006, Arts. 7 and 9.

parties to the treaty. With the exception of dual nationals, objections to the standing of natural persons are rare. Contrarily, the nationality of juridical persons raises more complex questions as IIAs lay down distinct criteria which apply independently or in their combination, namely the place of their incorporation, *siège social* or control over the entity.[16] In support of their claims of nationality in the arbitration, investors typically produce certificates or decisions issued by domestic authorities, validating their status under the applicable laws. Although tribunals tend to accord great weight to the interpretation of domestic law by State officials,[17] these legal opinions do not relieve arbitrators of their duty to determine the existence of their own jurisdiction if the claimant's nationality is challenged in the proceedings. In light of the *Kompetenz-Kompetenz* principle, they are thus empowered, even bound, to decide the issue of the claimant's nationality themselves.[18] Their decision is not binding outside of the specific case.[19]

The tribunals' jurisdiction *ratione personae* is finally affected by a temporal aspect. In a globalised economy, investors' nationality rarely remains static as it can potentially change during the lifecycle of their investment. In this regard, arbitrators have paid substantial attention to possession of the relevant nationality continuously on two dates; the date of the breach of the host state's treaty obligations which form the cause of action in the arbitration and the date of instituting the arbitral proceedings.

---

16 Dolzer, R. and Schreuer, C., *Principles of International Investment Law* (2008, Oxford University Press), pp. 47-52.

17 *Ioan Micula, Viorel Micula, S.C. European Food S.A, S.C. Starmill S.R.L. and S.C. Multipack S.R.L. v. Romania [I]*, ICSID Case No. ARB/05/20, Decision on Jurisdiction and Admissibility (24 Sep. 2008), para. 91; *Waguih Elie George Siag and Clorinda Vecchi v. The Arab Republic of Egypt*, ICSID Case No. ARB/05/15, Decision on Jurisdiction (11 April 2007), paras 144-145; *Hussein Nuaman Soufraki v. The United Arab Emirates*, ICSID Case No. ARB/02/7, Award (7 July 2004), para. 55.

18 Waibel, M., 'Investment Arbitration: Jurisdiction and Admissibility' *Legal Studies Research Paper Series*, Paper No. 9/2014, Feb. 2014, p. 21.

19 *Capital Financial Holdings Luxembourg S.A. v. Republic of Cameroon*, ICSID Case No. ARB/15/18, Award (22 June 2017), para. 82; *Société Civile Immobilière de Gaëta v. Republic of Guinea*, ICSID Case No. ARB/12/36, Award (21 Dec. 2015), para. 135.

20 *Alberto Carrizosa Gelzis, Enrique Carrizosa Gelzis, Felipe Carrizosa Gelzis v. Republic of Colombia*, PCA Case No. 2018-56, Award (7 May 2021), 176; *Sergei Viktorovich Pugachev v. The Russian Federation*, UNCITRAL, Award on Jurisdiction (18 June 2020), para. 437; *Central European Aluminium Company (CEAC) v. Montenegro*, ICSID Case No. ARB/14/8, Award (26 July 2016), para. 146; *Serafín García Armas and Karina García Gruber v. Bolivarian Republic of Venezuela*, PCA Case No. 2013-3, Decision on Jurisdiction (15 Dec. 2014), paras 657-658. Some tribunals have also considered the date of making the investment as the critical date. *See*, e.g., *Cem Cengiz Uzan v. Republic of Turkey*, SCC Case No. V 2014/023, Award (20 April 2016), para. 152.

20 The rationale behind this condition reflects the object and purpose of the investment protection system that seeks to promote economic cooperation and financial flows between individual countries. In the absence of this requirement, investors would be allowed to reorganise their investment and gain thereby access to a more favourable treaty regime even after the dispute has already arisen. Commentators have largely denounced this practice as abusive 'forum shopping'[21] and differentiated it from a legitimate restructuring of an investment which occurs at the time when no controversy between the investor and the host state is foreseeable. Where such actions were undertaken in bad faith, tribunals have found themselves unable to hear the case.[22]

Legal Capacity to Act

Standing of claimants in the arbitral proceedings is further dependent on their capacity to sue in their own name.[23] Generally, the capacity of a juridical person to perform acts and bring an action against another in defence of its own rights is governed by *lex societatis*. Depending on the jurisdiction, the connecting factor can be either the place of incorporation or the seat of the entity.[24] The capacity cannot be, however, expanded by the laws regulating the substantive obligations on which the respective claim is based.[25]

Although the capacity of a legal entity to sue in its own name can be curtailed on distinct statutory grounds, this issue has been discussed only sporadically in investment arbitration. It can arise though in disputes where

---

21 Voon, T., Mitchell, A. and Munro, J., 'Legal Responses to Corporate Manoeuvring in International Investment Arbitration' (2014) 5 *Journal of International Dispute Settlement*, pp. 41-42; Chieh, L., 'Resolving Nationality Planning Issue through the Application of the Doctrine of Piercing the Corporate Veil in International Investment Arbitration' (2016) 9(1) *Contemporary Asia Arbitration Journal*, p. 99; Feldman, M., 'Setting Limits on Corporate Nationality Planning in Investment Treaty Arbitration' (2012) 27(2) *ICSID Review—Foreign Investment Law Journal*, pp. 281-282.

22 *Lao Holdings N.V. v. Lao People's Democratic Republic*, ICSID Case No. ARB(AF)/12/6, Decision on Jurisdiction (21 Feb. 2014), para. 70; *Venezuela Holdings, B.V., et al (case formerly known as Mobil Corporation, Venezuela Holdings, B.V., et al.) v. Bolivarian Republic of Venezuela*, ICSID Case No. ARB/07/27, Decision on Jurisdiction (10 June 2010), paras 204-205; *Phoenix Action, Ltd. v. The Czech Republic*, ICSID Case No. ARB/06/5, Award (15 April 2009), paras 136-140.

23 Douglas, Z., *The International Law of Investment Claims* (2009, Cambridge University Press), p. 312.

24 *Ibid.*, p. 78.

25 Lord Collins of Mapesbury and Harris, J. Dicey, Morris & Collins on the Conflict of Laws (2018, Sweet & Maxwell), p. 1346.

the investment was made by a group of entities of a special corporate form. For instance, in *Impregilo*, the Italian investor attempted to pursue claims under two contracts for the construction of hydroelectric power facilities governed by the law of Pakistan on behalf of a joint venture organised in accordance with the law of Switzerland in which it participated.[26] Upon examining the nature of the joint venture, the tribunal pointed to the fact that the entity was a mere contractual partnership of four corporations which lacked a distinct legal personality both under the law of Switzerland as the *lex societatis* and the law of Pakistan as the *lex causae*.[27] Since the joint venture did not qualify as a 'juridical person' for the purposes of Article 25 of the ICSID Convention, the tribunal declined jurisdiction over its claims, adding that the limited legal capacity to sue another could not be bypassed by one of the joint venture members bringing the claims on its own behalf because the investment losses were sustained by the grouping as a whole.[28]

The Authority to Represent Claimant in the Arbitral Proceedings

Upon the declaration of insolvency, national jurisdictions differ as to the repercussions on the ability of insolvent juridical persons to manage their daily business operations, administer and dispose of their assets, or enforce their pecuniary claims. The scope of the powers of appointed insolvency administrators must be carefully evaluated with respect to not only the debtor's substantive rights, but also their procedural standing. The cases where the insolvency proceeds simultaneously with the arbitral proceedings, tribunals need to carefully consider also the investors' capacity to pursue legal actions in their own name, their right to appear as a party in the proceedings or authority to reach an out-of-court settlement.[29]

In practice, arbitrators have usually resorted first to the domestic laws governing the insolvency proceedings against the claimants as the primary

26 *Impregilo S.p.A. v. Islamic Republic of Pakistan*, ICSID Case No. ARB/03/3, Decision on Jurisdiction (22 April 2005), paras 13, 15-18.
27 *Ibid.*, paras 115-120.
28 *Ibid.*, paras 135-139.
29 One of the most recent initiatives mapping the distinct regulations across national jurisdictions has been launched under the auspices of the International Bar Association. *See* IBA Arbitration Committee, 'IBA Toolkit on Insolvency and Arbitration', *International Bar Association* (2021), especially paras 95-100, 105-112, 119-122.

reference point. In investment disputes, this should not be though the end of their inquiry, particularly in cases where the host state would be able to frustrate the claimant's participation in the arbitral proceedings by depriving it of its capacity to represent itself before the tribunal or select a counsel to act on its behalf. First, by virtue of a contractual relationship with the investor, the host state might be a creditor of the claimant, thus enjoying the right to initiate the opening of the insolvency proceedings against the investor and, once it is declared insolvent, attend the creditors' meeting and vote on any proposals related to the management of the estate, including the replacement of the insolvency administrator. In the absence of such liabilities, the host state could seek to impair the investor's case informally by pressuring the administrator to revoke a power of attorney granted to the claimant's counsels or withdraw an investment claim. This risk arguably increases when the respective investment, forming the subject matter of the dispute, was made through a subsidiary incorporated in the host state. In the event of its insolvency, the entity's administration would be, in turn, governed by the host state's laws and supervised by its courts.

As the following decisions illustrate, tribunals have appreciated the variety of scenarios of possible interferences with the claimant's capacity to appear in the arbitration and have a legal representation of its choice. There are, however, notable differences in the manner as to how they approached the issue of governing law to preserve both parties' due process rights.

Lex Societatis as the Governing Law

In most cases, the issue of the claimants' representation in the arbitral proceedings has been resolved in favour of *lex societatis* as the law governing the insolvency proceedings. This approach is consonant with the scope of IIAs that determine the characteristics of a qualified investor to benefit from the treaty protection but do not define the rules on the capacity of the investors to sue. The tribunals have acknowledged this limitation, noting that their jurisdiction is a matter of public international law and as such is regulated by international legal instruments whereas the capacity to appear in the arbitration and appoint a counsel is a matter of domestic law.

If the claimant was not incorporated under the laws of the host state and *lex societatis* was distinct from the rules defined by the respondent in the arbitration, the identification of the relevant domestic law would be the sole concern for the arbitrators. The lack of further inquiry reflected the fact that the claimants were not subject to the sovereign powers of the host state's authorities. There was thus no sign of a risk of the host state's interference into the insolvency proceedings against the claimant.[30] For instance, in *Teinver*, the tribunal did not consult the ICSID Convention and Arbitration Rules and reverted only to the Spanish Bankruptcy Act to determine the validity of a power of attorney granted to a counsel by the claimants' board of directors prior to their request for a voluntary re-organisation. Argentina objected that, upon declaring the claimants' insolvency, the original power of attorney extinguished and could be renewed only by a dated notification of the administrators in the form of a notarial deed based on a prior authorisation by the supervisory court.[31] As the court-appointed re-organisation administrators confirmed the effect of the procuration and ratified the counsels' actions,[32] the arbitrators agreed to dismiss Argentina's objection in its entirety, noting that it not only ran against the provisions of the Spanish Bankruptcy Act but was also delayed a number of years after the commencement of the re-organisations to the extent that the declaration of invalidity in accordance with Spanish law for any formal errors would be completely misplaced.[33]

Public International Law as the Governing Law

A different path was, in contrast, followed by the ad hoc Committee in the ICSID annulment proceedings in *Carnegie Minerals*. The application was

30 *See Teinver S.A., Transportes de Cercanías S.A. and Autobuses Urbanos del Sur S.A. v. The Argentine Republic* (ICSID Case No. ARB/09/1) and *Muhammet ap & Bankrupt Sehil Inçaat Endustri ve Ticaret Ltd. Sti. v. Turkmenistan* (ICSID Case No. ARB/12/6). Recently, the Tribunal in *PNB Banka v. Latvia* has also acknowledged the authority of a Latvian insolvency administrator to represent one of the Claimants in the arbitration following the opening of the insolvency proceedings despite the Claimant's objection regarding the administrator's conflict of interests. According to the public reports, this decision was made on a preliminary basis solely for the purposes of completing the submissions on the bifurcated issue while the parties were invited to present arguments on the Claimant's representation. *See* Bohmer, L. 'Analysis: Tribunal's Decision that a State-Appointed Insolvency Administrator Should Represent *PNB Banka* in ICSID Arbitration Prompts DQ Bid' *IA Reporter*, 26 Feb. 2020, available at: <https://www.iareporter.com/articles/revealed-tribunals-decision-that-a-state-appointed-insolvency-administrator-should-represent-pnb-banka-in-icsid-arbitration-prompts-challenge-to-all-three-tribunal-members/>.

31 *Teinver S.A., Transportes de Cercanías S.A. and Autobuses Urbanos del Sur S.A. v. The Argentine Republic*, ICSID Case No. ARB/09/1, Award (21 July 2017), paras 217 and 220.

32 *Ibid.*, paras 203-205, 214-215, 218-221 and 223.

33 *Ibid.*, paras 222-223.

filed by the claimant in the original proceedings who had fallen in liquidation by order of the High Court of Gambia four months before the commencement of the annulment case.

Shortly after the registration of the annulment application, Gambia requested Carnegie, a Gambian entity owned by an Australian corporate group, to provide the power of attorney authorising its counsel to represent it in the arbitration, considering that the powers to act for the insolvent company and contract on its behalf were vested with the liquidator.[34] Affirming its powers to decide the matter under Article 41 of the ICSID Convention,[35] the ad hoc Committee first turned to Rule 18 of the ICSID Arbitration Rules, which it interpreted as giving the parties an exclusive right to grant authority to legal counsel in the arbitration.[36] In the absence of any reference to the domestic law, the committee agreed with Carnegie that the question of legal representation of parties in ICSID proceedings falls within the ambit of the ICSID Convention, just like the question of who is a party to such proceedings in the first place.[37] In the committee's view, it would be absurd if an investor who is deemed a 'national of another contracting State' based on the agreement of the parties within the meaning of Article 25(2)(b) of the ICSID Convention was suddenly deprived of its right to choose its legal counsel because its representation in the arbitration would be effectively determined by the respondent state that had the power to appoint the company's liquidator in the first place.[38]

In its reasoning, the committee in *Carnegie Minerals* has indirectly touched the critical conflict between the policy concerns of insolvency law, seeking to maximise the pool of assets through centralised administration of the insolvent company by a certified professional, and the ability of the respondent state to potentially prevent investors from resorting to arbitration or interfere in the proceedings by controlling their legal representation. Although it arguably reached the appropriate conclusions, they seem to have relied on an overstretched interpretation of Rule 18 of the ICSID Arbitration Rules that merely speaks about the right of parties to be

34 *Carnegie Minerals (Gambia) Limited v. Republic of The Gambia* (ICSID Case No. ARB/09/19), Decision on Representation (7 Oct. 2016) ("Carnegie Decision"), paras 9 and 37.

35 Article 41 of the ICSID Convention reads: '(1) The Tribunal shall be the judge of its own competence. (2) Any objection by a party to the dispute that that dispute is not within the jurisdiction of the Centre, or for other reasons is not within the competence of the Tribunal, shall be considered by the Tribunal which shall determine whether to deal with it as a preliminary question or to join it to the merits of the dispute.'

36 Carnegie Decision, para. 41.

37 *Ibid.*, para. 43.

38 *Ibid.*, para. 44.

'represented or assisted' by counsel in the arbitration, not the right to choose them in disregard of any statutory limitations on the parties' legal capacity under *lex societatis*. The committee's reluctance to apply Gambian law is, furthermore, inconsistent with the role ascribed to it in determining Carnegie's nationality based on the place of its incorporation which would effectively prevent it from filing a claim against Gambia had it not been for the parties' agreement to treat the claimant as a foreign national in accordance with Article 25(2)(b) of the ICSID Convention. As the ICSID legal framework does not contain any rules on the terms of nationality or a person's capacity to act in law, it is difficult to understand why the tribunal pursued distinct legal routes without any detailed reasoning. Instead of expanding the scope of Rule 18 of the ICSID Arbitration Rules far beyond its letter, the arbitrators could have arguably invoked other legal safeguards against the risk of an abuse of power by the respondent state.

The Third Way?

A more nuanced reasoning, albeit with an identical result, was reportedly adopted by the tribunal in *BRIF* arbitration instituted by two Luxembourg-based companies against Serbia in April 2020. This arbitration followed a dispute related to the ownership of real estate plots in Belgrade, also allegedly involving accusations of an abuse of powers by Serbian officials.[39] Less than a year after the commencement of the arbitration, the claimants filed a series of urgent requests for temporary restraining orders in relation to the domestic proceedings against BRIF-TC, one of the claimants in the arbitration, initiated based on bankruptcy claims of the City of Belgrade and the Belgrade Land Development Public Agency.[40] Following the subsequent opening of the bankruptcy proceedings against BRIF-TC, the tribunal was required to consider its effects on the investor's legal representation in the arbitration.

---

39 Bohmer, L., 'Luxembourg-Based Investment Funds Initiate Treaty-Based Arbitration Against Serbia' *IA Reporter*, 27 April 2020, available at: <https://www.iareporter.com/articles/luxembourg-based-investment-funds-initiate-treaty-based-arbitration-against-serbia/>.

40 Charlotin, D., 'Revealed: Tribunal Decides that Appointment of Bankruptcy Administrator for Claimant Has No Impact on the Investor's Representation in ICSID Proceedings' *IA Reporter*, 10 Aug. 2021, available at: <https://www.iareporter.com/articles/revealed-icsid-tribunal-decides-that-appointment-of-bankruptcy-administrator-for-claimant-has-no-impact-on-the-investors-representation-in-icsid-proceedings/>.

Unlike their predecessors, the arbitrators agreed with Serbia that party representation in the arbitral proceedings was regulated by Serbian law as *lex societatis* of the claimants.[41] Their analysis, however, went further as they noted that any changes in the administration of the investor's business, resulting from its insolvency, could not influence the issue of party representation, which was frozen together with the foreign control over the company at the date of consent to arbitration by virtue of Article 25(2)(b) of the ICSID Convention.[42] As it seems, the tribunal attempted to balance the interests of both mechanisms. It is worth noting, however, that its reasoning was based on a questionable presumption that allowing the insolvency administrator to represent the insolvent investor in the arbitration would also amount to the shift in control over the investor for jurisdictional purposes. The following section shows that the dilemma of administrator acting as the principal or agent has been so far resolved contrary to such tribunal's proposition.

Principals Versus Agents

Considering the arbitral practice, the effects of an investor being placed under insolvency administration can materialise at all stages of the arbitration. While the claimant's insolvency might potentially strengthen its arguments on damages, some respondent states have suggested that it could equally prevent tribunals from exercising jurisdiction over a dispute. In their view, the critical factor is related to a preliminary issue as to who enjoys control over the claimant's operations. Since the criterion of control affects the nationality of legal entities in many IIAs, the statutory powers of the administrator to act on the claimant's behalf can also raise doubts regarding their qualification as a protected investor in accordance with the treaty terms.

The success of such jurisdictional objections depends on the time of opening of the insolvency proceedings. If administrators join the arbitration on behalf of the claimants that is already pending, they resume the power to represent the investor before a tribunal in conformity with *lex societatis* but their nationality remains irrelevant for the claimants' standing. This is a direct consequence of the rule that the tribunals' jurisdiction *ratione personae* is frozen at the date of parties' consent to arbitration.[43]

41 *Ibid.*
42 *Ibid.*
43 Douglas (n 16), para. 543.

Any later changes in the nationality of the investor fall outside the tribunals' review. In contrast, the most delicate period when the investor can enter insolvency is perhaps related to the commencement of the arbitration as the proceedings would have to be instituted by the insolvency administrator alone on the investor's behalf. Tribunals have repeatedly made clear that the administrators do not bring investment claims in their own name but as investors' agents. As a result, they concluded that the claimants' standing should be assessed separately from the nationality of their administrators.

Walter Bau v. Germany

The standing of an insolvency administrator is not expected to give rise to objections by the respondent state when their nationality is identical to the nationality of the insolvent investor. This outcome was confirmed by the approach of Thailand in the United Nations Commission on International Trade Law (UNCITRAL) arbitration initiated by a joint-stock company incorporated in Germany under the 2002 Germany-Thailand BIT. The dispute arose out of an investment into a joint venture to construct and operate a toll way from Bangkok to the Dong Muang airport which was thwarted following a series of steps by Thai authorities that refused to authorise the increase of toll rates and made improvements to the existing free highways, thus depriving the project of its profitability.[44]

In September 2005, the claimant filed a request for arbitration, alleging expropriation of its investment and violation of the fair and equitable treatment. Due to its insolvency, its claims were brought on its behalf by an insolvency administrator, an individual of German nationality.[45] The liquidation of the claimant went completely unnoticed for the purposes of the tribunal's jurisdiction. Thailand, however, filed an unsuccessful application for security for costs incurred in relation to the arbitration.[46]

The lack of any challenge to the claimant's standing at the jurisdictional stage is hardly surprising. First, the insolvency did not affect claimant's compliance with the expansive definition of an 'investor' in the BIT which refers, in respect of the Federal Republic of Germany, to any

44 *Werner Schneider, acting in his capacity as insolvency administrator of Walter Bau Ag (In Liquidation) v. Kingdom of Thailand*, UNCITRAL (formerly *Walter Bau AG (in liquidation) v. Kingdom of Thailand*), UNCITRAL, Partial Award on Jurisdiction (5 Oct. 2007), paras 1.48-1.59.

45 *Ibid.*, paras 1.6-1.8.

46 *Ibid.*, paras 1.27, 1.30.

> legal entities, including companies, corporations, business associations and other organizations, with or without legal personality, which are constituted or otherwise duly organized under the law of that Contracting Party and have their seat in the territory of that Contracting Party.[47]

Second, while the tribunal did not expressly comment on his role, the insolvency administrator was evidently understood as the claimant's agent enforcing its rights in the arbitration. This approach is consistent with the terms of the German Insolvency Code as the applicable law, designating administrators as the general representatives of insolvent companies who assume their authority to be a party to and conduct judicial or arbitral proceedings ex officio.[48] By virtue of its insolvency, Walter Bau thus lost the right to seek damages in the arbitration in its own name. It is of note that this limitation was reflected in neither the title of the case nor the definition of the claimant.[49]

Dirk Herzig as Insolvency Administrator over Assets of Unionmatex v. Turkmenistan

The insolvency of a German investor came up once again in the pending ICSID arbitration between Turkmenistan and a German limited liability corporation under the 1997 German-Turkmenistan BIT.[50] According to the publicly available reports, the dispute stems from a series of contracts

---

47 Treaty between the Kingdom of Thailand and the Federal Republic of Germany concerning the Encouragement and Reciprocal Protection of Investments, signed on 24 June 2002, entered into force on 20 Oct. 2004, Art. 1(3).

48 Insolvency Statute of 5 Oct. 1994 (Federal Law Gazette I page 2866), as last amended by Article 19 of the Act of 20 Dec. 2011 (Federal Law Gazette I page 2854), s. 80; Wagner, P. and Kramer, C., 'IBA Toolkit on Insolvency and Arbitration: National Report of Germany' *International Bar Association*, Jan. 2021, paras 65, 67.

49 This deficiency was avoided in *Inmaris Perestroika Sailing Maritime Services GmbH and Others v. Ukraine* (ICSID Case No. ARB/08/8) instituted by a group of four German companies against Ukraine under the 1993 Germany-Ukraine BIT, two of which were formally represented by a German insolvency administrator following their insolvency caused by the travel ban imposed by the Ukrainian authorities. The representation by the insolvency administrator did not raise any controversies at the jurisdictional stage because Ukraine presented objections only to the definition of a protected investment under the BIT and the ICSID Convention. *See Inmaris Perestroika Sailing Maritime Services GmbH and Others v. Ukraine*, ICSID Case No. ARB/08/8, Decision on Jurisdiction (8 March 2010), paras 31 and 60.

50 The case has earned reputation for the Tribunal's ruling ordering the insolvency administrator to post security for costs in light of Unionmatex's insolvency and the presence of a third-party funder. See *Dirk Herzig as Insolvency Administrator over the*

worth more than EUR 140 million concluded by Unionmatex and Turkmengallonumleri Cereals Products Association for the construction of a grain storage with processing facilities and two adjacent bakeries and cafes.[51] The project was supposed to be completed in 2011 but it foundered as the Turkmen authorities allegedly caused delays, failed to provide utility services to the building sites and pressured Unionmatex to renounce its claims for unpaid invoices.[52] Consequently, the investor has ceased its operations and fallen into insolvency under the supervision by a German insolvency administrator who instituted the arbitral proceedings.

Although the arbitration is still at the stage of a written procedure, it is clear from the public records that the insolvency administrator is facing an objection to its standing as the claimant under the applicable BIT based on the principles of beneficial ownership.[53] Without a full access to the parties' written submissions, one can assume that Turkmenistan challenges the link between the investment and the administrator who is not its legal owner but merely takes care of the investor's assets in accordance with the provisions of the German Insolvency Code on its behalf. Turkmenistan's pleading is reportedly inspired by the reasoning in *Blue Bank* where the tribunal declared that it did not have jurisdiction over a dispute between a Barbados-based trustee for the Qatar-Trust and Venezuela regarding an alleged expropriation of a stake in a 30-year concession redeveloping and operating the historic Humboldt Hotel and cable car in Avila mountain range close to the capital.[54] The trustee as the claimant in this case was found to lack any ownership title to the assets forming the protected investment, enjoying solely the power to manage and dispose of the trust estate in conformity with their statutory obligations under the

---

Assets of Unionmatex Industrieanlagen GmbH v. Turkmenistan, ICSID Case No. ARB/18/35, Decision on Security for Costs (27 Jan. 2020).

51 Peterson, L. E. and Williams Z., 'Turkmenistan Update: Award Rendered in Garanti Koza's BIT Arbitration; German Investor Files a Notice of Dispute' *IA Reporter*, 21 Dec. 2016, available at: <https://www.iareporter.com/articles/turkmenistan-update-award-rendered-in-garanti-kozas-bit-arbitration-german-investor-files-a-notice-of-dispute/>.

52 *Ibid.*

53 Bohmer, L., 'ICSID Tribunal Declines Request for Early Resolution of Bankruptcy-Related Claims; Turkmenistan's Jurisdictional Objections Are Also Joined to the Merits' *IA Reporter*, 7 May 2021, available at: <https://www.iareporter.com/articles/icsid-tribunal-declines-request-for-early-resolution-of-bankruptcy-related-claims-turkmenistans-jurisdictional-objections-are-also-joined-to-the-merits/>.

54 *Blue Bank International & Trust (Barbados) Ltd. v. Bolivarian Republic of Venezuela*, ICSID Case No. ARB 12/20, Award, 26 April 2017, para. 215. The application for annulment of the award filed by Blue Bank was dismissed in its entirety.

Barbados International Trusts Act.[55] The sui generis relationship was cited to be contrary to the terms of the 1994 Barbados-Venezuela BIT that conditioned the tribunal's jurisdiction *ratione personae* on the claimant having made an investment.[56] A similar requirement could be likely sought to be derived from the Germany-Turkmenistan BIT which otherwise adopts a broad formulation of a 'national' such as the Germany-Thailand BIT cited earlier,[57] and both Unionmatex and its insolvency administrator could arguably fit in the scope of the definition at first sight. Following the dismissal of the second application for bifurcation filed by Turkmenistan due to the advanced stage of the proceedings,[58] it remains to be seen how the tribunal reconciles the treaty terms with the administrator's powers under the German Insolvency Code.

Eskosol v. Italy

In comparison to the prior cases, treaty claims invoked by insolvency administrators holding a different nationality, than that of an insolvent investor, provided for more legal controversies. As follows from the ICSID arbitration instituted in December 2015 by an Italian joint stock company against Italy under the ECT, this assumption applies with even greater force when the claimant investor shares the nationality of the respondent state.

The proceedings concerned a €38.5 million investment into a 120 MW solar power plant project in Italy, made by a locally incorporated entity, owned by four Italian nationals and a Belgian company Blusun, holding 80% of its shares, in reliance on a feed-in tariffs regime fixed for the duration of 20 years.[59] In March 2011, Italy altered its regulatory framework, when it introduced the so-called Romani Decree, specifying that the existing tariff scheme would apply only to solar plants that entered into operation within two months of the decree's publication, following which only reduced feed-in tariffs would be granted.[60] As a result of these

55 *Ibid.*, paras 160-173.

56 *See* Agreement between the Government of Barbados and the Government of the Republic of Venezuela for the Promotion and Protection of Investments, signed on 15 July 1994, entered into force on 31 Oct. 1995, Art. 8(1).

57 *See* Section 3.1.

58 Bohmer (n 43).

59 *Eskosol S.p.A. in liquidazione v. Italian Republic*, ICSID Case No. ARB/15/50, Decision on Respondent's Application under Rule 41(5) (20 March 2017) ("Eskosol Decision under Rule 41(5)"), paras 20-24.

60 *Ibid.*, paras 25-26.

measures, the investor alleged to have been forced to abandon the project as not economically viable. Due to the inability to pay off its liabilities, the entity was declared insolvent in November 2013 and placed under receivership in accordance with Italian law.[61]

In the arbitration, Italy argued that Eskosol lacked standing to file claims under Article 25(2)(b) of the ICSID Convention[62] because it was controlled by an Italian bankruptcy receiver on the date of the commencement of the proceedings and, thus, did not satisfy the requirement of foreign control[63] within the meaning of Article 26(7) of the ECT.[64] In contrast, Eskosol opposed Italy's reliance on the date of consent to the arbitration, arguing instead that the date of the emergence of the dispute was decisive under the ECT, at which time its foreign control by a Belgian company was undisputed.[65] Apart from that, Eskosol argued that the mere fact of entering into bankruptcy could not affect existence of that control, because otherwise Italy would be able to prevent any ICSID arbitration by bankrupting every would-be claimant.[66]

The tribunal addressed this jurisdictional objection at two stages. In its Decision on Rule 41(5) Objection,[67] it first recalled the terms of Article 25(2)(b) of the ICSID Convention, noting that it included two elements: first, the subjective agreement of the parties to treat the investor as foreign despite it having the host state's nationality on the date of consent to arbitration, and second, the objective existence of foreign control.[68]

The arbitrators had no concern finding that Article 26(7) of the ECT constituted such agreement, and that its terms were satisfied as Eskosol

---

61 *Ibid.*, para. 27.

62 Art. 25(2)(b) of the ICSID Convention provides an alternative definition of a 'national of another Contracting State' for juridical persons which includes legal entities with the nationality of a State party to the ICSID Convention distinct from the respondent State or with 'the nationality of the Contracting State party to the dispute on that date and which, because of foreign control, the parties have agreed should be treated as a national of another Contracting State for the purposes of this Convention'.

63 Eskosol Decision under Rule 41(5), paras 52-61.

64 Art. 26(7) of the ECT clarifies that for the purposes of Art. 25(2)(b) of the ICSID Convention, a juridical person which holds the nationality of the respondent State qualifies as a 'national of another Contracting State' provided that 'before a dispute between it and that Contracting Party arises, [it] is controlled by Investors of another Contracting Party'.

65 Eskosol Decision under Rule 41(5), paras 76-77.

66 *Ibid.*, paras 71-74.

67 Rule 41(5) of the ICSID Arbitration Rules entitles parties to the arbitration to seek a dismissal of claims based on an objection that they are manifestly without legal merit. This objection must be raised no later than 30 days following the constitution of the tribunal and, in any event, before its first session.

68 *Ibid.*, para. 85.

was incorporated in Italy and was under foreign control before the dispute arose.[69] As to the objective requirement, the tribunal pointed out that the ICSID Convention was silent on whether the foreign control over the claimant had to continue until the date of the commencement of the arbitration as Italy advocated.[70] While literal textual interpretation would suggest otherwise, the arbitrators referred to other provisions of the ICSID Convention as the context[71] where the date of consent was by contrast relevant.[72] In light of the potentially serious doctrinal ramifications for future cases, the tribunal ultimately refused to make a final say on this 'novel and complex' issue in summary dismissal proceedings.[73]

Before closing the discussion on the critical date, the tribunal, however, admitted that the outcome would be only relevant if Eskosol's bankruptcy had overridden the foreign control by its 80% Belgian shareholder. It thus reverted to the provisions of the ECT and its definition of 'control' in the joint understanding listing non-exhaustively various financial and structural factors.[74] It observed that Italy did not provide any support for its assertion that Eskosol's insolvency alone displaced whatever control that previously existed, except for a reference to its bankruptcy law.[75] For the tribunal, the foreign control under the ICSID Convention was, nevertheless, a question of international law, not domestic law, and it would run contrary to the purpose of the treaty if a possibly temporary bankruptcy, which could have been caused by the respondent state's actions, deprived the investor of an access to ICSID.[76]

While the arbitrators agreed to revisit these findings in the full proceedings, the award largely followed the teleological interpretation of the

69 *Ibid.*, paras 87-88.
70 *Ibid.*, para. 91.
71 *Ibid.*, paras 92-95.
72 *See*, e.g., Art. 26 of the ICSID Convention where the date of consent is critical for precluding resort to any other remedy in parallel to the arbitration.
73 Eskosol Decision under Rule 41(5), paras 98-99.
74 Final Act of the European Energy Charter Conference, Understanding with respect to Art. 1(6). The Understanding stresses the need to examine the particular circumstances in each situation, especially the following factors: '(a) financial interest, including equity interest, in the Investment; (b) ability to exercise substantial in influence over the management and operation of the Investment; and (c) ability to exercise substantial influence over the selection of members of the board of directors or any other managing body'.
75 Eskosol Decision under Rule 41(5), paras 104-106.
76 *Ibid.*, paras 106-107.

treaties.[77] The tribunal again ascribed great weigh to the effects of potentially abusive bankruptcy but corroborated its ruling with a further inquiry into the powers of bankruptcy receivers under Italian law. It admitted that a receiver temporarily exercises influence over the company's assets under the supervision of a bankruptcy court,[78] but they do not do so on their own behalf, acting rather as a 'trustee or agent' for persons having an interest in the insolvent company who retain residual control even after the opening of the receivership procedure.[79] Resolving the conundrum of the receiver's status in the arbitration, the tribunal thus concluded that his nationality was not determinative for Eskosol's standing in the arbitration.

Safeguards Against the Abuse of Insolvency Proceedings

The comments of tribunals, which had to address the interplay between arbitration and insolvency, reveal that arbitrators expressed great concern regarding the possible abuse of powers by respondent states which could seek to derail the arbitral proceedings, stripping investors of their capacity to pursue their claims and ability to duly present their case before a tribunal. This risk not only can materialise when the state is in the position of the claimant's creditor, thus being entitled to file for its insolvency proceedings but also has been repeatedly cited in cases when the claimant's insolvency was governed by *lex societatis* of the host state, and the insolvent investor, in turn, fell under the administration by a host state's national. Ironically, the observation can be contrasted with the prevailing view that, except for insolvency courts,[80] actions of insolvency administrators are generally not attributable to a state because they are statutorily obliged to represent insolvent debtors in an independent and impartial manner.[81] Tribunals can, nevertheless, derive the state's responsibility

77 *Eskosol S.p.A. in liquidazione v. Italian Republic*, ICSID Case No. ARB/15/50, Award (4 Sep. 2020) ("Eskosol Award"), paras 236-237.

78 Upon the publication of the bankruptcy decree, the bankrupt entity is deprived of its right to administer and dispose of all assets in its possession and loses its standing in the civil proceedings related to the rights in the bankruptcy estate. *See* Italy's Royal Decree No. 267 of 16 March 1942, as amended, Arts. 42-43.

79 Eskosol Award, paras 234-235.

80 *Georg Gavrilovic and Gavrilovic d.o.o. v. Republic of Croatia*, ICSID Case No. ARB/12/39, Award (25 July 2018), paras 796-803.

81 *Plama Consortium Limited v. Republic of Bulgaria*, ICSID Case No. ARB/03/24, Award (27Aug. 2008) para. 253; Peter Franz Vocklinghaus v. Czech Republic, UNCITRAL, Final Award (19 Sep. 2011), paras 188-189; *Jan Oostergetel and Theodora*

either for the excess of powers by a state official unlawfully interfering in the claimant's insolvency in accordance with Article 7 of the ILC Articles, or, where the investor provides evidence of the state's instructions, directions or control, indirectly by attributing the actions of the insolvency administrator to the state under Article 8 of the ILC Articles.[82]

The question remains whether in such situations, insolvent investors have any legal tools at their disposal to defend themselves against the state's actions. The first option is the filing of an application for provisional measures in the form of a non-aggravation order, which can adapt to a variety of interferences. For instance, in *Muhammet Cap & Sehil*, the interim relief request against Turkmenistan followed the opening of bankruptcy proceedings against the Turkish-based corporate claimant during the ICSID arbitration.[83] In accordance with Turkish law, Sehil's creditors were invited to register their pecuniary claims against the company. In 2017, Turkmenistan submitted to Turkish courts its petition, seeking to enforce a claim overlapping with its counterclaim in the arbitration.[84] By joining the insolvency proceedings, Turkmenistan was arguably feared to have the opportunity to access some of the confidential Sehil's records related to the arbitration and through its participation in the board of creditors subsequently influence Sehil's management of the proceedings. For these reasons, the tribunal ordered Turkmen authorities to inform Turkish courts about the pendency of the ICSID case and refrain from intervening into Sehil's legal representation.[85]

A similar course of action prompted two urgent requests for restraining orders against Serbia in *BRIF* when one of the claimants was summoned to a hearing based on insolvency claims filed by the City of Belgrade and the

---

Laurentius v. Slovak Republic, UNCITRAL, Award (23 April 2012), para. 157; *Yukos Universal Limited (Isle of Man) v. The Russian Federation*, UNCITRAL, PCA Case No. 2005-04/AA227, Final Award (18 July 2014), para. 1480; *MNSS B.V. and Recupero Credito Acciaio N.V. v. Montenegro*, ICSID Case No. ARB(AF)/12/8, Award (4 May 2016), paras 313-316.

82 ILC, *Draft Articles on Diplomatic Protection*, 2006, Arts. 7 and 8.

83 Bohmer, L., 'Analysis: Arbitrators Hearing Large-Scale Construction Dispute Decline to Broaden Their Jurisdiction Beyond Expropriation Claim, and Dismiss the Case on Merits' *IA Reporter*, 12 May 2021, available at: <https://www.iareporter.com/articles/analysis-arbitrators-hearing-large-scale-construction-dispute-see-no-evidence-that-claims-were-assigned-to-third-party-funder-decline-to-broaden-their-jurisdiction-beyond-expropriation-claim-and-di/>.

84 *Ibid.*

85 *Ibid.*

Belgrade Land Development Public Agency.[86] The claimant first attempted to suspend the domestic proceedings or, in the alternative, postpone the hearing, criticising the short notice it had received to appear before Serbian courts.[87] While the tribunal refused to interfere with the insolvency procedure, it sided with the claimant that, through its instrumentalities, Serbia could aggravate the dispute submitted to the arbitration.[88] It concluded that Serbian authorities should refrain from adopting any measures related to the claimant's insolvency that would undermine the ICSID proceedings.[89]

Although provisional measures are apt to swiftly react to potentially harmful actions of the respondent state, their necessity and urgency are notoriously difficult to prove. Tribunals have refused to grant them lightly,[90] paying special attention to the balance of interests of both parties to the arbitration.[91] Furthermore, the ICSID Convention does not establish any formal mechanism for the enforcement of provisional measures orders, and their violation can be penalised merely by drawing adverse inferences on certain points in the dispute[92] or imposing costs of arbitration on the disobedient party.[93] In ad hoc arbitrations governed by the UNCITRAL Arbitration Rules, some decisions on provisional measures in the form of partial awards can be hypothetically enforced under the New York Convention[94] while the enforceability of others will depend on the

86 Charlotin (n 30).

87 *Ibid.*

88 *Ibid.*

89 *Ibid.*

90 *Maffezini v. The Kingdom of Spain,* ICSID Case No. ARB/97/7, Procedural Order No. 2 (28 Oct. 1999), para. 10; *Plama Consortium Limited v. Republic of Bulgaria*, ICSID Case No. ARB/03/24, Order (6 Sep. 2005), para. 38; *Phoenix Action, Ltd. v. The Czech Republic*, ICSID Case No. ARB/06/5, Decision on Provisional Measures (6 April 2007) para 33.

91 *See*, e.g., *Gerald International Limited v. Republic of Sierra Leone*, ICSID Case No. ARB/19/31/, Procedural Order No. 2 (28 July 2020), para. 182; *Hydro S.r.l. and others v. Republic of Albania*, ICSID Case No. ARB/15/28, Order on Provisional Measures (3 March 2016), para. 3.37; *Nova Group Investments, B.V. v. Romania*, ICSID Case No. ARB/16/19, Procedural Order No. 7 (29 March 2017), para. 250.

92 *AGIP SpA v. People's Republic of the Congo* (1979) 1 ICSID Reports 306, 317; *Yaung Chi Oo Trading Pte Ltd v. Myanmar* (2002) 8 ICSID Reports 456, 461.

93 *Maritime International Nominees Establishment v. Guinea* (1988) 4 ICSID Reports 3, 69, 77.

94 Convention on the Recognition and Enforcement of Foreign Arbitral Awards, signed on 10 June 1958, entered into force on 7 June 1959, Art. III. The provision requires each contracting State to 'recognize arbitral awards as binding and enforce them,' without specifying the nature of the award. Cf. Veeder, V. V. 'Provisional and Conservatory

legislation in the respective jurisdiction.[95] In the light of these shortcomings, arbitrators may rather prefer using their inherent powers to preserve the parties' equality of arms and address the conflict of interests of the respondent state related to the investor's insolvency through the abuse of rights doctrine, or more broadly, the principle of good faith and the maxim that no party should be permitted to benefit from its own wrong. Since such rules are common to many national legal systems[96] and have been equally recognised by the International Court of Justice,[97] they may be invoked by tribunals as general principles of law, irrespective of the seat of arbitration or the applicable law. Given their purpose of looking beyond the black letter law, they are perfectly suited also in scenarios when the respondent state would engage in tactics that formally does not violate any hard rule but is, nevertheless, illegitimate for its negative effects on the due process rights of the parties in the arbitration. From a practical perspective, the claimants may struggle in discharging its burden of proof as the threshold to find an abuse of rights or bad faith is generally high. Owing to their duty to guarantee fairness of the proceedings, tribunals alone should be more attentive to any signs of intrusions into the administration of insolvent claimants and examine in detail the specifics of insolvency legislation in the relevant jurisdictions to assess their impact on the arbitral proceedings.

Conclusion

Insolvency brings new complexities in the assessment of claimants' standing to pursue their investment claims. Depending on the applicable insolvency law, arbitrators must carefully examine to what extent an insolvency procedure affects investors' capacity to enforce their rights in their own name and represent themselves in the proceedings. As the above discussed

Measures in Enforcing Arbitration Awards Under The New York Convention: Experience and Prospects', UN Publication Sales No. E.99.V.2, A/CN.9(063)/A664 (1999, United Nations), p. 21.

95 Castello, J. E. and Chahine, R. 'Enforcement of Interim Measures' In: Gaillard, E.; Kaiser, G. E. and Siino, B. (eds.), *The Guide to Challenging and Enforcing Arbitral Awards* (2021, Law Business Research), p. 112.

96 Gaillard, E. 'Abuse of Process in International Arbitration' (2017) 32(1) *ICSID Review—Foreign Investment Law Journal*, pp. 32-33.

97 *See*, e.g., *Fisheries Case (United Kingdom v. Norway)* [1951] ICJ Rep 3; *Case of Certain Norwegian Loans (France v. Norway)* [1957] ICJ Rep 9; *Nottebohm Case (Liechtenstein v. Guatemala)* [1955] ICJ Rep 1; *Gabčikovo-Nagymaros Project (Hungary v. Slovakia)* [1997] ICJ Rep 7.

case law shows, tribunals have been reluctant to limit their review to domestic insolvency rules only but paid due regard to the possible conflict of interests on the part of host states. In their view, the investment protection regime would become largely ineffective if host states could point to investors' insolvency, which they might have even caused, to deprive them of their right to access international arbitration and avoid the legal consequences of their own unlawful conduct. To resolve this conflict, tribunals have adopted distinct legal approaches. Although it may be too soon to draw any conclusions, the general legal principle that no one should take advantage of their own wrong seems to provide a useful guidance in such situations.

On (Non) Binding Nature of Pre-insolvency Arbitration Agreements When Avoiding an Underlying Transaction, Executory Contracts, and Anti-suit Injunctions in Support of Arbitration Against Foreign Insolvency Debtors: News from England and Canada

V. Lazić
Associate Professor. Utrecht University and Senior Researcher T.M.C. Asser Institute The Hague
P. Chauhan
Associate Professor, Jindal Global Law School; Phd Candidate Maastricht University Co-Founder Arbinsol

Introduction [1]

The interplay between arbitration and insolvency, once a rather neglected area of law, has become a topical issue nowadays. Cross-border implications and conflict of laws method have been the subjects of a particular attention in the literature. A majority view is to look for solutions in characterisation and the use of conflict of laws with respect to the points of

1 In this chapter, Professor Lazić wrote parts 'Introduction', 'Points of Interaction Between Insolvency and Arbitration', 'Nature and Underlying Purpose of "Avoidance Powers" of the Trustee', 'Non-binding Nature upon the Trustee in Insolvency When Exercising "Avoidance Powers"', 'Binding Nature of Arbitration Clauses in Avoidance Transactions: Case Law in England' and 'Conclusions', whereas part 'Anti-suit Injunctions' is co-written by Lazić and Chauhan. Chauhan is the sole author of the parts entitled Executory Contracts: *Petrowest Corporation v. Peace River Hydro Partners*' and 'Other views'.

interaction.[2] One of the present authors in her earlier publication[3] expressed the view that conflict of laws method is inappropriate and unhelpful particularly for arbitrators. Widely criticised decisions reaching opposing conclusions in *Syska v. Vivendi* of both English[4] and Swiss[5] courts are clear examples. The Swiss judgment, on one hand, illustrates the inadequacy of an attempt to 'qualify' the opening of insolvency proceedings in the terms and concepts of arbitration law (such as, capacity, arbitrability, and binding nature/validity of an arbitration agreement). After a 'qualification' of the matter as a 'capacity', the Swiss court erroneously applied all consequences of insolvency law, including an invalidity of the arbitration agreement. On the other hand, the judgment of the English court proves how relevant it is to recognise effects of foreign insolvencies both by arbitrators and by courts. It further demonstrates that regrettably such a recognition is not ensured even when an international legal instrument such as the EU Insolvency Regulation is in place.[6]

Considering that English courts found their ways[7] to hold provisions on suspension of proceedings inapplicable to arbitration even when the Insolvency Regulation so required, it would not be much of a surprise if no or limited effect would be given to foreign insolvencies in the absence of such a legal instrument.[8] A recent decision in *Riverrock*,[9] on an allegedly binding nature of arbitration agreements upon a trustee in insolvency proceedings when exercising the so-called avoidance powers, is rather unique and distinct from both case law and literature in other jurisdictions. Moreover, the English court issued an anti-suit injunction against a foreign

2 *See*, e.g., Kröll, S., Chapter 18, 'Arbitration & Insolvency', Selected Conflict of Laws Problems, Mistelis, L & D.M. Lew J. (eds.) in *Conflict of Laws in International Commercial Arbitration*, (2019), p. 658.

3 Lazić, V., Cross-Border Insolvency and Arbitration: Which Consequences of Insolvency Proceedings Should be Given Effect in Arbitration?', in Kröll, S. Mistelis, L.A, Perales Viscasillas, P., Rogers V., (eds.), *International Arbitration and International Commercial Law: Synergy, Convergence and Evolution*, Liber Amicorum Eric Bergsten, Kluwer Law International (2011), pp. 337-363.

4 Judgment of Mr Justice Christopher Clarke in High Court of Justice, Queen's Bench Division, Commercial Court, *Syska v. Vivendi Universal SA et al* (2008) EWHC 2155 (Comm) (2 Oct. 2008). Court of Appeal (Civil Division) Judgment of 9 July 2009, *Syska v. Vivendi Universal SA et al* (2009) 28 EG 84, (2009) EWCA Civ 677.

5 *Bundesgericht/Tribunal Fédéral* (T 1/2 4A_428/2008) 31 March 2009.

6 *See*, e.g., *Syska v. Vivendi*, *supra*, n. 2 and an earlier rendered judgment in *Mazur Media Ltd v. Mazur Media GmbH* (2005) 1 Lloyd's Rep. 41.

7 *Ibid.*

8 It is outside of the scope of this chapter to discuss the attitude of English courts in general regarding foreign insolvency proceedings.

9 *Riverrock Securities Ltd v. International Bank of St Petersburg (Joint Stock Company)*, (2020) EWHC 2483 (Comm).

court proceeding in support of arbitration seated in England. Considering that England is a rather popular 'seat' of arbitration, any such designation of the seat will trigger jurisdiction of English courts to 'determine any question on as to substantive jurisdiction of the tribunal' under Section 32(1) of the 1996 English Arbitration Act.[10] Besides, English courts have been issuing anti-suit injunctions to restrain foreign proceedings in support of arbitration, whether or not a claim is accompanied by a request for a decision under Section 32(1) of the Arbitration Act. Since an increase of insolvencies due to the pandemic crisis may be expected, the courts in England are likely to be deciding on the points of interaction between insolvency and arbitration more often. The present contribution in its first part examines not only the legal reasoning primarily followed in the *Riverrock* and *Nori Holding* judgments, but also views expressed in a subsequent case, to assess the appropriateness of the holding and examines how likely it is to be followed in the future.

This chapter also examines another point of intersection between insolvency and arbitration – a binding or non-binding nature of arbitration clauses contained in the so-called executory contracts. The analysis is inspired by a recent decision of the Court of Appeal of British Columbia in *Petrowest* case.[11] The court held that even acceptance of the underlying contract did not necessarily imply that the trustee would be bound by an arbitration clause contained therein. Similar to the exceptional nature of the holding in English courts, this decision also departs from the prevailing views in case law and literature in other jurisdictions.

Points of Interaction Between Insolvency and Arbitration

A comparative analysis[12] shows that provisions of insolvency law may, in most general terms, affect not only arbitrators' jurisdiction, but also the

10 Similar provisions on the possibility to apply for a decision on issues of jurisdiction, including a decision on the validity of an arbitration agreement can be found under the USA Federal Arbitration Act (Sects. 4 and 206) and German arbitration law (Art. 1032(2) of the German Code of Civil Procedure).

11 *Petrowest Corporation v. Peace River Hydro Partners*, 2020 BCCA 339 (CanLII) Court of Appeal for British Columbia, 30 Nov. 2020.

12 *See*, e.g., Lazić, V., *Insolvency Proceedings and Commercial Arbitration*, International Arbitration Law Library, Kluwer Law International, 1999, The Hague – London – Boston, p. 381; International Bar Association *Toolkit on Insolvency and Arbitration, Part I: Impact of Insolvency Proceedings on the Ability to Commence or Continue Arbitration,* March 2021, pp. 9-11, available at https://www.ibanet.org/MediaHandler?id=087B4D4A-B82E-4FAC-817F-64EE50091D66.

manner in which arbitral proceedings are conducted. Only in a very limited number of jurisdictions does opening of insolvency proceedings of itself invalidates arbitration agreements previously concluded by a debtor. Such example could be found in Polish insolvency law in force at the time of arbitral proceedings taking place in Switzerland and England in *Syska v. Vivendi*.[13] This is a rather exceptional approach and there is luckily a trend to abolish such a consequence when amending the law,[14] since they do not necessarily serve the purposes and aims of insolvency laws.

Most likely will an opening of insolvency raise the issues of objective arbitrability in respect of insolvency matters either because of the 'conflicting jurisdictions' between the courts and arbitrators over certain matters or due to a nature of the claim or both. Besides, vesting the right of management and disposal of the estate with the trustee will result in the need to apply provisions concerning his or her position and powers especially relating to pending legal actions and those to be initiated, the possibility of concluding new arbitration agreements, as well as those provisions that relate to initiating new proceedings arising out of special powers given by the insolvency laws. The latter include 'avoidance powers' of certain pre-insolvency transactions considered being detrimental to the estate and the right to assume or reject 'executory contract'. Indeed, among most important questions is the enforceability of previously concluded arbitration agreements contained in transactions with respect to which legal proceedings that are to be instituted either on behalf or against the estate.

Although a comparative study may point to some notable differences among insolvency laws and particularities of the interaction with arbitration, there are some common denominators, especially as far as underlying purposes of insolvency laws are concerned. The same holds true for some concepts that are commonly found in comparative insolvency laws. It is not to suggest that they are regulated in an identical manner, but they usually serve the same or similar purposes and aims. This is particularly so with

---

13 Art. 142 of the Polish Act of 28 Feb. 2003—Law on Insolvency and Restructuring regulated the declaration of bankruptcy proceedings with the option of concluding an arrangement. A corresponding provision in the context of declaration of bankruptcy with liquidation of the bankrupt's assets was found in Art. 147. The wording of the provisions of Arts 142 and 147 is identical.

14 For example, this provision was omitted when Spanish law on insolvency was revised. The same holds true for the Polish law and Art. 142 of the former Polish Bankruptcy and Reorganisation Act (Prawo upadlosciowe I naprawcze) of 28. 02. 2003, Dz. U. No 60, Pos. 535, repealed by virtue of Art. 428(80) of the Act 15. 05. 2015; Dz. U. Pos. 978.

respect to two concepts primarily addressed in this contribution – avoidance powers and executory contracts.

Nature and Underlying Purpose of 'Avoidance Powers' of the Trustee

The mechanism of avoiding a pre bankruptcy transaction entered into between the debtor and a creditor, by the insolvency trustee on account of it being prejudicial to the rights of other creditors has been termed as an avoidance power or claw back of retrospective transactions. Avoidance powers reverse opportunistic and value destroying behaviour usually faced by debtors in the zone of insolvency such as asset dilution, asset substitution, or debt dilution and prevents the race to the debtors' assets when insolvency looms.[15] These transactions may be treated as void or illegal under different insolvency systems so that the transfer by the debtor may be recovered by the trustee. There are different types of transactions which may be subject to the trustee's avoidance powers. They may be differently termed in various legal systems. Here are some examples: transfers in intentional fraud, transfers at an undervalue, preferential payments to select creditors, invalid security interests,[16] unfair preferences, transactions at an undervalue,[17] or fraudulent conveyances.[18]

Among jurisdictions there may be a divergence in the practice or implementation of the avoidance provisions due to their different legal traditions or prevailing underlying purposes. However they are outweighed by the similarities with respect to the consequence and aims of an avoidance action, which is to invalidate the transaction.[19] The essential elements of any statutory scheme are to treat creditors in accordance with the ranking of the insolvency law, as well as to prevent transactions which diminish the value of the assets of the debtor and avoidance powers are one such mechanism.[20] The purpose of any insolvency regime is limited not

15 Gurrea-Martínez, A. (Aurelio), 'The Avoidance of Pre-Bankruptcy Transactions: An Economic and Comparative Approach', 93 *Chicago-Kent Law Review* Issue 3 (2018), p. 714.

16 Westbrook, J.L., *A Global View of Business Insolvency Systems, with Booth*, C.D., Paulus, C.G. and Rajak, H. (eds.), Washington D.C., Martinus Nijhoff (2010), p. 125.

17 *Larsen Oil and Gas Pte Ltd v. Petropod Ltd* (2011) SGCA 21, para 4(a) referring to the relevant insolvency and company law of Singapore.

18 *Ibid*, para 7.

19 Moustaira, E., Chapter 4 – European Union, International Insolvency Law – National Laws and International Texts, Springer, (2019), p. 57.

20 *See* generally Chan, H. (Ho) L., 'Conflict of Laws in Insolvency Transaction Avoidance', 20 *Singapore Academy of Law Journal* (2008), p. 346.

only to a *pari passu* distribution among ordinary non-secured non-preferred creditors, but also to the preservation of the debtor's estate. Reversing transactions which are detrimental to the general body of creditors by the insolvency trustee are an integral aspect of an insolvency legislation. They are usually referred to as core issues, which may be decided only by the court of appropriate jurisdiction.[21] Identified in different legislations, it is the power of the trustee to bring insolvency *pauliana* actions before the competent court.[22]

Non-binding Nature upon the Trustee in Insolvency When Exercising 'Avoidance Powers'

In contrast to often different views on several aspects of intersection between arbitration and insolvency, no controversies are encountered with respect to 'avoidance powers'. It is generally undisputed that a trustee cannot be bound by arbitration agreements contained in transactions entered by the debtor which are subject to impeachment by the trustee. There are numerous and rather obvious reasons for which a trustee cannot possibly be bound by arbitration agreements when pursuing such claims.

Most compelling is the fact that these causes of action are established by insolvency laws that defines conditions under which certain transactions may be invalidated. They are created by the insolvency law, and by the same law they are vested with the trustee. Such actions may be pursued only after a commencement of insolvency proceedings and may be instituted solely within this context. Thus, the legal actions which the trustee pursues with the aim of having such transactions invalidated have their source in insolvency law. As such they qualify as pure or 'core' insolvency disputes, i.e., those which emanate directly from an insolvency legislation and as such by their very nature may not bind the trustee. On the other hand, non-core insolvency disputes may include ancillary agreements to which the debtor is a party, but which are not central to the insolvency process. Such disputes are arbitrable and fall within the scope of the arbitration agreement.[23]

An example of following this line of argumentation in reaching the conclusion on a non-binding nature of arbitration clauses in contracts subject to avoidance under insolvency law can be seen in the judgment of

21 Kirgis, P. F., 'Arbitration, Bankruptcy and Public Policy: A Contractarian Analysis', *17 American Bankruptcy Institute of Law Review* 14 (2009), p. 510.

22 Westbrook, *Supra*, p. 116.

23 Kröll *supra*.

the Singapore Court of Appeal in the case of *Larsen Oil & Gas Pte Ltd. v. Petropod Ltd.*[24] The case revolved around avoidance claims in an insolvency proceeding and a request to stay the proceeding by invoking an arbitration clause contained in the underlying transaction that was subject to the avoidance action. The court first examined the scope of the arbitration clause holding that the avoidance actions are independent of the nature of the relationship between the parties.[25] It held that an arbitration clause must be construed broadly, but the broad construction is better for cases where there exist private claims which are subject to arbitration and do not affect third parties, reflective of the core and non-core distinction. Such a broad construction was held not to apply to avoidance claims.

The court then focuses its analysis on the subject-matter arbitrability and bases its decision predominantly on the non-arbitrability of avoidance actions. It holds first that non-arbitrability results either from the intention of a legislator to preclude resolving the particular type of dispute in question in arbitration or from 'an inherent conflict between arbitration and the public policy considerations involved in that particular type of dispute'.[26] Relating to insolvency matters, it draws the distinction between 'disputes involving an insolvent company that stem from its pre-insolvency rights and obligations, and those that arise only upon the onset of insolvency due to the operation of the insolvency regime'.[27] It concludes that the latter should be treated 'per se as non-arbitrable even if the parties expressly included them within the scope of the arbitration agreement'.[28] In contrast, the former are binding on liquidators who have stepped into the shoes of insolvent companies, even though not themselves been the parties to such agreements. Yet even when the clauses are binding as a matter of principle, there may be policy considerations that justify holding them ineffective.[29] The court concludes that avoidance actions are not arbitrable as they are in essence insolvency issues.

Even though it can and often in the literature and jurisprudence it is discussed within the issue of 'objective arbitrability', the issue of a binding nature of previously concluded arbitration agreements should be distinguished from the question whether a trustee can enter into an arbitration agreement with respect to such matters. The latter is of a lesser importance

24 *Larsen Oil and Gas Pte Ltd v. Petropod Ltd* (2011) SGCA 21.
25 *Ibid.*, para 10.
26 *Ibid.*, para 44.
27 *Ibid.*, para 45.
28 *Ibid.*, para 46.
29 *Ibid.*, para 47.

considering that a trustee will most likely need to obtain necessary approvals for the court and/or creditors' committee, depending on insolvency law in a particular legal system.

In addition, a non-binding nature of arbitration agreements in these types of actions does not solely follow from considerations pertaining to 'objective non arbitrability', even though these claims, as purely insolvency issues are generally considered non-arbitrable. In particular, causes of actions that the trustee pursues in this type of actions are not causes of actions that can belong or have even belonged to the debtor. In other words, these are not causes of action that a trustee 'inherited' from the debtor as a contracting party to the transaction and which he or she pursues instead of the debtor due to his or her lack of legal capacity. Not at all do they belong to the debtor as a party to the contract. Also, it should be emphasised that this is not a matter of the scope of arbitration clause. Even if, in a hardly conceivable case, an arbitration clause was expressly to provide that it would extent to avoidance of transactions in case of insolvency, such a stipulation would obviously have no effect and would not be able to bind the trustee. In fact, this would be an attempt to extend an arbitration clause to a third party, which is a party neither to the underlying contract nor to the arbitration clause. The right to avoid transactions according to insolvency law is not a right which can belong to the debtor and of which he or she can freely dispose.

Examples of following this line of argumentation can be found in case law in the USA and Australia. The US Court of Appeals for the Third Circuit in *Hays v. Merrill Lynch, Pierce, Fenner & Smith Inc* [30] held that the fraudulent conveyance and constructive trust claims under Section 544(b) of the Bankruptcy Code 'are not arbitrable under the arbitration clause, because they are not derivative of the debtor and the trustee is accordingly not bound' with respect to them.[31]

A similar line of reasoning was followed in the judgment of an Australian Court per Barett J. in *New Cap Reinsurance Corporation Limited v. A E Grant & Ors, Lloyd's Syndicate No 991*.[32] When deciding on an avoidance action under the Australian Corporations Act of 2001, the court reasoned as follows:

> [E]ven on the most generous interpretation of the words "[a]ll matters in difference between the parties arising under, out of or in

---

30 *Hays v. Merrill Lynch, Pierce, Fenner & Smith Inc.*, 885 F.2d 1149 (3d Cir. 1989).

31 *Ibid.*, p. 1153.

32 *New Cap Reinsurance Corporation Limited v. A E Grant & Ors, Lloyd's Syndicate No 991*, (2009) NSWSC 662.

> connection with this Reinsurance," they do not extend to the present proceeding under s 588FF(1) of the Corporations Act in which the liquidator of one party to the reinsurance contract seeks an order for the payment of money to that contracting party by the other contracting party. This proceeding has nothing to do with the reinsurance contract. It is a proceeding upon a statutory cause of action maintainable by the liquidator of one of the former contracting parties. The cause of action is not available to the contracting party itself. Its liquidator, when suing upon the statutory cause of action, does not attempt to enforce some right of the contracting party.

A similar trend and understanding on a non-binding nature of arbitration clauses in such disputes can be found in the literature and case law of other legal systems.[33] This is not surprising, considering that a non-binding nature follows from the basic principle of arbitration which presupposes the existence of a valid arbitration agreement *between the parties*. This holds true for actions both in and outside insolvency proceedings. Avoidance transactions in insolvency proceedings are in civil law legal systems referred to as 'bankruptcy *pauliana*' or 'insolvency *pauliana*'. Causes of action in ordinary *actio pauliana* (outside insolvency proceedings) belong to a third party against both the debtor and the debtor's contracting party for entering into a transaction detrimental to that third party. It is quite obvious that the latter cannot possibly be bound by an arbitration clause contained in the transaction the avoidance of which is sought. Consequently, by no means can an arbitral tribunal properly establish jurisdiction against such a third party.

---

33 *See*, e.g., *IBA Toolkit on Insolvency and Arbitration Questionnaire, National Report of England & Wales*, Jan. 2021, paras 67-69, pp. 17-18, available at https://www.ibanet.org/MediaHandler?id=FC0D06DA-7D96-49AE-AC90-D13027976B80; *IBA Toolkit on Insolvency and Arbitration Questionnaire, National Report of The Netherlands,* Jan. 2021, paras 62-63, pp. 23-24, available at https://www.ibanet.org/MediaHandler?id=8B0FA391-B50D-4039-9156-98514254B7AE; *IBA Toolkit on Insolvency and Arbitration Questionnaire, National Report of France*, Jan. 2021, paras 61-62, pp. 15-16, available at https://www.ibanet.org/MediaHandler?id=097400CE-C218-4FA4-9114-88A2BC57960D; *IBA Toolkit on Insolvency and Arbitration Questionnaire, National Report of Germany*, Jan. 2021, paras 57-58, p. 14, available at https://www.ibanet.org/MediaHandler?id=7C3981B3-B3C2-4912-810A-D1EA92F6531D; *IBA Toolkit on Insolvency and Arbitration Questionnaire, National Report of Singapore*, Jan. 2021, paras 23, p. 8, available at https://www.ibanet.org/MediaHandler?id=B20D6283-BE13-44FF-8D2B-A3B110B80A7C; *IBA Toolkit on Insolvency and Arbitration Questionnaire, National Report of the United States of America*, Jan. 2021, para 28, p. 11, available at https://www.ibanet.org/MediaHandler?id=8A157F9D-7590-4CF4-B7F4-EB2CDDF3AA20.

The same line of reasoning is to be followed in the context of 'insolvency *pauliana*'. The trustee does not pursue avoidance transactions as a successor of the debtor who is a party to the contract subject to impeachment. Such actions must be distinguished from claims arising from an allegedly fraudulent behaviour of a debtor's contracting party, which clearly do belong to the debtor.

What appears problematic in practice is when the trustee pursues both types of actions in one proceeding – those that are 'inherited' from the debtor and those pursued in the exercise of its powers to avoid certain transactions according to insolvency law.[34] Most importantly, not all actions of the trustee aiming at avoiding certain transactions are genuine 'avoidance powers' within the meaning of insolvency law, regardless of been 'labelled' as such. In such a case if the claims are dismissed under the insolvency law, so that transaction is not found by the court to be an 'avoidable transaction', the trustee should be considered as bound by an arbitration clause if wishing to avoid the underlying transactions for other reasons. Of course, the condition is always that the clause is otherwise valid and that the cause of actions does not have its source in the insolvency law.[35]

As illustrated in the text that follows, it is rather a nature of actions that might have led the English Court in *Nori Holdings*[36] to reach a decision which, at the first appearance, seems to depart from the prevailing views in case law and in the literature. The *Nori Holdings* judgment at least correctly raised that point stating that a mere labelling a claim does not alter the nature of the dispute. Unfortunately, however, the *Riverrock* judgment reached a decision which is in stark contradiction with the prevailing view. It did not follow up on the reasoning of the *Nori Holdings* judgment on that point, even though otherwise relied heavily on it. Most regrettable is the express qualification of the claim as avoidance actions within the meaning of insolvency law in the *Riverrock* judgment and the conclusion on the binding nature of arbitration agreements contained therein on the insolvency administrator.

---

34 This is exactly the state of facts in a judgment that preceded the *Riverrock* case, as it is discussed in the next portion.

35 *See*, e.g., decision of the USA Bankruptcy Court in *Dunes Hotel Associates v. Hyatt Corp.*, 194 B.R. 967 (Bankr. D.S.Car. 1995), holding that there is no reason to refuse arbitration when all the Bankruptcy Code claims were dismissed, if the arbitration agreement is otherwise enforceable.

36 Judgment of 6 June 2018, Nori Holdings Ltd & Ors v Public Joint-Stock Company 'Bank Otkritie Financial Corporation' | [2018] WLR(D) 343, viewed at https://www.casemine.com/judgement/uk/5b2898012c94e06b9e19ed4b.

Binding Nature of Arbitration Clauses in Avoidance Transactions: Case Law in England

The opinion expressed by the English Court in *Riverrock* is in stark opposition to *Larsen Oil and Gas Pte Ltd v. Petroprod Ltd*, decided by the Singapore Court of Appeal, as well as with relevant case law in other jurisdictions. Both cases originated from avoidance transactions but met with different fate in two popular arbitration venues. It is therefore interesting to trace the sources of such opposing conclusions reached by the courts in two jurisdictions both frequently designated as places of arbitration.

The *Riverrock* judgment has been the subject matter of intense discussions of late. The high court while granting an anti-suit injunction under the Senior Courts Act held that an insolvency administrator is bound by an arbitration clause contained in the transaction subject to avoidance under the insolvency law. The parties in the dispute concluded nine contracts wherein Riverrock sold securities in the form of credit linked notes to International Bank of St. Petersburg (hereinafter 'the bank') issued by UBS AG. The effect of the transactions was to transfer the credit risk arising under certain loans held by UBS AG to the holder of the notes, i.e., to the bank. In addition to the Riverrock, the bank and UBS AG, a transaction involved also a Cypriot company, a minority shareholder in the bank. The notes were subject to the governing law and jurisdiction of England and Wales. The contracts contained an arbitration clause providing for the seat in London to be conducted in accordance with the LCIA Rules. On 24 September 2019, the bank was declared insolvent with Deposit Insurance Agency (DIA) appointed as its receiver. In the context of insolvency proceedings, the bank filed in St. Petersburg seeking invalidation of certain contracts with Riverrock on the basis of avoidance provisions of the Bankruptcy law of the Russian Federation and on the basis of the Civil Code for the 'abuse of rights'. Subsequently, one of the bank's creditors filed a claim in St. Petersburg for the annulment of the contracts under the Bankruptcy law. The court at St. Petersburg ordered Riverrock to respond to the complaint. In turn, Riverrock filed a request for an anti-suit injunction before the High Court in England to restrict the proceedings in Russia and to refer the parties to arbitration.

From paragraphs 50 to 54, it can be concluded that the high court was not convinced that the causes of action belonged to the administrator regardless of the fact that the claims were based on the insolvency law. There seem to be two major reasons for this conclusion. First, it concluded that the party in the proceedings was the bank and not an administrator in insolvency.[37] Consequently, in the view of the court, the causes of actions are those that may be instituted by the debtor (the bank), since 'the administrator or liquidator will generally have supplanted the previous management of the company, which will not retain any power of independent action in relation to the contract in issue'.[38] Thus, the fact that the bank was a party in all court proceedings was decisive for the high court to reach its conclusion and distinguish the present case from the reasoning in *Larsen Oil and Gas Pte Ltd v. Petroprod Ltd.* This was deduced from the fact that the claims were being pursued by the bank and not the DIA. In this context the court, while assessing the scope of the claims brought by the bank under the Russian Bankruptcy law, interestingly held that the claims were a simple claim for abuse of rights. The court did not engage in any analysis of a possible division of the right to dispose and administer the debtor's estate between the management and the appointed administrator under the Russian insolvency law. Presumably, the qualification of the action as a claim for abuse of rights was the basis of the conclusion that the claims were pursued by the bank and not the DIA. It was not questioned how an insolvent debtor can under the applicable insolvency law be entitled to pursue legal actions on behalf of the estate.

Most problematic is the reasoning in paragraphs 74-76. First, what is stated in paragraph 74 is entirely incompatible with the reasoning reached previously relating to causes of action belonging to the bank as a debtor. In contrast to the previous conclusion, the high court here holds that the causes of actions are genuine insolvency claims of avoidance powers that may be exercised solely by an administrator. The court does not explain how the claims can be qualified at the same time both as claims for abuse of rights and as avoidance actions. Curiously enough, the high court even makes a parallel with English law, holding that under English law such avoidance claims would be the matters of insolvency law, but concludes that it does not render the claim automatically non-arbitrable under English law as *lex arbitri* and as the law governing the arbitration agreement. This is the most regrettable conclusion and an erroneous and misleading message to arbitration and insolvency specialist alike.

37 *Riverrock*, para 50(iv), stating that 'IBSP gave undertakings to this Court to adjourn a hearing in the St Petersburg Action and "not to take any steps to pursue, progress or prosecute the Russian Claims or the Russian Proceedings," and delivered on those undertakings, which is scarcely consistent with the assertion that the St Petersburg Action is being brought by someone else.'

38 *Ibid.*, para 54.

The reasoning of the court relating to the trend of English courts generally to favour arbitration and uphold arbitration agreements is here omitted, as moot and irrelevant in the circumstances of the present case. The same holds true regarding the reference to *Fiona Trust,*[39] being a leading authority on the separability of an arbitration clause. Indeed, English law has adopted a generous approach when interpreting arbitration agreements. However, English courts expressly reject the theories aiming at extending a binding effect of arbitration agreement to the so-called non-signatories,[40] such as the 'groups of companies doctrine'. As already addressed, considering the nature of avoidance actions the trustee cannot be considered as a 'signatory to the arbitration agreement', in contrast to other causes of action which are 'inherited' from the debtor and derivative of the debtor's rights and obligations. Thus, in the circumstances of the present case it would have been more appropriate to refer to *Peterson Farms* judgment then to *Fiona Trust.*

It is now opportune to discuss the *Nori Holdings*[41] judgment which finds excessive reliance in the *Riverrock* case. In *Nori Holdings*, the court was requested to issue an anti-suit injunction to restrain proceedings in Cyprus and Russia commenced in order to set aside certain transactions in breach of an arbitration clause.

The bank incorporated under the Russian law entered into loan agreements with many companies incorporated under the law of Cyprus and Russia. The agreements were governed by Russian law and provided for jurisdiction of the Moscow Arbitrazh Court. They were secured by pledges of shares which were given in the form of five Pledge Agreements. The latter were governed by the law of Cyprus and provided for arbitration in London under the LCIA Rules. By agreements dated 9 and 10 August 2017, the parties terminated the Pledge Agreements. They were governed by the law of Cyprus and contained identical arbitration clauses. The purpose of the termination was a replacement of short-term loans secured by pledges with long-term unsecured bonds. Only three weeks later on 29 August 2017, the Central Bank of Russia appointed a temporary administrator under the Bankruptcy Code with the purpose of financial rehabilitation aimed at preventing bankruptcy. On 12 December 2017, the Central

39 *Fiona Trust & Holding Corporation v. Privalov* (2007) UKHL 40.

40 *See*, *Peterson Farms Inc. v. C&M Farming* Ltd (2004) EWCH 121 (comm) 4 Feb. 2004. For a comment on the judgment, *see* Woolhouse, S. (Sarita) P., 'Groups of Companies Doctrine and English Arbitration Law', 20 Arbitration International Issue 4 (2004), pp. 435-443.

41 *Nori, supra* n. 36.

Bank of Russia nationalised the bank and soon thereafter appointed a new management whereby the temporary administration ceased. On 31 October 2017, the bank acting by the temporary administrator commenced proceedings before the courts in Russia seeking the invalidation and reversal of all August transactions, including the Termination Agreements. The bank alleged that it was the victim of a fraud which resulted in a loss of US$ 500 Million. The purpose was to restore the bank to the position it had been before these transactions.

Apart from instituting 10 arbitrations against the bank, for a declaration that the termination was valid, the claimants filed anti-suit injunction to restrain the Russian proceedings, as well as subsequently commenced proceedings against the claimant in Cyprus. In the latter proceedings, the bank sought the annulment of the August transactions as a result of a fraudulent conspiracy to defraud and restoring the Pledge agreements. Thus, the claims of the bank were based on both the Bankruptcy Law and the Civil Code of Russia. The bank argued, *inter alia*, that the arbitration clause did not extend to an insolvency claim to avoid a transaction at an undervalue and/or that such claims were not arbitrable.

The court rejected to follow the reasoning in the *Larsen Oil*[42] in the context of interpreting an arbitration clause and relied on *Fulham*[43] instead. It concluded that the wording of arbitration clause was sufficiently broad so as to extend to claims arising in the context of insolvency proceedings.[44] When deciding on the objection of non-arbitrability, the court correctly held it necessary to focus on 'the nature of the particular claim',[45] whereby holding it irrelevant whether the claim can be qualified as an insolvency claim under Russian law. The court approached the dispute as one of substance over form and qualified it as a simpliciter case of fraud carried out by the claimant, which the tribunal was capable of deciding. Most substantial arguments are as follows:

> In this case the parties' dispute is a straightforward factual dispute whether the August transactions constitute *a fraud carried out on the Bank* to replace valuable secured loans with worthless bonds. If so, the Bank will have a claim to avoid those transactions and to require the claimants to reinstate the position in which it was before they were carried out. A variety of *legal labels* can be and have been attached to that claim, including *the labels of transaction with*

42 *Larsen Oil* [2011] SGCA 21.
43 *Fulham*, [2011] EWCA Civ 855 [2012] Ch 333.
44 *Nori,* para 60.
45 *Ibid.*, para 62.

> *unequal consideration* and abuse of rights under Russian law and conspiracy to defraud under Cypriot law. But in each case the essential dispute is the same, regardless of the *label*. This is a dispute that arbitrators can determine.[46] (emphasis added)

Thus, the court obviously assessed that the claims were not avoidance actions proper within the meaning of insolvency law but were merely 'labelled' as such. Instead, they are pure claims that belong to a party to the contract. The wording emphasised *supra*, as well as the wording 'whether the *claimants defrauded the Bank*'[47] illustrate that the claims in the case at hand are pure civil law claims that one contracting party may file against another contracting party. They are not true avoidance actions created under the insolvency law and vested upon the trustee. Furthermore, the court rightly points out that in the present case there is 'no remedy claimed such as a winding up order which would affect the status of the Bank or which would affect the position of third parties as to take the case beyond the consensually derived jurisdiction of arbitrators'. Indeed, the reorganisation proceedings were in the meantime terminated. The last part of the wording implies that a different line of argumentation could apply when there would be a debtor in insolvency proceedings.

In the opinion of the authors, *Nori Holdings* is a well-reasoned judgment when compared with *Riverrock*, since it does not hold that arbitration clauses are enforceable in true cases when the trustee would pursue true avoidance actions. In contrast, the *Riverrock* judgment does not *examine* the nature of all claims but qualifies them in an unclear and contradictory manner. Thus, it is not possible to state with certainty whether or not some of the claims were avoidance actions proper. Moreover, the reasoning of the *Riverrock* Court makes it even irrelevant, implying that the same line of reasoning applies regardless of the nature of the claim. This is the major shortcoming of the ruling: expressly qualifying the claim as a genuine avoidance action, confirming that in the English insolvency law there is a corresponding concept and concluding that arbitration clauses have binding effect on the trustee. Herewith the court sends a conceptually incorrect, erroneous, and misleading message, thereby unnecessarily further complicating the understanding of the intersection between arbitration and insolvency.

---

46 *Ibid.*, para 63.
47 *Ibid.*, para 64.

Anti-suit Injunctions

Both courts were requested to order anti-suit injunctions to restrain court proceedings commenced abroad in order to support the effectiveness of arbitration agreements. The requests were granted in both cases. However, the court in *Nori Holding* rejected to issue anti-suit injunctions to restrain the proceedings in Cyprus as an EU Member State in light of the CJEU *West Tankers*[48] judgment. The latter has held the anti-suit injunction to be incompatible with the EU law.

In doing so, the court in *Nori Holding* criticised and rightly rejected the Opinion of the Advocate General in CJEU *Gazprom* case,[49] invoked by the claimants. The advocate general surprisingly argued that Recital (12) in the Revised Brussels Ibis Regulation[50] allegedly reversed the CJEU *West Tankers* ruling given under the Brussels I Regulation, so that the anti-suit injunctions would become available when ordered in support to arbitration. The court rejected this line of argumentation, holding the CJEU decision in *West Tankers* to be good law which precludes anti-suit injunctions to restrain proceedings in an EU Member State. Considering that the opinion of the advocate general finds no support either in the revised text of the Regulation or in the CJEU case law,[51] it is to be met with approval that it has been rejected also by English courts.[52]

Indeed, the relevant CJEU decision had no relevance regarding UK courts issuing anti-suit injunctions aimed at restraining claimants to pursue litigations in non-EU Member States. Thus, shortly after the CJEU judgment in *West Tankers* case had been brought, UK courts continued with

---

48 CJEU Judgment of 10 Feb. 2009, Case C-185/07 *Allianz SpA/Generali Assicurazioni Generali ApA v. West Tankers, Inc.*, ECLI:EU:C:2009:69. *See also*, earlier cases of the CJEU holding anti-suit injunctions incompatible with the EU legislation, Judgment of 9 Dec. 2003, (2003) ECR I-14693 *Erich Gasser GmbH v. MISAT Srl,* and Judgment of 27 April 2004, (2004) ECR I-3589 *Turner v. Grovit.*

49 CJEU Judgment of 13 May 2015, Case C-536/13, *Gazprom OAO v. Lietuvos Respublika,* ECLI:EU:C:2015:316.

50 Council Regulation (EU) No 1215/2012 of the European Parliament and of the Council of 12 Dec. 2012 [2012] OJ L351/1.

51 See the criticism on the Advocate General Opinion, Lazić, V. and Stuij, S., 'Brussels I bis in Relation to Other Instruments on the Global Level, in Brussels Ibis Regulation', in Lazić, V. & Stuij, S. (eds.), *Brussels Ibis Regulation: Changes and Challenges of the Renewed Procedural Scheme*, Asser Press/Springer Publishing, 2017, pp. 119-152, at pp. 144-145.

52 The Court in *Nori Holding* in para 91 of the judgment concluded that the Opinion of the Advocate General was fundamentally flawed.

orders restraining legal proceedings in non-EU Member States.[53] Even though anti-suit injunctions could be considered as violating the 1958 New York Convention,[54] the UK courts do continue to issue them in support to arbitration. In accordance with the Withdrawal Agreement,[55] after the expiry of the 'transitional period' on 31 December 2020, the EU private international law instruments will no longer apply in the UK or more precisely they will apply to the extend defined in the Withdrawal Agreement. Indeed, it includes both the Brussels Ibis Regulation[56] and the Insolvency Regulation.[57] Consequently, the UK courts are no longer restricted by the relevant CJEU case law from issuing anti-suit injunctions to restrain litigations in the EU Member States. Thus, that could also be against foreign insolvency debtors or the trustees of such debtors in breach of arbitration agreements. Whether or not will the UK courts be doing so remains to be seen. It seems that courts in some EU Member States have started to use comparable 'means' to restrain UK anti-suit injunctions,[58] even though the concept of anti-suit injunctions as such is unknown in civil

---

53 *See*, e.g., High Court of Justice, Queen's Bench Division, Commercial Court, 7 May 2009, *Roger Shashouaetal. v. Mukesh Sharma*, [2009] EWHC 957 (comm.); See also, High Court of Justice, Queen's Bench Division, Commercial Court, 22 Dec. 2009, *Transfield Shipping Inc. v. Chiping Xinfa Huayau Alumina Co. Ltd*, (2009) EWHC 3642 (comm.).

54 One of the present authors argued that anti-suit injunctions are contrary to Art. II of the New York Convention in an earlier publication V. Lazić, 'The Commission' Proposal to Amend the Arbitration Exception in the EC Jurisdiction Regulation: How "Much Ado About Nothing" can end up in a "Comedy of Errors" and in Anti-suit Injunctions Brussels-style', *Journal of International Arbitration* 29, no. 1, Feb. (2012) pp. 19-48.

55 Agreement on the withdrawal of the United Kingdom of Great Britain and Northern Ireland from the European Union and the European Atomic Energy Community (2019/C 384 I/01) (hereinafter: 'Withdrawal Agreement'). It was agreed on 17 Oct. 2019, signed on 24 Jan. 2020 and entered into force on 1 Feb. 2020.

56 Council Regulation (EU) No 1215/2012 of the European Parliament and of the Council of 12 Dec. 2012 OJ L351/1. According to Arts 67(1)(a) and 61(1)(b), the Regulation will cease to apply in the UK to determine international jurisdiction and to enforce judgments rendered in the EU Member States in proceedings instituted on or after 1 Jan. 2021.

57 Regulation (EU) 2015/848 of the European Parliament and of the Council of 20 May 2015 on insolvency proceedings (OJ L 141, 5.6.2015, p. 19). According to Art. 67(3)©, the Regulation shall apply to insolvency proceedings, and actions referred to in Art. 6(1) of that Regulation, provided that the main proceedings were opened before the end of the transition period.

58 *See*, e.g., *Oberlandesgericht München*, 12 Dec. 2019 and the comment of the decision by M. Lehman, 'Anti-Anti-Suit Injunctions by German Courts – What Goes Around, Comes Around' available at Anti-Anti-Suit Injunctions by German Courts – What Goes Around, Comes Around – EAPIL; *see also*, *Cour d'appel de Paris*, 3 March 2020 and the commentary by G. Cuniberti, Paris Court Issues Anti Suit Injunctions', available at Paris Court Issues Anti Anti Suit Injunction – EAPIL.

law jurisdiction. Such developments may influence decisions of the UK courts when choosing the most appropriate means to support arbitrations.[59]

In conclusion, in the opinion of the authors, *Nori Holdings* is a well-reasoned judgment when compared to *Riverrock*, primarily on the intersection part, but also on the use of anti-suit injunctions. Certainly, better approach than the *Riverrock* was observed recently in *Louis Dreyfus*,[60] relating to the request for anti-suit injunctions in favour of arbitration proceedings. The claimant did not object to the jurisdiction of the Russian Courts insofar as it pertained to the invalidation of the debtor's transaction as it was undervalued and to the detriment of the debtor.[61] The objection to jurisdiction was with respect to claim for payments arising out of underlying and distinct commercial transactions governed by English Law containing mandatory arbitration agreement. Thus, this case is not an example of holding arbitration clauses binding upon the trustee in insolvency, since all claims were contractual claims derivative of the debtor.

Executory Contracts: *Petrowest Corporation v. Peace River Hydro Partners*[62]

The jurisprudence relating to executory contracts may seem comparatively straightforward but is vexed with technicalities. To a layman it is a simple acceptance or rejection of a contract, which contains an arbitration clause, however it is the opposite. If an executory contract is assumed, then the trustee or debtor in possession performs the contract, making any necessary payments out of the estate as administrative expenses. If it is rejected, then the other party to the contract is entitled to damages, to be paid out of the estate upon distribution on the same basis as any other unsecured claim. Recognising the derivative action, the administrator being bound to arbitration agreement, should he choose to perform it? The rejection of an executory contract raises a question on the fate of the arbitration agreement. A rejection would result in the claim being treated as a pre-petition

59 On the possible ways to be taken by UK courts in the future, *see* Hartely, T., 'Arbitration and the Brussels I Regulation – Before and After Brexit', *Journal of Private International Law*, (2021) 17:1, pp. 53-73, p. 57 *et seq.*

60 *Louis Dreyfus Company Suisse S.A. v. International Bank of St. Petersburg* (Joint-Stock Company) (A Company in liquidation in The Russian Federation [2021] EWHC 1039 (Comm).

61 *Ibid.*, para 40.

62 *Petrowest Corporation v. Peace River Hydro Partners*, 2020 BCCA 339 (Court of Appeal for British Columbia).

claim.[63] However, does rejection of the contract also result in the rejection of the arbitration agreement? Does the arbitration agreement survive the rejection by virtue of separability? One of us has assessed it in great detail.[64] It has been suggested that the following line of reasoning may be adopted for the enforceability of the arbitration agreement[65]:

(a) When a trustee rejects the main contract, the other party is entitled to claim damages.
(b) The claim is a pre-petition claim against the estate.
(c) Whether the amount of damages arising from the rejection may be decided in an arbitration given, depends on the subject-matter arbitrability of claims contested in the verification procedure in a particular legal system. As a matter of principle, such claims may be arbitrable, even though in some jurisdictions it may be subject to an approval of the court. The latter may be regarded to have a discretion when deciding on that issue in some legal systems.

As seen in *Merrill Lynch*,[66] the court enforced the arbitration agreement binding the trustees to the pre-petition executory contracts. However, in a recent decision, the separability aspect of an executory contract and its binding nature on the administrator were explored, where the line of reasoning needs relooking. In *Petrowest* the appellant challenged an order by the chambers judge dismissing an application for a stay of proceedings under section 15(2) of the British Columbia Arbitration Act. The respondent debtor was placed in receivership under the supervision of the court-ordered respondent receiver. The receiver pursued claims under several agreements, which the appellants argued were subject to mandatory arbitration clauses. The court of first instance found that section 15 of the Arbitration Act had been engaged, but that the court retained inherent jurisdiction pursuant to section 183 of the Bankruptcy and Insolvency Act to decline to order the stay, notwithstanding the mandatory language of the Arbitration Act.

The appeal was dismissed. The reason for dismissal however, is noteworthy. The appellate court held that the party which initiated the proceedings was not Petrowest but the receiver and discarded the previous court's

63 Zunshine, Z., 'Pre-Petition Arbitration Agreements and Hays & Co. v. Merrill Lynch'; 7 *Journal on Dispute Resolution Issue* 1 (1991), p. 165.

64 Lazić, V., *Insolvency Proceedings and Commercial Arbitration*, International Arbitration Law Library, Kluwer Law International, 1999, p. 195.

65 *Ibid*., p. 196.

66 *Hays v. Merrill Lynch, Pierce, Fenner & Smith Inc*, 885 F.2d 1149 (3d Cir. 1989).

dictum that the receiver was bound by the arbitration clause.[67] The respondent stated, ' … unlike a trustee, the debtor's assets do not vest in the receiver, who must bring action in the debtor's name … they maintain that a court-appointed receiver is not bound by the contracts of the debtor corporation, and in particular, is not bound by, or a party to, the mandatory arbitration clauses … They then argue that because the receiver is not a party to the arbitration agreements, the arbitration agreements are inoperable.'[68]

While considering the parties' submissions on separability, the respondent submitted that separability is irrelevant given the power of the receiver to disclaim contracts generally; the appellants contended that separability does not permit the receiver to avoid arbitration agreements. The court found that 'it is open to the receiver to disclaim the arbitration agreements notwithstanding that it has adopted the containing contracts for the purpose of suing on them. This flows from the receiver's particular powers and position, and the separability of the arbitration agreements'.[69] Further, the court went on to hold 'the action has not been commenced by a party to the arbitration agreements within the meaning of section 15(1) of the Act, and in any event, due to the receiver's disclaimer, the arbitration agreements have become "void, inoperative or incapable of being performed" within the meaning of section 15(2)'.[70]

Other Views

In many legal systems, the acceptance of the contract would imply the acceptance of all provisions, including the arbitration clause. Here are some examples.

In Austria, insolvency administrators are bound by arbitration agreements which an insolvent party has entered into with third parties prior to commencement of insolvency. They would not be bound if the rights of the administrator arise directly from the Austrian Insolvency Act, or the person of the administrator.[71] If a contract is rescinded by the insolvency administrator and legal validity of this rescission is disputed, then the arbitration agreement contained in the contract continues to exist. In addition, if the

---

67 *Petrowest*, para 45.
68 *Ibid.*, paras 34-35.
69 *Ibid.*, para 55.
70 *Ibid.*, para 56.
71 Neuburger P, 'Arbitration and Insolvency: Dispute Resolution' (*OBLIN*, 8 Aug. 2021) <https://oblin.at/newsletter/arbitration-and-insolvency/> accessed 7 Sep. 2021.

insolvency administrator chooses to perform the executory contract, he or she is bound by the arbitration clause.[72]Under Article 37 of the Dutch Bankruptcy Act, the trustee has been given the power to refrain from performing executory contracts. If the trustee accepts the executory contract, the arbitration clause in it will also be accepted; if it is repudiated, and the claim for damages is contested, that shall be resolved in arbitration.[73] The trustee can enter into agreements for the proper management of the estate which include arbitration agreements.[74]

In the UK, the trustee under sec 349 A(3) of the Insolvency Act has to apply to the court to refer the case to arbitration. It is a discretionary power of the court and not per se vested in the trustee. However, there is no authority which settles the position of the trustee in the bankruptcy decision to disclaim a contract that contains an arbitration agreement.[75] It has been suggested that the trustee/liquidator must specifically disclaim the arbitration agreement rather than disclaiming the contract in which the arbitration agreement is contained.[76]

Two lines of arguments appear here. One, considering the arbitration agreement itself as an executory contract and reject it as a whole, another pertains to separability. However, this line of argumentation cannot be maintained, considering that a rejection of the executory contract results in a claim for damages which can be filed in the insolvency proceedings. Thus, no such claim would be available when an arbitration clause would be rejected.[77] Rejection as a whole may be problematic, for a simple reason that the administrator derived the claim from the debtor which contained a promise to refer future disputes to arbitration. The discretion would lie with the administrator to decide whether initiating arbitration would be beneficial for the estate, including aspects of costs.

While considering the arbitration agreement separable, suggestion has been made to extend it to mean an executory contract, which would give

72 *Ibid.*

73 *IBA Toolkit on Insolvency and Arbitration Questionnaire, National Report of The Netherlands,* Jan. 2021, paras 62-63, pp. 23-24, available at https://www.ibanet.org/MediaHandler?id=8B0FA391-B50D-4039-9156-98514254B7AE.

74 *Ibid.*, p. 24.

75 *IBA Toolkit on Insolvency and Arbitration Questionnaire, National Report of England & Wales*, Jan. 2021, paras 67-69, pp. 17-18, available at https://www.ibanet.org/MediaHandler?id=FC0D06DA-7D96-49AE-AC90-D13027976B80.

76 *Ibid.* pp. 14-15.

77 Westbrook, J. L., 'The Coming Encounter: International Arbitration and Bankruptcy', 67 *Minn. Law Review* (1989), pp. 227 *et seq.*

the administrator control over its enforcement.[78] This extrapolation may not lead to any result. We have observed instances where the courts have referred parties to arbitration in executory contracts, the decision of the administrator must be given primacy over counterparty arguments to initiate arbitration. This, however, comes with a caveat that contracts must not be assumed or rejected at will, although a pro-arbitration arbitration approach of the courts does play a determinative role. Segregation of core and non-core proceedings has been suggested to decide the enforceability of an arbitration clause.[79]

Conclusions

In this complex area of law, a non-binding nature of arbitration clauses on the trustee when pursuing avoidance actions under the insolvency law is the least controversial and approached in almost unanimous manner in a comparative law overview. The same can be said for an arbitration clause contained in an executory contract that is accepted or assumed by the trustee. Decisions on certain aspects of the intersections between arbitration and insolvency discussed in this contribution depart substantially from these prevailing views in theory and practice. This particularly holds true for the *Riverrock* and *Petrowest* judgments. As such they will certainly further complicate the understanding of the interaction between insolvency and arbitration by both arbitrators and insolvency practitioners.

By invoking the principle of separability as a reason to reject an arbitration clause in an accepted executory contract in the *Petrowest* judgment regrettably reverses the operation of this basic principle. The underlying purpose of separability is to uphold the validity and effectiveness of an arbitration clause in a voidable contract if the clause itself is

78 *See,* Brookner, J. S. & Blacker, M. S. '*The Rejectability of Arbitration Clauses*', 26 *American Bankruptcy Institute Journal* 1, 77 (April 2007) ('The reciprocal future obligation (of the arbitration clause) would appear to make the arbitration clause executory and would thus subject arbitration clause to independent assumption or rejection.') at 98 in Kirgis, P. F., 'Arbitration, Bankruptcy and Public Policy: A Contractarian Analysis', 17 *American Bankruptcy Institute of Law Review* 14 (2009), p. 521.

79 *See* Resnick, A. N., 'The Enforceability of Arbitration Clauses in Bankruptcy', 15 *American Bankruptcy Institute Law Review* 183, 194 (2007) (classifying trustee claims against third parties non-core because they 'do not present any bankruptcy issues') at 43 in Kirgis, P. F., 'Arbitration, Bankruptcy and Public Policy: A Contractarian Analysis', 17 *American Bankruptcy Institute of Law Review* 14 (2009), p. 510.

valid and enforceable. A reliance of the severability principle to *invalidate* a valid arbitration clause in *a valid (accepted) contract* is an apparent paradox and probably will not be easily understood by arbitration lawyers.

In a similar vein, insolvency and arbitration lawyers alike will have difficulties in following the line of argumentation in the *Riverrock* judgment. In an attempt to trace the motives and basis for the conclusions, it seems that a true nature of claims is the source of the difficulty. Particularly problematic is when the trustee pursues different causes of action – those pertaining to insolvency law and pure civil law actions. The *Nori Holdings* judgment approaches the problem in an appropriate manner by engaging in the determination of the true nature of the action. It is regrettable indeed that the *Riverrock* judgment did not follow the same approach and did not attempt to determine the true nature of the claims. Most inappropriate is the conclusion that a distinction between the claims is unnecessary or rather that it would not make a difference for the decision of the court. This is the most erroneous and misleading message.

Another important aspect is the absence of a recognition of foreign insolvency proceedings in both *Nori Holding* and *Riverrock* cases. In neither of them the recognition was requested, but generally a giving effect to foreign insolvency proceedings, when they are genuine insolvency proceedings, is an important aspect not only within the intersection between arbitration and insolvency, but more generally with the view of enhancing a cooperation in cross-border situations. It is therefore crucial that regulating cross-border insolvency becomes the part of the legislative framework in many jurisdictions. It is hardly conceivable that English courts would apply the reasoning of the *Riverrock* judgment in cases when insolvency proceedings are opened in the UK, but hopefully it will also not be followed in cases in which certain effects of foreign insolvencies are recognised in the UK.

Considering that England is a popular arbitration venue and that the number of insolvencies is likely to increase in the current pandemic crisis, the UK courts will even more often encounter the challenge of dealing with the interplay between insolvency and arbitration. Whether or not there will be any change in issuing anti-suit injunction in support to arbitration in general and more specifically against foreign insolvency trustees remains to be seen. Particularly interesting will it be to see the position of the UK courts with respect to proceedings before the courts of the EU Member States. Considering that the UK is no longer an EU Member State, the CJEU case law is no longer a hurdle for the UK courts to issue anti-suit injunctions to restrain these proceedings, as well.

The "Wonderland" of Insolvency and Arbitration: "Re-cohabitation" of the Duo as an Inevitable Destiny (Pre-award Phase)

Mahmoud M. Moghrabi
PhD in Law, Assistant Professor Kuwait International Law School
Kuwait
Nadim M. Al Jisr
LLM in Law Lawyer at Mohammad & Abbad Al Jisr Law Office
Lebanon

Introduction

Imagination creates reality.

Richard Wagner

None disagrees about the distinguished impact of literary work in society through criticisms, guidance, and reforms. This fact materialized in the value messages of the famous fantasy book *Alice's Adventures in Wonderland,* affectionately known to most people as "Alice in Wonderland." "Alice," who believes that the world is orderly and stable, learns from her experiences, ultimately becomes more mature emotionally, and faces her problems in the way she interprets different situations she confronts, by regaining sight of her identity. The "strange and crazy land" within its characters reflects in many ways challenges and difficulties in daily life: a "White Rabbit" who suffers from general anxiety disorder "I'm late," often unable to distinguish right from wrong, yet would be the first one to "blow the whistle" if things do not go his way, a "hole" where everything begins, which symbolizes a "gate" into a new world of adventures, a "Queen of Hearts" who takes control with absolute rule and execution, affected by egotism and narcissist syndrome "head off," a "Cheshire Cat" affected by schizophrenia as he disappears and reappears distorting reality around him and subsequently driving other characters in the story to madness, and a "mushroom" in the pocket at the end of the story, that represents how to face the fear and take on responsibility by simply "growing up."[1]

Imagination is a mirror of reality. Thus, the wonderland Alice steps into resembles, to a great extent, the wonderland legal professionals and courts have stepped into when discussing and examining the dialectic relation or interplay between insolvency and arbitration, especially in the era of the new unknown territories—"the pandemic."

The COVID-19 has forced businesses to adapt to a new world order and continues to do so. Businesses are trying to survive the COVID-19 caused disruption in the economy by radically changing their operations, while the sword of "Damocles" hangs over their heads; it is expected to lead many corporations to insolvency,[2] as well as trigger an increase in the number of commercial disputes.[3] Once again, maybe more dramatically, "Insolvency and Arbitration" have returned on the menu of the international arbitration community.[4] In describing their relations,[5] the court in *United States Lines*

1 Gabrielle Maletto: Alice's adventures in wonderland, website https://alicesadventuresin wonderlandd.weebly.com/; Maria Giulia Marini : so much inside Alice in wonderland for medical humanities Post published: Aug. 2, 2018 https://www.medicinana rrativa.eu/so-much-inside-alice-wonderland-for-medical-humanities.

2 The term "insolvency" shall be used to encompass all proceedings with the goal of liquidating assets of an insolvent debtor in favor of its creditors foreseen and/or organized by the state—regardless of the various national terminologies employed. Markert, L. (2009). Arbitrating in the financial crisis: Insolvency and public policy versus arbitration and party autonomy which law governs. Contemporary Asia Arbitration Journal 2(2), 217.

3 "Insolvency and Arbitration: What Issues Arise?" article posted on July 4, 2020. https://www.acerislaw.com/insolvency-and-arbitration-what-issues-arise/; Ayca Bengu Koksal, A Tale of Two Proceedings: Arbitration and Insolvency, article posted on Nov. 16, 2020, https://www.mondaq.com/turkey/arbitration-dispute-resolution/1006244/a-tale-of-two-proceedings-arbitration-and-insolvency; James Rogers, Paul Stothard: Insolvency and international arbitration: Tension between competing public policy interests, International arbitration report Published by Norton Rose Fulbright – Issue 14 – June 2020, p. 10.

4 Wolfgang Kuhn: Arbitration Insolvency and Arbitration, dispute resolution 5(2).204. Until Aug. 16, 2020, more than 125 corporations (many of them household names) appear on this list. Hank Tucker, Coronavirus Bankruptcy Tracker: These Major Companies are failing Amid the Shutdown, Forbes (May 3, 2020), https://www.forbes.com/sites/hanktucker/2020/05/03/coronavirus-bankruptcy-tracker-these-major-companies-are-failing-amid-the-shutdown/#33c68fb23425 (last visited Aug. 16, 2020). *See also* 'Litigations Trends Survey' (16th edition) (Norton Rose Fullbright 2020), p. 17.

5 E.g., Domitille Baizeau, Arbitration and Insolvency: Issues of Applicable Law in: Christoph Moller/Antonio Rigozzi (eds.), New Developments in International Commercial Arbitration, Zurich 2009, 97; Laurent Levy, Arbitration and Bankruptcy: Bankruptcy of Arbitration?, Dispute Resolution International, 5 (2011) 1, 2011, p. 103

case (1999), concluded that it "...presents a conflict of near polar extremes."[6] Elsewhere, the description was never less harsh or accurate; i.e., it is compared to a "dilemma of two diverging systems,"[7] "conflict of near polar extremes,"[8] "strange bedfellows,"[9] "nuclear threat,"[10] a "mismatched, incompatible, antagonistic couple,"[11] "two strong heads of business law"[12] and so on.

Accordingly, three main questions arise when admiring these metaphors that aptly encapsulate the inherent tension between the two regimes:

(1) Why whenever arbitration meets insolvency, a major risk of practical concerns appears?
(2) When do these problems and concerns arise?
(3) How can this endless battle ever be resolved?

---

et seq.; Richard Millett: Cross-Border Insolvency and Arbitration: A Collision of Spheres?, Dispute Resolution International, 5 (2011) 1, p. 113 et seq.; Sara Nadeau-Seguin: when Bankruptcy and Arbitration Meet: A Look at Recent ICC Practice, Dispute Resolution International, 5 (2011) 1, p. 79 et seq.; Georg Naegeli: Bankruptcy and Arbitration—What Should Prevail? The Impact of Bankruptcy on Pending Arbitral Proceedings, in: Christian Klausegger et al. (eds.), Austrian Yearbook on International Arbitration, Vienna 2010, p. 193 et seq.; Gabrielle Kaufmann-Kohler, Laurent Levy, Sabina Sacco: The Survival of the Arbitration Agreement and Arbitration Proceedings in Cases of Cross-Border Insolvency: An Analysis from the Swiss Perspective, Les Cahiers de L'Arbitrage. The Paris Journal of International Arbitration, 2 (2010), p. 371 et seq.; Stefan Krill, Arbitration and Insolvency—Selected Conflict of Law Problems, in: Stefan Krill/Franco Ferrari (eds.), Conflict of Laws in International Arbitration, Munich 2010, p. 211 et seq.

6 United States Lines, 197 F 3d 631 (640) (2d Civ 1999); *see also Sonatrach v. Distrigas, Corp*, 80 BR 606 (610). (D. Mass 1987).

7 Philipp Wagner : Insolvency and Arbitration, posted on June 21, 2018, https://wagner-arbitration.com/en/journal/insolvency-law-and-arbitration/.

8 Corporate Disputes e-magazine dedicated to the latest developments in corporate and commercial disputes. Kirkland & Ellis International LLP, Oct-Dec 2017 issue, https://www.corporatedisputesmagazine.com/arbitration-and-insolvency-still-two-near-polar-extremes.

9 Jelena Bezarevic Pajic, and Vanja Tica, Moravcevic Vojnovic in cooperation with Schoenherr: When Arbitration Meets Insolvency in Montenegro – Can They Coexist? CEE Legal Matters, Year 3, Issue 6, Dec. 2016, p. 85.

10 Ishaan Madaan and Chauhan Prakhar; A Dialogue on International Arbitration and Insolvency; Kluwer arbitration blog, posted on Sep. 6, 2020.

11 Sylvain Marchand: Arbitrage et insolvabilité: tribulations d'un couple mal assorti. In: Nouveautés en matière de faillite transfrontalière; et les banques et les assurance face aux tiers: Actes de la 28e journée de droit international privé du 27 mai 2016 à Lausanne. Genève : Schulthess éd. romandes, 2016, p. 48.

12 Bruno cressard: État des lieux de l'articulation entre deux fortes têtes du droit des affaires, 23 juillet 2018 : Lettre de l'AFA (Association For Arbitration) n°28 | Juillet 2018 | Arbitrage et procédures collectives.

In addition, an arsenal of sub-questions surfaces: does the arbitration agreement concluded by the debtor before the commencement of insolvency proceedings become invalid or incapable of being performed in insolvency? Are pending arbitrations or ancillary court proceedings automatically stayed due to the insolvency of a party and under what circumstances may such proceedings be resumed? How should the conflicting interests be balanced in practice to achieve an efficient outcome for the users of arbitration agreements?

In fact, there is no consistency in terms of the various issues that arise when insolvency and international arbitration clash.[13] The reason they make such an "odd" couple is the different underlying policies, objectives, and purposes they stand for[14] throughout the various decisional stages and spheres of the problem. The approach to interpret the relation between arbitration and insolvency depends, as Manuel Fons[15] argued, on two factors: (1) whether the analysis is conducted by arbitrators or by national courts, and (2) whether the intersection is approached from the point of view of arbitration law or insolvency law.

The scene becomes expressive and complex within in between the divergent approaches taken by different national legal systems; some jurisdictions purport to prohibit individual proceedings, including arbitration, involving the debtor all together; some prohibit arbitration only in some circumstances or authorize the conduct of arbitration subject to various limitations and procedural adaptations; and others posit that insolvency should not affect arbitration at all. An additional group of states simply have no well-defined regime, or even no regime at all, necessitating a case-by-case analysis and response.[16]

From the perspective of an arbitration tribunal, it may be unclear to what extent a national regime purporting to regulate the effects of insolvency on arbitration should impact the arbitration at all, particularly when the seat of the arbitration is located outside the jurisdiction conducting the

13 'Insolvency and Arbitration: What Issues Arise?' article posted on July 4, 2020. https://www.acerislaw.com/insolvency-and-arbitration-what-issues-arise/.

14 Duncan Gorst and Josh Redman, associates at Hogan Lovells: Insolvency and arbitration during coronavirus (Covid-19), analysis was first published on Lexis®PSL on Nov. 13, 2020.

15 Manuel Penades Fons: Cross-border insolvency and international commercial arbitration, PhD thesis submitted at the University of Valencia (Spain) in July 2015, electronic copy available at: https://ssrn.com/abstract=3472328.

16 Courtney Lotfi, Isabel Lightbody: the overlap between insolvency proceedings and arbitration: the potential abuse and inconsistent result, TDM Special Issue, Vol (19), Issue (1), January 2022.

insolvency proceedings. In these cases, the co-existence of national approaches frequently raises conflict of laws questions that add a layer of complexity to the legal issues posed by the insolvency of a party to an arbitration at the domestic level. Moreover, the divergence of approaches in the arbitral law of various jurisdictions—for example, with respect to anti-arbitration injunctions, evaluating the legal capacity of a party to arbitrate, or the state's power to regulate domestic versus non-domestic arbitrations—may present further issues for arbitrators.[17]

On the other hand, cross-border insolvency by itself represents a separate problematic ground; it occurs when a debtor has assets in more than one state, or when debtor's creditors are not from the state where the insolvency proceeding is taking place.[18] This is invariably the case when large multinational companies apply for creditor protection, although these companies rarely operate under the same corporate entity internationally.[19] Instead, they rely on foreign incorporated subsidiaries that are created for tax, governance, or limitation of liability purposes. These complex corporate structures create difficulties for courts tasked with overseeing the insolvency proceedings, the main goals of which are to maximize the value of the debtor's worldwide assets, to protect debtor and creditor rights and to facilitate just administration of the proceedings.[20] The fragmented corporate structure creates a tension between the need for uniformity in international insolvency law to achieve these goals and the reality that a court's jurisdiction is territorially defined.

The basic issue that arises, as a result of the interplay between insolvency and arbitration before the issuance of the arbitral award, relates to the impact insolvency proceedings commenced for one party to an arbitration agreement have on the arbitration process. In other words, will the insolvency proceedings impose an automatic moratorium that comes into force and prevents the commencement or continuation of any "legal process," including arbitration? Or does it invoke a standalone moratorium which a

---

17 IBA, Toolkit on Insolvency and arbitration, IBA Arbitration committee, International Bar Association, 2021, p. 2.

18 EU, Library of the European Parliament, Cross-Border Insolvency Law in the EU (Library Briefing) by Rafal Manko (Feb. 21, 2013) at 1, online: http://www.europarl.europa.eu/RegData/bibliotheque/briefing/2013/130476/LDM_BRI(2013)130476_REV1_EN.pdf.

19 Allan L. Gropper: The Arbitration of Cross-Border Insolvencies" (2012) 86 Am Bank LJ 201 at 203 [Gropper].

20 World Bank, Principles and Guidelines for Effective Insolvency and Creditor Rights Systems (April 2001) at 53 online: http://www.worldbank.org/ifa/ipg_eng.pdf.

person or company can apply for provided that certain conditions or requirements are met?

In this chapter, we seek to address the renewed conflict between universalism and territorialism.

Rules Governing the Dialectic Relation Between Insolvency and Arbitration

A "Ticklish" Approach

The heart of the arbitration process lies in its delocalized nature and privity of the contract within the existence of party autonomy and independence from the state. Arbitrations are often conducted behind closed doors.[21]

In contrast, the insolvency process reflects a centralized, formalistic, accountable, and to a certain extent state-managed procedure governed by mandatory substantive and procedural law provisions designed with domestic economic objectives, aiming to support a state's economic, social, and political goals.[22] In many jurisdictions, various principles of insolvency law are part of domestic and international public policy, "*a cross-road where all the elements of the Legal System in question meet*"[23]

21 Lucila Marchini (Herbert Smith Freehills LLP): Arbitration And Insolvency: An Overview From Latin America, Kluwer Arbitration Blog, posted on Nov. 8, 2020.

22 "Policy goals" or "public interests" are used with the understanding that the interests of not just two parties to a transaction, but the interests of the public at large or of certain interested groups are concerned. For the public interests involved in insolvency proceedings, Gabrielle Kaufmann-Kohler & Laurent levy, Insolvency and International Arbitration in: The challenges of insolvency law reform in the 21st century 257, 275 (Henry Peter et al. eds., 2006). These public interests can—but do not necessarily have to—amount to a question of "public policy" or "order public." The latter denote fundamental legal principles or notions of justice, a departure from which would be incompatible with the respective national legal or economic system, *see also* Ishaaan Madaan: Insolvency and international arbitration, Kluwer Arbitration Blog, posted on June 15, 2020.

23 Klaus Sachs: Behind Closed doors: The impact of arbitral decisions and ADR/ mediation processes in the insolvency arena 'in Restructuring among the Ruins'. A Conference presented by the Insolvency, Restructuring and Creditors' Rights Committee of the IBA Insolvency, Restructuring and Creditors' Rights Section May 7-9, 2006 Athens, Greece. Alexander J. BĚLOHLÁVEK: Impact of Insolvency of a Party on Pending Arbitration Proceedings in Czech Republic, England and Switzerland and Other Countries, Yearbook on International Arbitration, p. 145; M. Roth, M. Giestlinger, eds., EAP, Berlin, 2010. Domitille Baizeau: Arbitration and Insolvency:

ensuring clear rules, predictable outcomes, and effective dispute resolution.

To better understand the impact of insolvency proceedings on international arbitration, it is worth reviewing the regulations in national laws of various jurisdictions (operating under different legal systems) and examine whether these regulations refer to the interplay between both proceedings on the domestic level and on the international level.

Domestic Regulations

The legal system a country adopts differs from one jurisdiction to another. The two well-known legal systems globally are the Common Law System and the Civil Law System. Hence, the rules under one legal system may differ from those under the other. Thus, we divide the study of domestic regulations into two categories: (1) regulations of jurisdictions adopting the Common Law Rules (here, the United Kingdom and the United States of America) and (2) regulations of jurisdictions adopting the Civil Law Rules (here, a selection of countries from different regions).

Common Law Rules:

United Kingdom

For nearly 17 years, insolvency and its administration were regulated under the Enterprise Act of 2003. However, the United Kingdom has recently reformed the insolvency framework with the enactment of the Corporate Insolvency and Governance Act of 2020. The law brings the changes seen as necessary to support the struggling businesses as they deal with the economic fallout from COVID-19. Nonetheless, the changes are not temporary. They are permanent. This means, the new changes will transform and shape the way creditors and debtors—facing or suffering from financial difficulties—interact with each other moving forward.[24]

One of the key areas the legislation focuses on is moratorium on legal proceedings, which will help prevent creditors initiating certain actions

---

Issues of Applicable Law, in: Christoph Müller/Antonio Rigozzi (eds.), New Developments in International Commercial Arbitration, Zurich/Basel/Geneva 2009, 97. Samantha Jayne Lord, "'When Two Polar Extremes Collide: An Exploration into the Effects of Insolvency on International Arbitration" (2012) 15 International Trade and Business Law Review 316, 319.

24 Corporate Insolvency and Governance Act 2020: A lifeline for struggling businesses in the United Kingdom – the most significant insolvency reforms for a generation – Allen & Overy Bulletin, Oct. 2020.

against the company for a specified duration. The provisions will provide businesses with a statutory breathing space from creditors within which to formulate a restructuring plan to help rescue the suffering business. The moratorium will last for an initial period of 20 business days from the day when it is ordered by an insolvency court, with an ability to be extended for further periods up to one year or more. For as long as the moratorium applies, it will prevent the enforcement of securities, commencement of insolvency proceedings, or other legal proceedings against the company.

Article (21/e) of the Corporate Insolvency and Governance Act 2020 states that:

> no legal process (including legal proceedings, execution, distress or diligence) may be instituted, carried out or continued against the company or its property except:
>
> (i) employment tribunal proceedings or any legal process arising out of such proceedings,
> (ii) proceedings, not within sub-paragraph (i), involving a claim between an employer and a worker, or
> (iii) a legal process instituted, carried out or continued with the permission of the court.

Even though the provisions of the above referenced article do not refer to arbitration per se, it is understood that the scope of the general term "legal process" does, in fact, include arbitration proceedings. Hence, the topic is examined by reference to three distinct stages:

(1) Arbitration proceedings commencing after the insolvency process (post-insolvency).
(2) Arbitration proceedings commencing prior to the insolvency process (pre-insolvency) and before issuing the arbitral award.
(3) Arbitration proceedings commenced prior to the insolvency process and the arbitral award issued but not enforced or recognized.

Based on the above interpretation of Article (21/e) of the Corporate Insolvency and Governance Act 2020, arbitration proceedings—being qualified as "legal process"—will be stayed in the first and second stages referred to above, due to the moratorium introduced by the new Act, unless a leave or exemption is granted by the court in this regard.

In reference to the third stage, an unenforced or unrecognized award is equivalent to a domestic judgment. In most circumstances, when a company has not paid an award and enters an insolvency process, the payment of the award will be resolved through the insolvency rules relating to distributions to creditors, unless the company survives.[25] Therefore, since the new standalone moratorium prevents certain enforcement actions and the commencement/continuation of legal proceedings against the company, the unenforced or unrecognized award will be treated as an established claim.

United States of America

In the United States, insolvencies are governed by the Bankruptcy Code. In general, arbitration, mediation, and other forms of alternative dispute resolution may not be used to administer or adjudicate matters that are before a bankruptcy court.[26] Therefore, it can be clearly noticed that tension exists between a legal presumption in favor of the enforceability of arbitration agreements and the broad jurisdiction that bankruptcy courts have over all proceedings arising in, under, or related to the Bankruptcy Code.[27]

The approach that bankruptcy courts have often adopted searches for the existence or satisfaction of four main factors to decide whether to enforce an arbitration clause or retain jurisdiction. These factors are

(1) Whether parties agreed to arbitrate.
(2) What is the scope of the agreements.
(3) Whether Congress intended the claims to be non-arbitrable.
(4) If some claims are arbitrable, the court must decide whether to stay the proceedings pending the outcome of the arbitration.

Nonetheless, even if the four criteria mentioned above are satisfied, bankruptcy courts may choose to retain jurisdiction for institutional legitimacy reasons such as a desire to uphold authority of the bankruptcy courts to oversee bankruptcy matters and the right of the debtor to file for bankruptcy.[28] Hence, we note that bankruptcy courts often differentiate between two types of disputes. On one hand, there are core disputes wherein a claim to be arbitrated is a claim that arises solely because the debtor is in bankruptcy; the courts will not enforce an arbitration clause. On the other hand, there are non-core disputes wherein the claim exists

25 Stephenson, Hothi, Impact of restructuring and insolvency on arbitration (Part 2), 10 July 2020, Practical Law Arbitration Blog (http://arbitrationblog.practicallaw.com/impact-of-restructuring-and-insolvency-on-arbitration-part-2/).

26 Adam Brenneman, Pamela Arce, Pablo Mori Bregante, David Schwartz, You have options: The use of alternative dispute resolution in insolvency proceedings, Emerging Markets Restructuring Journal, Issue No. 3, Spring 2017.

27 *Ibid.*

28 *Ibid.*

outside of the debtor's bankruptcy; the courts are most likely to enforce the arbitration agreement.[29]

Civil Law Rules

The majority of the countries/jurisdictions across the world have what can be described as primarily civil law systems. Therefore, we will be listing briefly the legal stance for the interplay between insolvency and arbitration for a number of jurisdictions from Latin America, Europe, the Middle East, and North African region.

Latin America

Argentina

As per the provisions of the Argentinian Insolvency Law (Law No. 24522 of 1995), the declaration of insolvency/bankruptcy leads to the arbitration clauses becoming "inapplicable."[30] This provision is clearly stipulated in Article 134 of the Argentinian Insolvency Law (as amended) which states that "The declaration of bankruptcy renders the arbitration clauses agreed with the debtor inapplicable, unless the arbitration or arbitration court has been constituted before the judgment is issued." In other words, the parties are not allowed to initiate arbitration proceedings to resolve their dispute if one of them has already been declared bankrupt or insolvent. However, if the arbitration proceedings commenced or the arbitral tribunal was already appointed before the declaration of bankruptcy, then the arbitration proceedings will resume after the bankruptcy declaration to reach an award.

Article 134 further continues to mention that the judge may authorize the trustee (who is a representative of the bankrupt party) to agree on the arbitration in particular cases or to allow the formation of an arbitral tribunal or appointment of an arbitrator.

Chile

The new Chilean Insolvency Law (Law No. 20.720 of 2013) was enacted to promote reorganizations as an alternative to liquidations. A lot of reforms were introduced to the provisions of the existing bankruptcy

---

29 *Ibid.*

30 Lucila Marchini, Arbitration and insolvency: An overview from Latin America, Kluwer Arbitration Blog, Nov. 8, 2020.

regime with the aim of simplification, but most importantly that of facilitating the financing of insolvent companies. As a result, specialized insolvency courts were created.[31]

The new Chilean Insolvency Law incorporates the figure of "Insolvency Arbitration." as a channel for dispute resolution. Chapter 7 of this law provides for the possibility to arbitrate both liquidation and reorganization proceedings. With regards to the reorganization proceedings, the debtor's consent is required in addition to two-thirds of creditor's liabilities. Regarding the liquidation proceedings, the debtor's consent is not needed and only a two-thirds majority vote of the verified claims is required to resort to arbitration.

In both cases, the arbitration procedure—once approved—is binding on all creditors, including those who did not consent from the start.[32]

Insolvency arbitration decision may be appealed, unless the parties agree otherwise. However, despite the adoption of this modern alternative by Chile, there are no known insolvency proceedings involving international creditors that have chosen to use arbitration.[33]

Peru

Unlike most jurisdictions in Latin America, Peru adopts administrative bankruptcy proceedings only, and courts have limited jurisdiction. These bankruptcy proceedings are handled and supervised by a specialized agency called the "National Institute for the Defense of Free Competition and the Protection of Intellectual Property."[34]

Articles 73 and 79 of the General Bankruptcy Law of Peru (Law No. 27809 of 2002) stipulate that the creditors have the option to decide that all disputes arising from the reorganization plan or the liquidation agreement will be subject to arbitration. However, the law does not contemplate the administration of bankruptcy proceedings themselves through arbitration. Thus, under the Peruvian Insolvency System, the bankruptcy proceedings themselves, and ancillary matters (such as recognition of credits and ranking of claims) cannot be handled through arbitration.[35]

---

31 Adam Brenneman, Pamela Arce, Pablo Mori Bregante, David Schwartz, You have options: The use of alternative dispute resolution in insolvency proceedings, Emerging Markets Restructuring Journal, Issue No. 3, Spring 2017.

32 *Ibid.*

33 *Ibid.*

34 *Ibid.*

35 *Ibid.*

The existence of a default under an ordinary reorganization plan cannot be arbitrated. Consequently, in the Peruvian insolvency system, the ability of creditors to elect arbitration under a restructuring proceeding is limited to controversies that are not related to a default on the payment terms set forth in the plan.[36]

In case of a dispute related to the execution of the pre-packaged agreement, including the debtor's default, both the creditors and debtor have the right to choose arbitration as the mechanism for resolution of such disputes.[37]

Europe

France

Being part of the European Union (EU) and subject to its regulations means that when the question of pending arbitration proceedings is raised during insolvency, one should refer to Article 18 of the EU Regulation No. 2015/848 stipulating that "the effects of insolvency proceedings on a pending law suit or pending arbitral proceedings concerning an asset or a right which forms part of the debtor's insolvency estate shall be governed solely by the law of the member state in which that lawsuit is pending or in which the arbitral tribunal has its seat."[38] In other words, it is important to refer to the insolvency provisions applied in France and their impact on pending arbitration proceedings.

According to Article L622-22 of the French Commercial Code, pending legal proceedings are stayed until the pursuing creditor has declared his or her debt in the insolvency proceedings. Therefore, arbitration proceedings may be resumed only for the purpose of certifying the existence of the debt and its quantity or amount. As a result, the arbitral tribunal will only be competent or capable to rule to determine whether the debt exists, and if so, to determine its amount. Yet, the arbitral tribunal will not be able to issue an order for payment against the insolvent party. In practice, this may mean that the arbitral tribunal's jurisdiction may be curtailed by the exclusive jurisdiction of the Insolvency Judge over the disputes and claims arising from or relating to the insolvency proceedings.

---

36 *Ibid.*

37 *Ibid.*

38 Roland Ziadé, Claudia Cavicchioli and Anne de Mazières, Cross-border Guide on the Impact of Insolvency on International Arbitration – Linklaters Insights, March 25, 2021.

Moreover, in the event the arbitration was initiated by the insolvent party, then the proceedings shall be suspended pursuant to Article (369) of the French Civil Procedure Code.

The question remains whether arbitration proceedings may be commenced against an insolvent party. Pursuant to Article L622-21 of the French Commercial Code, opening insolvency proceedings suspends and prohibits legal proceedings by any creditor seeking damages and termination of contract for default on payments against the debtor. The French Supreme Court has confirmed, in this regard, that the insolvency judge is bound by the principle of "competence-competence" and must, in such circumstances, defer the matter of the debt's existence, and its amount, to the arbitral tribunal.[39]

Middle East and North Africa

Although not all the countries of the Middle East and Northern African region have enacted or promulgated independent insolvency legislation, a few of them (Kingdom of Bahrain,[40] United Arab Emirates,[41] and the Hashemite Kingdom of Jordan[42]) have stand-alone Insolvency Laws.

---

39 Cass. Com. 2 Juin 2004, 02-18.700; Cass . Com. 25 Novembre 2008, 7-21.888; Cass. Civ. 1er Avril 2015, 14-14.552; Cass. Com. 3 Mai 2016, 14-28.982, in Bruno Cressard, État des lieux de l'articulation entre deux fortes têtes du droit des affaires, 23 juillet 2018 : Lettre de l'AFA (Association For Arbitration) n°28 | Juillet 2018 | Arbitrage et procédures collectives.

40 The insolvency regulations in Bahrain are split between two laws, the first being the Central Bank and Financial Institutions Law (No. 64 of 2006, issued on Sep. 6, 2006 and published in the Official Gazette, Issue No. 2755 (Supplement), Sep. 6, 2006. In force since Sep. 7, 2006); and the second being the Restructuring and Insolvency Law (No. 22 of 2018. Issued on May 30, 2018 and published in the official gazette, issue No. 3369, June 7, 2018. In force since Dec. 5, 2018. Amended once in 2020). The difference between the two laws is that the Insolvency Law applies to any company that is not licensed by the Central Bank, whereas the Central Bank and Financial Institutions Law applies to companies licensed by the Central Bank.

41 Federal Decree by Law No. 19 of 2019. Issued on Aug. 29, 2019 and published in the official gazette, issue No. 661 (Supplement), Aug. 29, 2019. In force since Nov. 28, 2019.

42 The Jordanian legislator has adopted the UNCITRAL Model Law on Cross-border Insolvency and enacted its Insolvency Law (No. 21 of 2018. Issue on May 7, 2018 and published in the official gazette, issue No. 5514, May 16, 2018. In force since Nov. 13, 2018).

Other countries (such as Kingdom of Saudi Arabia,[43] the Arab Republic of Egypt,[44] Kuwait,[45] Qatar,[46] and the Sultanate of Oman[47]) regulate insolvency within the provisions of Bankruptcy Laws, Commercial and/or Civil Codes as well as Commercial Companies Codes.

We look at two examples of these countries:

United Arab Emirates

The Insolvency Law that the United Arab Emirates has promulgated is also aligned with the international best practices, following the steps of mature and developed economies in establishing a clear legal and regulatory framework for insolvency.

Like many other pieces of legislation, the UAE Insolvency Law makes a general reference to the stay of legal proceedings. Articles (51), (52), and (67) dictate that when insolvency proceedings are commenced, existing or new lawsuits, execution and criminal proceedings are stayed or suspended. The exception to this general rule would be creditors with secured or preferential debts. They may, after pursuing permission from the competent court overlooking the insolvency proceedings, execute on their securities.

The law does not make any clear or direct reference to the effect of commencing insolvency proceedings on arbitration. However, the interpretation of the term "execution" could also mean the application to enforce any arbitral award against the insolvent party. In this event, the execution process is stayed by virtue of the articles referenced earlier.

---

43 The Saudi Bankruptcy Law (Royal Decree No. M/50 of 1439H. Issued on 28/5/1439H (corresponding to Feb. 14, 2018). Published in the official gazette, issue No. 4712, Feb. 23, 2018. In force since Aug. 22, 2018).

44 In Egypt, insolvency is regulated by the provisions in the Egyptian Civil Code of 1948 (Law No. 131 of 1948. Issue on July 16, 1948 and published in the official gazette, issue No. 108 BIS, July 29, 1948. In force as of Oct. 15, 1949); whereas bankruptcy is regulated under the provisions of the Egyptian Commercial Code (Law No. 17 of 1999, issued on May 17, 1999 and published in the official gazette, issue No. 19 BIS, May 17, 1999. In Force since Oct. 1, 1999).

45 The Kuwait Bankruptcy Law (No. 71 of 2020. Issued on Oct. 15, 2020 and published in the official gazette, issue No. 1506, Oct. 25, 2020. In force since Jan. 24, 2021).

46 The bankruptcy regime in Qatar is regulated by the provisions of Articles (606 to (846) of the Commercial Code (Law No. 27 of 2006. Issued on July 27,2006 and published in the official gazette, issue No. 2, Nov. 13, 2006. In force since May 13, 2007).

47 The Oman Bankruptcy Law (Royal Decree No. 53 of 2019. Issued on July 1, 2019. Published in the official gazette, issue No. 1300, July 7, 2019. In force since July 7, 2020).

Kuwait

Bankruptcy in Kuwait has always been regulated under the provisions of the Commercial Code. However, a little over a year ago, a new bankruptcy law was enacted. It is seen as an important legal update given it also used international bankruptcy and insolvency regulations as a benchmark.

Nonetheless, the Kuwait bankruptcy law differentiates between three situations where claims are suspended or stayed. These situations are

(1) In the event a decision to open the preventive settlement procedures is rendered, Article (61) of Kuwait bankruptcy law provides that the suspension of claims happens for a limited period (3 months). However, the period is renewable as long as the total period of suspension or stay does not exceed six months.
(2) In the event a decision to commence the restructuring procedures is rendered, Article (102) provides that all claims shall be suspended as of the day following the issuance of the decision and until the date the restructuring plan is approved and ratified.
(3) In the event a decision to commence the bankruptcy proceedings is rendered, Article (166) provides that no new or existing lawsuits may examined and ruled upon except for those relating to:
    (a) Assets and dispositions to which the debtor's prohibition does not extend.
    (b) Procedures stipulated in the bankruptcy law that are legally authorized.
    (c) Criminal lawsuits.

It is clearly noticeable from the above two examples, and similarly when examining provisions of legislation from different jurisdictions across the region, that most legislation do not make a clear or direct reference to arbitration proceedings in the event insolvency and/or bankruptcy was declared. The provision referring to the stay of legal proceedings (lawsuits, judicial and execution proceedings, etc.) exists in all the laws (insolvency or bankruptcy) without, however, making a clear reference to arbitral proceedings.

The only exception to the above would be the case of Jordan since it adopted the provisions of the United Nations Commission on International Trade Law (UNCITRAL) Model Law on Cross-border Insolvency that do, in fact, reference arbitration (and mediation) in Article (23).

International Regulations

When examining the provisions or regulations on the domestic level, in the preceding paragraphs, we noticed that most of the laws/legislation (in most jurisdiction showcased), fail to refer to arbitration as an independent "legal process" when stipulating the stay of procedures against an insolvent debtor. Most legislation, when referencing the stay or suspension of procedures, uses general terms that may—or may not—include arbitration as a stand-alone judicial or legal process that may be initiated against an insolvent debtor.

Having said that, it is clearly noticeable that recent laws and regulations enacted to organize the insolvency regime used international practices and the UN Model Law on Cross-border insolvency as benchmark. Therefore, the question that remains is: did these international regulations reference arbitration in the stay of proceedings? If not, in what way then can international regulations provisions be interpreted?

In the following paragraphs, we have a close look on two of the main international regulations concerning insolvency. The first is the UNCITRAL Model Law on Cross-Border Insolvency (and its interpretive guide of 2013). The second is the EU Insolvency Regulation of 2015.

UNCITRAL Model Law on Cross-Border Insolvency

The international community has acknowledged the importance of the insolvency phenomenon since the previous century.[48] They have focused their efforts on formulating, a legal framework comprehensively and effectively in order to achieve the desired goals of protecting the investment projects and helping investors avoid bankruptcy.

International efforts in this regard resulted in the development of the UNCITRAL Legislative Guide on Insolvency Law. In its four parts, it provides a reference tool for use by national authorities and legislative bodies, while they prepare new laws and regulations, or review their adequacy in a manner that achieves a balance between addressing the debtor's financial distress—in the fastest and most efficient way possible—and the interests of the various parties directly concerned with

---

48 The insolvency system is subject to legislative regulation in most countries, and we mention from that: chapter 11 of the US Federal Bankruptcy Act (1978), articles (L611-4 to L611-15) of the French Trade Act (2005), the German Insolvency Act (1999), the UAE Insolvency Law (2019), the Bahrain Reorganization and Bankruptcy Law (2018), the Oman Bankruptcy Law (2019) and the Kuwait Bankruptcy Law (2020).

that financial distress. This includes creditors and other parties who have an interest in the debtor's commercial business, in addition to the public policy considerations such as employment and tax matters.

UNCITRAL issued in 1997 the UNCITRAL Model Law on Cross-border Insolvency, its interpretive guide (2013) and its application from a judicial perspective (2011). The judicial perspective is mainly concerned with identifying the issues that may arise in connection with a request for recognition or cooperation under the Model Law. It examines measures used by various courts in states that have enacted legislation based on the Model Law.

Paragraph 180 of the Guide to Enactment and Interpretation of the UNCITRAL Model Law on Cross-Border Insolvency provides that "sub-paragraph 1 *(a)* (of Article 20 of the Model Law) by not distinguishing between various kinds of individual action, also covers actions before an arbitral tribunal. Thus, Article 20 establishes a mandatory limitation to the effectiveness of an arbitration agreement. This limitation is added to other possible limitations restricting the freedom of the parties to agree to arbitration that may exist under national law."[49] Nonetheless, there may exist a difficulty in enforcing the stay such as the event the arbitration does not take place in either the enacting state (of either parties) or the state of the main proceeding. Apart from that, the interest of the parties may be a reason for allowing the arbitral proceedings to continue, the right to commence individual actions or proceedings will not be affected by the stay to the extent that such actions or proceedings are necessary to preserve a claim against the debtor. This occurs in the case the scope of the stay is subject to certain provisions of the law of the enacting state relating to insolvency that apply to exceptions, limitations, modifications, or termination of the stay (sub-paragraph 2 of Article 20 of the Model Law).

European Union Insolvency Regulations (2000 and 2015)

In the interpretation of the European Insolvency Regulations (referred to hereafter as "EIR"), scholars have expressed two main points of view:

The first position adopts a wide interpretation of the rules of the EIR (namely Articles 4.2(f) and 15 or Regulation No. 1346/2000). This position is encapsulated in the judgment of the English Court of Appeal in *Elektrim v. Vivendi*.

49 UNCITRAL Model Law on Cross-Border Insolvency Law with Guide to Enactment and Interpretation, United Nations, New York 2014, p. 84.

According to this position, the law applicable to the effects of insolvency on arbitration should be determined by Articles 4.2(f)[50] (*under the new provisions of the Recast Insolvency Regulations EIR 848/2015, it is Article 7.2.f*) and 15[51] (*under the new provisions of the Recast Insolvency Regulations EIR 848/2015, it is Article 18)* of the EIR 1346/2000, provided that the arbitration proceedings have not yet started at the time the insolvency of one of the parties has been declared. Therefore, the *lex fori concursus (law of the State of the opening of insolvency proceedings)* will govern the consequences of insolvency on the arbitration process (including the validity and operability of the arbitration agreement). To the contrary, if the arbitration proceedings were already pending at the time the insolvency was declared, the law of the seat of the arbitration (*lex loci arbitri*) will be applicable and thus regulate the effects of insolvency.[52]

The second position adopts a narrow interpretation based on the issues of *vis attractiva concursus* (i.e., questions that relate to the scope of the jurisdiction of the insolvency court). Defining the limits of the *vis attractiva concursus* has been a subject of various cases before the Court of Justice of the European Union. According to the court's case law, when the claim is the consequence of insolvency proceedings or is directly related to it, then it should be characterized as an action of insolvency nature. Therefore, in applying the rules of the EIR, the competence to decide on these claims is exclusive to the Member State where the collective proceedings have been initiated. In contrary, when the subject matter of the action is of civil or commercial nature, then there is no mandatory *vis attractiva concursus* imposed by the EIR.[53]

---

50 EIR 1346/2000, Art. 4:

> "1 …
> 2. The law of the State of opening of proceedings shall determine the conditions for opening of those proceedings, their conduct and their closure. It shall determine in particular:
>   (a) …
>   …
>   (f) the effects of the insolvency proceedings on proceedings brought by individual creditors, with the exception of lawsuits pending." Under the new provisions of the Recast Insolvency Regulations (EIR 848/2015), it is art. 7.2.f.

51 EIR 1346/2000, Art. 15: "The effects of insolvency proceedings on a lawsuit pending concerning an asset or a right of which the debtor has been divested shall be governed solely by the law of the Member State in which the lawsuit is pending."

52 Manuel Penades Fons, Cross-border insolvency and international commercial arbitration, PHD Thesis submitted at the University of Valencia (Spain) in July 2015, electronic copy available at: https//ssrn.com/abstract=3472328.

53 *Ibid.*

The court's case law reminds of the approach US courts have adopted (explained earlier here) when differentiating between the "core" and "non-core" insolvency issues related to insolvency.

It is worth noting here that a new directive (2019/1023, June 20, 2019) was issued by the European Parliament and Council of the European Union concerning the *preventive restructuring frameworks, on discharge of debt and disqualifications, and on measures to increase the efficiency of procedures concerning restructuring, insolvency and discharge of debt.* The directive, now in force (as of 17 July 2021), aims to remove obstacles to the exercise of fundamental freedoms (such as the free movement of capital) by ensuring that viable enterprises and entrepreneurs that are in financial difficulties have access to effective national preventive restructuring frameworks which enable them to continue operating.[54] Therefore, the directive in Article 6 (stay of individual enforcement claims) stipulates that Member States shall ensure that debtors can benefit from a stay of individual enforcement actions to support the negotiations of a restructuring plan in a preventive restructuring framework (art 6.1). The directive continues to mention, under the provisions of the same article, that the stay of individual enforcement actions can cover all types of claims, including secured claims and preferential claims (Article 6.2).

What this new directive seems to miss clarifying is whether the stay will apply to arbitration proceedings commenced against the debtor (party to an arbitration agreement or contract with a clause in dispute resolution by arbitration). Even though the text used in Article 6 is broad and general (all types of claims), however it may be construed that the broad implication of the term does, in fact, include the "claim" to enforce a favorable arbitral award before national courts against the insolvent party.

The directive came into force on July 17, 2021. Therefore, this will be an area for legal practitioners to watch and monitor closely to see how the Court of Justice of the European Union will respond to claims of stay of arbitration proceedings commenced before or after the enforcement of the directive that may affect the discussion or negotiation of the debtor's restructuring plan.

---

54 The objective as mentioned in the text of the EU Directive 2019/1023, June 20, 2019.

The Evolution of Jurisprudence and Courts' Approach: Lessons Learned

Having reviewed the domestic and international regulation that touch upon the issues or legal questions arising from the clash between insolvency proceedings and international arbitration, it is important to read through the different approaches that courts, across different jurisdictions, have taken regarding the interplay between insolvency and arbitration and understand the background of some of their key and defining judgments.

However, before we start our roller coaster ride through the different judgments, it is important to understand that most of the judgments examined cases that related to two main sets of legal points that may be grouped as follows:

(A) Capacity, Validity, and Arbitrability.
(B) Good Faith and the abused referral to arbitration.

Capacity, Validity, and Arbitrability:

The question of capacity and validity of the arbitration agreement has always been raised when faced with insolvency proceedings, requesting a stay or suspension of arbitration (as a legal process) against the insolvent party. Therefore, the application of general rules varied between courts from different jurisdictions. In the following text, we look at key judgments that had a significant impact on the legal scene relating to the interaction between insolvency and international arbitration.

Elektrim SA v. Vivendi (2009):

The Swiss Federal Supreme Court was presented, in March 2009, with an interim award on jurisdiction rendered by the arbitral[55] tribunal dealing with the impact of cross-border insolvency on its competence to hear the case. In such an interim award, the arbitral tribunal decided to discontinue proceedings against a Polish entity (*Elektrim SA*), which had fallen into bankruptcy after the initiation of the arbitration proceedings.

55 Daniel Eisele and Tamir Livschitz, The impact of cross-border insolvency on international arbitration: A Swiss view, Expert Guide: Litigation & Dispute Resolution, Aug. 2013.

Pursuant to Article 142 of the Polish Bankruptcy Law,[56] the law of the place of incorporation of *Elektrim SA*, any arbitration agreement concluded by a bankrupt entity is deemed to lose its legal effect, and, thus, arbitral proceedings shall be discontinued. Consequently, the arbitral tribunal decided that, since *Elektrim SA* had fallen into bankruptcy, it then lost its legal capacity to arbitrate and thus the lack of the subjective arbitrability automatically resulted in the lack of jurisdiction of the arbitral tribunal over *Elektrim SA*.

The Swiss Federal Supreme Court upheld the interim award in appeal,[57] holding that pursuant to the Swiss conflict of laws rules, Articles 154[58] and 155/c[59] of the Private International Law Act (PILA), the legal capacity of an entity or corporation is governed by the law of the entity or corporation's place of incorporation. Hence, reverting to the Polish Law (place of incorporation of *Elektrim SA*), and stipulating that any arbitration clause lost its legal effect with respect to the bankrupt party, the arbitral tribunal rightfully rejected its jurisdiction over the bankrupt *Elektrim SA*.[60]

After the widespread criticism[61] of the *Elektrim v. Vivendi* judgment, the Swiss Federal Court ceased the opportunity to revisit its decision in 2012 (case reference 4A_50/2012, October 16, 2012[62]), to clarify—and in essence to retract—its previous position expressed in the *Elektrim v.*

56 Article 142 of the Polish Bankruptcy Law (PKSG, Act of 28 Feb. 2003): "Any arbitration clause concluded by a bankrupt shall lose its legal effect as at the date bankruptcy is declared and any pending arbitration proceedings shall be discontinued."

57 Judgment of 31 March 2009, *Vivendi S.A. v. Deutsche Telekom*, AG, 28 ASA, Bull. 104 (Swiss Fed. Trib) (201).

58 Art. 154:

> "1. Companies shall be governed by the law of the State under which they are organized if they satisfy the publication or registration requirements of that law or, if there are no such requirements, if they are organized according to the law of that State.
> 2. A company which fails to meet these conditions shall be governed by the law of the State in which it is administered in fact."

59 Art. 155: "Except as set forth in Art 156 to 161, the law applicable to the company shall govern in particular:

a. The legal nature of the company;
b. …
c. The legal capacity and the capacity to act;
d. … "

60 Daniel Eisele and Tamir Livschitz, The impact of cross-border insolvency on international arbitration.

61 Karrer: Views on the decision by the Swiss Supreme Court of 31 March 2009, *Vivendi S.A. v. Deutsche Telekom*, AG, 28 ASA, Bull. 111.111 (2010)

62 Judgment of 16 October 2012, 31 ASA Bull. 354,366 (Swiss Fed. Trib) (2013)

Vivendi judgment. It adopted another approach towards the dispute presented to it in following a two-step method:

> The first step was to separate the question of the validity of the arbitration clause from the question of legal capacity. It noted that, pursuant to the provisions of Swiss law, an arbitration clause shall be considered valid if it corresponded either to the law chosen by the parties, to the law applicable to the dispute or to the Swiss law (Article 178/2 PILA). Hence, an arbitration clause would be considered valid because it is not affected by the opening of a bankruptcy proceeding and remains binding on the bankruptcy administrator.[63]
>
> Although an arbitration agreement/clause may be considered invalid due to the party's incapacity, however, the Swiss Federal Court tried to differentiate the two concepts from each other because the "incapacity" of the insolvent/bankrupt party (pursuant to Article 142 of the Polish Bankruptcy Law) was not present at the time of signing the arbitration agreement or agreement containing the arbitration clause. It existed after the agreement was signed by the insolvent party (not insolvent at the time of signing).
>
> In contrast, if we compare the above with the provisions of Article V of the New York Convention of 1958, we notice the similarity in the approach adopted by the Convention in reference to the enforcement of arbitral awards. Article V identifies the conditions under which the enforcement of an arbitral award may be refused. One of the listed conditions is the "parties' capacity." A lack of capacity of either parties is valid grounds for courts to refuse the enforcement of an arbitral award. However, two special notes must be cleared as a result:
>
>> First, Article V(1)(a) provides that the parties' capacity must be determined by reference to the law "applicable to them." However, the provision does not specify the choice of law rules relevant to this determination, leaving it to the court of the enforcement state to deal with any conflicts of law rules.

63 Daniel Eisele and Tamir Livschitz The Impact of Cross-border Insolvency on International Arbitration: A Swiss View, Expert Guide Litigation & Dispute Resolution, August 2013.

> Second, Article V(1)(a) of the New York Convention is restricted to lack of capacity to enter into the agreement at the time it was made. It does not deal with any lack of capacity to enter into the underlying contract, or lack of proper representation during the arbitral proceedings.

The second step was in the differentiation between the new case and the *Elektrim* case. The court stated that the pertinent provisions in Portuguese law related to the validity of the arbitration clause and not the question of legal capacity (of a bankrupt party).

2. Fulham Football Club (1987) Ltd v. Richards (2011):

The arbitrability of claims and remedies in accordance with the provisions of company and insolvency laws was one of the key points that examined by courts under the English Law. This judgment reflects the position under the English Law.[64]

In dismissing an appeal, the English Court of Appeal concluded that it was a case where there was no express provision in either the UK Arbitration Act of 1996 or the UK Companies Act 2006 which excluded arbitration as a means of resolving this type of shareholder dispute. Therefore, there was no reason why the dispute should not be arbitrated. This, ultimately, raised the question of whether there was an implicit restriction or some inherent reason why unfair prejudice claims should not be arbitrable.

The case concerned an unfair prejudice petition brought by Fulham Football Club regarding allegations that Sir David Richards, chairman of the Football Association Premier League (FAPL), had acted as an unauthorized agent with respect to the transfer of Peter Crouch from Portsmouth to Tottenham Hotspur Football & Athletic Company Limited (aka Tottenham), to the detriment of Fulham. The FAPL was created to give the Premier League commercial independence. Each of the clubs in the Premier League holds one share in the FAPL, and these shares cannot be traded or sold and are only transferred upon relegation of a club.

Rather than going to arbitration, Fulham brought court proceedings against Sir Richards and FAPL seeking an injunction prohibiting Sir

64 Ayca Bengu Koksal, A Tale of Two Proceedings: Arbitration and Insolvency, Nov. 16, 2020, published on https://www.mondaq.com/turkey/arbitration-dispute-resolution/1006244/a-tale-of-two-proceedings-arbitration-and-insolvency.

Richards from acting as unauthorized agent in the future and requesting his removal as the FAPL chairman. The grounds on which Fulham based its proceedings were

(1) the subject matter was not arbitrable; and
(2) the arbitration clause in question should be construed as to exclude a dispute about unfair prejudice.

In dealing with this question, Patten LJ (delivering the leading judgment of the Court of Appeal) differentiated between the "subject matter" of the dispute, the allegation of unfair prejudice, which he held was clearly arbitrable, and the remedies which might be granted as a result.[65]

In the absence of any statutory restriction or rule of public policy preventing the parties from agreeing to submit certain types of claims to arbitration, it was impossible to read any limitation into the wide language of the arbitration clause. Therefore, when deciding whether a corporate dispute, i.e., the "subject matter," was arbitrable or not, the question to consider was whether the claim brought attracted "a degree of state intervention and public interest such as to make it inappropriate for disposal by anything other than judicial process."

The wide expressions of "all disputes" and "all differences" should be given their natural meaning.

The High Court in England, in a recent judgment issued on 23 September 2020, in the matter of *Riverrock Securities Limited v International Bank of St Petersburg (Joint Stock Company)*, held and confirmed the pro-arbitration approach of the English courts in holding parties to their agreement to arbitrate when the latter is broad enough to cover the claims under dispute.[66]

(3) *Nori Holding Limited v. Bank Otkritie Financial Corporation (PJSC) (2018)*

The decision of the English Court of Appeal in this case revisited the question whether the court of one EU Member State can grant an anti-suit injunction where one of the parties has started legal proceedings in another EU Member State in disregard of an existing arbitration agreement. The

65 Fulham Football Club (1987) Ltd. V. Richards and others, (2011) EWCA cvi 955 (21 July 2011).

66 Velislava Hristova and Boris Praštalo, Arbitrating insolvency disputes? The English High Court showcases its pro-arbitration stance once again, Kluwer Arbitration Blog, Nov.19, 2020.

main question that was addressed by the English Court was whether an injunction can or should be granted to restrain proceedings brought in accordance with the insolvency law of a foreign state to set aside a transaction at an undervalue.

The case Nori Holdings is the first reported decision by the English courts on this issue since the Recast Brussels Regulation[67] came into force. This regulation sought to clarify the issue of conflicts of jurisdiction and the recognition and enforcement of judgments between the courts of EU Member States.[68]

The claimants in the anti-suit proceeding, which were companies incorporated in Cyprus and BVI that owned real estate in Russia, had entered into several loan agreements with a Russian bank (the defendant), which were secured by pledges of shares. While the loan agreements were governed by the laws of Russia, the share pledge agreements were governed by the laws of Cyprus. Moreover, most of the referred agreements included an arbitration clause that provided for disputes to be resolved by arbitration in London.

In 2017, the bank's short-term secured loans were replaced with long-term unsecured bonds. Despite the claimants' arguments that the new arrangements were a legitimate commercial restructuring, the bank initiated legal proceedings in both Russia and Cyprus for civil fraud and insolvency. However, the claimants sought to enforce the arbitration clause in the agreements. They argued that in light of an arbitration clause, the bank should not be permitted to proceed with the legal proceedings in Russian and Cyprus.

The bank asserted that the proceedings (Russian Court) were not in breach of the arbitration agreements because

(1) the arbitration clause should be construed as not applicable to an insolvency claim; and
(2) such claims (insolvency related) are in principle not arbitrable.

The decision in *Nori Holdings* upholds the European Court of Justice's position[69] that an EU court's ability to determine its own jurisdiction, when

67 EU Regulation No. 1215/2012.
68 Edward Attenborough and Mark Sanders, English Commercial Court confirms West Tankers decision on EU anti-suit injunctions, White & Case, 19 June 2018, published on: https://www.whitecase.com/publications/alert/english-commercial-court-confirms-west-tankers-decision-eu-anti-suit-injunctions.
69 *Allianz SpA and Generali Assicurazioni Generali SpA v. West Tankers Inc.*, Case C-185/07, [2009] ECR. I-663.

it is perceived as a dispute potentially subject to an arbitration clause, trumps the enforcement of the said clause by another EU court. As a result, the English Court refused to grant the anti-suit injunction (submitted by Nori Holdings) to enforce arbitration clauses. The court, however, also ordered the discontinuance of the proceedings before the Russian Court while allowing the Cyprus proceedings (also initiated by the Russian Bank) to continue.

Larsen Oil and Gas Pte Ltd v. Petropod Ltd (2011)

This judgment was rendered in 2011. It explains the position under the Singaporean Law.[70] In *Larsen Oil and Gas Pte Ltd v. Petropod Ltd (in liquidation)* (2011) SGCA 21, the Singapore Court of Appeal refused to grant a stay of the liquidators' court-initiated preference claims arising under a management agreement containing an arbitration clause. Despite the accepted strong judicial inclination in favor of arbitration, it was held that preference claims were not contemplated by the parties at the time of contracting and consequently did not fall within the scope of the arbitration agreement.[71]

However, the court went even further and held that statutory insolvency claims were generally non-arbitrable (which was endorsed in *Fulham*).

The English Court undertook a detailed examination of the authorities under both English Law and Singaporean Law. The conclusion it reached can be summarized as follows:

(1) In the absence of express exclusion of disputes of any kind, from the terms of the arbitration clause, the words should be understood to "mean what they say." There is no good reason to imply any limitation to the clause's effect or inclusion of insolvency proceedings. Therefore, the dispute was held as arbitrable.

(2) Contrary to the Singaporean law, the English law does not operate with the presumption that claims made in the context of insolvency will fall outside the scope of the arbitration clause/agreement. The court affirmed that the dispute was a straightforward factual dispute as to whether the bank was defrauded to replace valuable secured loans with non-valuable bonds.

(3) With reference to the claim that the subject matter was non-arbitrable, the court valued substance over form. Therefore, the

70 Matthew Crawford, Insolvency and Arbitration, published on https://www.ritanz.org.nz/insolvency-and-arbitration.

71 *Ibid.*

arbitrators could decide whether the claimants had defrauded the bank and grant, if so, the required remedy the damaged party is entitled to.

The Larsen case drew a distinction between claims arising within the insolvency where there is a presumption of non-arbitrability, and claims arising from pre-insolvency rights where the presumption is reversed. For the court to rule on the claim as "non-arbitrable," it needed express exclusion from arbitration. However, the court relied on the scope of the arbitration clause/agreement to issue its decision.

Good Faith v. the Abuse of Referral to Arbitration

Winding-up petitions resemble "quick sands." They are tricky when it comes to the relationship between insolvency and arbitration. The veracity of the claim of insolvency is of big importance. Professor Mistelis states that an allegation of insolvency should be evidenced before the tribunal. The tribunal is then entrusted with the duty of verifying both the allegations and the implications of such insolvency proceedings under domestic law. Another point of view presented by Professor Shaughnessy states, court insolvency proceedings provide ample proof of the existence of such a situation and allegations of impunity must be demonstrated, too.[72] However, actual practice has led to a different approach.

The Traditional Approach: Restrictive Framework to Arbitrate:

The traditional approach was that the courts will only dismiss an insolvency petition in favor of arbitration if the opposing debtor is able to prove that it has a *bona fide* defense on substantial grounds to the underlying debt. In practice, this meant that the courts would grant the creditor his application to wind up the debtor if the debtor has failed to pay a debt without a credible defense, and without requiring the parties to first arbitrate.[73]

The English Courts, however, broke this traditional approach. As per a recent judgment from 2014, the court decided that arbitration prevails, and the court should only exercise its discretion to dismiss the winding-up petition where it has been presented based on a contractual debt where the contract contains an arbitration clause. This was the position of the court of

72 Ishaan Madaan and Chauhan Prakhar: A Dialogue on International Arbitration and Insolvency.

73 Sarah Thomas, Jessica Chan: The Effect of Arbitration Clauses on Winding Up Petitions: Arbitration Come What May, Nov. 2019, published on http://www.hk-lawyer.org/content/effect-arbitration-clauses-winding-petitions-arbitration-come-what-may.

appeal in the famous case known as "Salford Estates" (2014).[74] Unanimously, the court stated that

> [T]he intention of the legislature in enacting the 1996 Act was to exclude the court's jurisdiction to give summary judgment… it would be anomalous, in the circumstances, for the Companies Court to conduct a summary judgment type analysis of liability for an unadmitted debt, on which a winding up petition is grounded, when the creditor has agreed to refer any dispute relating to the debt to arbitration. Exercise of the discretion otherwise than consistently with the policy underlying the 1996 Act would inevitably encourage parties to an arbitration agreement – as a standard tactic – to by-pass the arbitration agreement and the 1996 Act by presenting a winding up petition.

The court reasoned that the absence of an admission of the petitioning debt sufficed to constitute a "dispute" under the Arbitration Act 1996. "Dispute" is defined to include "any difference." The court concluded that the arbitration agreement covered the dispute as to petitioning debt and thus stayed the petition so that the parties would be compelled to resolve their "dispute" by arbitration. The approach effectively places insolvent debtors who are party to an arbitration agreement in a favored position compared to other insolvent debtors by enabling them to stave off insolvency proceedings.

However, a division emerged over the purportedly "pro-arbitration" approach in Salford Estates in the case law of certain current and former Commonwealth jurisdictions that consider English authorities to be highly persuasive.[75] For instance, the position of the Hong Kong court was remarkable. The contrast started with the "Lasmos" case (2018).[76]

---

74 *Salford Estates (No 2) Ltd v. Altomart Ltd (No 2)* [2015] Ch 589. *See also* Eco Measure Market Exchange Ltd (2015) BCC 877.

75 See the position of the Eastern Caribbean Court of Appeal in *Jinpeng Group Ltd v. Peak Hotels and Resorts Ltd*, BVI HCMAP 2014/0025 and 2015/0003. Also see in Singapore, The High Court of The Republic Of Singapore, BDG v. BDH [2016] 5 SLR 977; Supreme Court of Singapore, *AnAn Group (Singapore) Pte Ltd v. VTB Bank* (Public Joint Stock Company) [2020] SGCA 33. For more details see Sarah Thomas, Jessica Chan: But Ka Chon v. Interactive Brokers LLC, Case Updates Bankruptcy, Sep. 2019, http://www.hk-lawyer.org/content/ka-chon-v-interactive-brokers-llc; Nandakumar Ponniya, Richard Allen: Singapore Court of Appeal Clarifies Relationship Between Insolvency and Arbitration Regimes, May 6, 2020 https://restructuring.bakermckenzie.com/2020/05/06/singapore-singapore-court-of-appeal-clarifies-relationship-between-insolvency-and-arbitration-regimes/.

76 *Lasmos Ltd v. Southwest Bauxite (HK) Ltd* (2018) 2 HKLRD 449.

Prior to the "Lasmos" case, the position of the Hong Kong courts was very clear.[77] When faced with a petition submitted based on insolvency grounds, with the debt relied upon arising from a contract containing an arbitration clause, the court would require the debtor to demonstrate that there is a "*bona fide dispute in substance*" for the purpose of persuading the court to exercise its discretion to either stay or dismiss a petition in favor of arbitration.

It has been construed that there is a valid reasoning behind this approach: When a debtor is insolvent, the winding-up petition would engage the court's jurisdiction, and the latter would be required to consider the interest of all creditors of the debtor and not just the interest of the petitioner. Permitting a debtor to dismiss a petition with relative ease even when there is no "real" dispute to be arbitrated, however, could have the effect of allowing an insolvent debtor to continue trading and incur further debts, thus prejudicing the rights of all creditors.

In the "Lasmos" case, the Honorable Mr. Justice Harris ("Harris J") in the Court of First Instance decided to depart from the prior Hong Kong first instance authorities and broadly followed the English Court of Appeal's approach in Salford Estates. Harris J considered that, previously, the Hong Kong authorities had failed to give enough weight to the policy underlying the Arbitration Ordinance, i.e., encouraging and supporting party autonomy in determining the means by which a dispute arising between them should be resolved. Citing Salford Estates and its related authorities and the Singaporean authority BDG versus BDH,[78] Harris J held that the courts should generally dismiss an insolvency petition in favor of arbitration when the following three requirements are met:

(1) The opposing debtor disputes the petitioning debt (it is sufficient for the debtor to show that the debt is not admitted).
(2) The contract under which the petitioning debt is alleged to arise contains an arbitration clause that covers any dispute relating to the debt.

77 *Hollmet AG & Anr v. Meridian Success Metal Supplies Ltd* [1997] HKLRD 828; Re Sky Datamann (Hong Kong) Ltd (unreported, HCCW 487/2001, Jan. 29, 2002); Re Jade Union Investment Ltd (unreported, HCCW 400/2003, March 5, 2004); Re Southern Beauty Materials Holding (HK) Co Ltd (unreported, HCCW 281/2007, 13 Feb. 2008); and Re Quicksilver Glorious Sun JV Ltd [2014] 4 HKLRD 759 in Robin Darton, Tim Au: Arbitration clauses and insolvency proceedings revisited, Sep. 12, 2019, https://www.tannerdewitt.com/legal-update-arbitration-clause-insolvency-proceedings/

78 *BDG v. BDH* (2016) SGHC 211; Darius Chan, Sidharrth B Rajagopal: To stay or not to stay? A clash of arbitration and insolvency regimes. (2021). Journal of International Arbitration. 38, (4), p. 473.

(3) The opposing debtor takes steps required under the arbitration clause to commence the contractually mandated dispute resolution process.[79]

Similar to "Salford Estates," the "Lasmos" approach establishes a substantial obstacle to winding up petitions in respect of debts arising under agreements containing an arbitration clause, with the additional requirement (derived from BDG versus BDH) that the opposing debtor must have taken a step towards formal dispute resolution. If the creditor and debtor have an arbitration agreement, then the insolvent debtor can stave off insolvency proceedings by simply not admitting the underlying debt and force the creditor to arbitrate.

The Moderate Approach: A Justified Reservation

However, recently, in the "But Ka Chon" case (2019),[80] the Court of Appeal succinctly summarized the position of Lasmos and adopted a rather moderate approach. Due to the importance and novelty of this judgment, we believe it will be useful to include more details on it.

Mr. But was one of Interactive Brokers LLC's customers. Among other instruments, he traded in currency future contracts, including a contract relating to the differential between the Euro and the Swiss Francs ("CHF"). In January 2015, the Swiss National Bank unexpectedly lifted the "peg" that hitherto had existed as between the CHF and the Euro. The result was a rapid move in the market. Mr. But incurred substantial losses on his trading positions as a result. Thus, he refused to compensate for the resulting shortfall on his account. Accordingly, Interactive Brokers subsequently issued a statutory demand against him for such amount. Mr. But then made an application to set aside the statutory demand pursuant to Rules 47 and 48 of the Bankruptcy Rules (Cap. 6A) ("BR"). He relied on several grounds claiming that there is a "*bona fide* dispute with substance" based on alleged misrepresentations (made by Interactive Brokers LLC) when he opened his account.

As the underlying contract contained an arbitration clause, Mr. But also relied on Salford in requesting to set aside the application. However, his application was unsuccessful.

Mr. Butt had argued that (1) he had a defense and counterclaim based on misrepresentation, and (2) the court should follow the Salford Estates

79 *Thomas, Chan: But Ka Chon v. Interactive Brokers LLC.*
80 *But Ka Chon v. Interactive Brokers LLC* [2019] HKCA 873.

approach and set aside the statutory demand without any need for him to show that the debt was a "*bona fide* dispute" on substantial grounds.[81]

The Court of First Instance, Deputy High Court Judge Yee dismissed the claim on misrepresentation of the facts and decided to follow the pre-*Lasmos* approach. He noted that the *Lasmos* decision "*made a substantial departure from previous authorities at first instance in Hong Kong*." He also held that there was no "genuine dispute" to be arbitrated and that the alleged dispute was "*thoroughly bad and has no merit*." The judge further noted that even if the Lasmos approach was to be applied, he would not have set aside the statutory demand because the debtor had not commenced arbitration for more than four years and had no genuine intention of doing so.

It must be noted that Deputy High Court Judge Yee considered the Lasmos case, and the approach adopted in it, to be inapplicable because Mr. But's application was based on Rule 48(5)(b) of the Bankruptcy Rules (BR). This rule states that the court may grant the application to set aside a statutory demand if the debt is disputed on grounds which appear to the court to be substantial. By relying on these provisions, the decision "*sought by the parties*" was whether there was a "*bona fide* dispute" on substantial grounds.[82]

On appeal, the court agreed with the Court of First Instance's finding that there is no "dispute" to be arbitrated, and that the allegations of misrepresentation were ill founded. The "Lasmos" approach represents a substantial reduction in the creditors' statutory right since it requires the courts to exercise discretion in favor of arbitration only if all three requirements are met, save in wholly exceptional circumstances.[83]

The Court of Appeal in Mr. But's case continued to discuss the appropriateness of the Lasmos approach on an *obiter* basis, given "*the importance of this issue to insolvency proceedings*." The court also gave considerable weight to the existence of an arbitration agreement and recognized that the possibility of exercising discretion in a manner inconsistent with

---

81 *Thomas, Chan: But Ka Chon v. Interactive Brokers LLC*.

82 *Ibid.*

83 *See But Ka Chon v. Interactive Brokers LLC* [2019] HKCA 873 para 62: '62. Third, Lasmos (which followed Salford) decided that the discretion under the insolvency legislation should be exercised in only one way [when an arbitration clause is present]: the petition should "generally be dismissed" save in "exceptional circumstances," upon satisfaction of these three requirements: if the petitioning debt is not admitted (it is settled law that this is regarded as a dispute sufficient for the purpose of arbitration, without regard to the quality of the dispute or substantive merits); the dispute is covered by an arbitration clause; and the alleged debtor has taken steps to commence arbitration."

pro-arbitration policy might encourage parties to bypass an arbitration agreement. The Honorable Kwan V-P expressed clearly that she had "reservations if the discretion under the insolvency legislation should be exercised only one way to substantially curtail the right of a creditor to present a petition ... considerable weight should be given to the factor of arbitration in the exercise of the discretion [to dismiss or stay a petition]."[84]

In the same context, the ICC case *Casa v. Cambio*[85] illustrates the claimants attempt to take advantage of the national insolvency rules to evade or suspend arbitration proceedings that commenced in France. When a counterclaim was filed, the claimant asked the tribunal to decline jurisdiction due to its insolvency which rendered the dispute non-arbitrable. Effectively, the tribunal rejected the claimant's arguments and stated that "*bankruptcy proceedings is not in itself sufficient to render a dispute non-arbitrable per se ... .*"

Another case can be cited in this context, *Société Nationale Algerienne v. Distrigas Corp*[86]. In this judgment, the US Courts firmly took a position in favor of arbitration by stating that "*while international arbitration will require a temporary and limited incursion into the bankruptcy court's exclusive jurisdiction bailiwick, no bankruptcy policies will suffer adverse impact but rather that the US reputation in the international business community stood to suffer if the arbitration agreement was disregarded ... .*"

Reverting back to the case of Mr. Butt, it is clearly noticeable that recent approaches by courts aim to take a balanced position between insolvency and arbitration. The scale cannot be tipped completely to either sides. This will entail "injustice" to either parties. In the same context, the court cannot set aside or suspend arbitration proceedings simply for the fact that a party filed for or claimed the existence of insolvency. In doing so, courts will allow parties to "abuse" their rights or capability to claim the existence of insolvency to get away with arbitration proceedings, especially if the subject matter or dispute is not in their favor. Therefore, an "equitable" approach is crucial to prevent the "abusive" referral to insolvency proceedings/international agreements. The significance of such approaches lies in the fact that an insolvent party – subject to unfavorable claims and within ambiguous approaches by courts – will not give up or

---

84 Darton, Au: Arbitration clauses and insolvency proceedings revisited.

85 ICC Interim Award No. 6697 (1992).

86 *Société Nationale Algérienne Pour la recherche. v. Distrigas Corp*, 80. B.R. 606, 614(D.Mass 1987) at 614, p. 615.

hesitate to benefit from the "incongruities to their advantages."[87] All attempts by courts/tribunals to recognize jurisdiction are indeed useful; however, they may be more proactive or effective. Currently, arbitration seems to be put under the "mercy" of insolvency proceedings[88]. Therefore, it is significant that court exercise discretion to address the issue of "abuse" referral to insolvency, that may be exercised by aggrieved parties from unfavorable positions or awards, provided that a few fundamental principles are taken into consideration such as: good faith, *pacta sunt servanda*, in order to moderate its application and respect the parties' legitimate expectations against domestic insolvency objectives such as public policies[89]. Otherwise, in an era of controversial approach within Insolvency regime, an automatic "prejudging" of violating public policies just because a tribunal decided correctly to disregard an insolvency law, will definitively "undermine" the estimated friendly coexistence with arbitration.

Conclusion

A real paradox is the desire to reconcile two systems that are brought together by mere "contradiction." This resembles the attempt to mix oil and water, or to bring an elephant into a room, or to make the sun rise from the West.

This paradox gains a new dimension in the COVID-19 pandemic "era," where the world of economics and business seeks ways to heal its wounds by mobilizing all its local and international procedures and tools, with arbitration obviously topping its list.

It appears that, this time, the clash between arbitration and insolvency that most economic entities are facing has reached a dangerous level of obstruction and threat to arbitration process. This may imply that arbitration might be stripped off its strengths by suspending its proceedings or raising questions concerning the capacity to arbitrate and the validity of the

87 Courtney Lotfi, Isabel Lightbody: ibid. Jonathan Sutcliffe, James Rogers: Effect of party insolvency on arbitration proceedings: Pause for thought in testing times (Arbitration, The International Journal of Arbitration, Mediation and Dispute management, 2010), p. 276.

88 Courtney Lotfi, Isabel Lightbody: ibid. *see also* ICC case N.1350(1975). ICC case N.2139(1975). ICC case N.4415(1984). ICC case N.5996(1991). ICC case N.6057(1991). ICC case N.11028(2002). Award in SCAI case N.25 of 25 January 2016.

89 Courtney Lotfi, Isabel Lightbody: *ibid.*

arbitral agreement, ending with creating new problems related to the financing of the arbitral procedures.

It is beneficial, at this point, to raise the "red flag" to first draw attention and second to direct ideas towards a specific goal, now a priority in today's practical world, that ensures cohabitation and harmony between the "insolvency" situation with sovereign origins and the philosophy of "arbitration" with global features. The main pillar of this new goal would be a "new and modern set" of legal rules and regulations, both local and international, that aims to regulate, with precision, the various aspects of this relationship.

If the mushroom in Alice's pocket has helped her wake up from her dream, we believe that a special "mushroom recipe" that promotes the coexistence between insolvency and arbitration is not far-fetched.

Crossroads of Insolvency and Arbitration in Italy

Roberto Oliva
Partner, Pavia e Ansaldo law firm, Milan

Introduction

Under Italian law, a dispute can be referred to an arbitral tribunal if the parties are allowed to dispose of its subject matter. This general rule only faces limited exceptions and limitations (e.g., concerning certain labor disputes).

There is no clear definition of what is a disposable right. There are at least two lines of cases with respect to certain rights in corporate matters, such as the right to challenge a resolution approving the company's financial statements.[1]If a state court or an arbitral tribunal is satisfied that a right is disposable, then they will also find that the relevant dispute can be referred to arbitration. In this context, a good thumb rule is that all commercial disputes may be referred to arbitration.

Recent studies also found that Italian State Courts support arbitration and that usually uphold awards.[2] Indeed, in 2007-2014, out of 99 decisions issued by four major Courts of Appeal (the Courts of Milan, Turin, Genoa, and Brescia), in proceedings for the setting aside of arbitration awards, only four decisions granted the claimant's request: 95 awards out of 99 were upheld.

In addition, Italian law does not require Italian parties to submit their disputes to domestic arbitration. In other words, an entirely domestic case (between Italian parties, concerning a contract entered into in Italy and to be fulfilled in Italy) may be deferred to an overseas-seating arbitral tribunal (once again, with possible limited exceptions and limitations: for instance, in corporate matters).[3]

---

1 *See* R. Oliva, *Corporate Arbitration*, in *Arbitration in Italy*, 2020, pp. 29-31.
2 A. Ross, *Italian judges tend to uphold awards, research shows*, GAR, 2016.
3 Italian scholars did not carefully explore the issue, a few exceptions apart; the sole reported precedent is very liberal and only indicates some limited exceptions, however concerning the formal validity of the arbitration agreement: Court of Appeal of Genoa, decision July 9, 2020, Number 649, in *Arbitration in Italy*, 2020, pp. 16-18.

Italian law does not strictly follow United Nations Commission on International Trade Law (UNCITRAL) Model Law. For instance, to date Italian arbitral tribunals do not usually have jurisdiction to issue interim orders (they only have that jurisdiction in the matter of corporate arbitration and only to order the stay of a resolution passed by a company's general meeting or board of directors).[4] Nonetheless, for several years Italian Parliament has been supporting ADR mechanisms (and arbitration among them), trying to reduce the caseload of state courts (and therefore improve their efficiency).

In that same perspective, the reform of Articles 806-840 of Italian Code of Civil Procedure, which took place in 2006, could be regarded.

That reform contains interesting provisions: for instance, it expressly addresses the issues of multi-party arbitration (Italian Code of Civil Procedure, Article 816-quater) and intervention/joinder of a third party (Italian Code of Civil Procedure, Article 816-quinquies). It also expressly states that arbitration awards have the same effects as a judgment issued by a state court (Italian Code of Civil Procedure, Article 824-bis). However, a state court's exequatur is still required to enforce the award (Italian Code of Civil Procedure, Article 825).

If we would like to understand the purpose of enacting the reform mentioned above, we should look at Article 808-quater of Italian Code of Civil Procedure. This article contains a construction rule. If a doubt arises as to the scope of an arbitration agreement, it must be construed in the broadest possible manner. Indeed, it has to be construed as "extending to all disputes arising from the contract or from the relationship to which the agreement refers."

In conclusion, it appears that Italian law follows a facilitative approach: if the parties wish to have their disputes settled by arbitration, then they should be allowed to do so. In the matter of private law, Italian state courts hold exclusive jurisdiction over a limited number of cases; over a few exceptional cases, if we regard commercial and corporate disputes. Moreover, even if the wording of the arbitration agreement is not crystal clear, the parties are allowed to have their disputes settled by arbitration, and if

---

4 Italian Parliament has recently approved a law delegating the Government to issue one or more legislative decrees aimed at reforming Italian civil procedural law and, in particular, at extending precautionary jurisdiction of Italian-seated arbitral tribunals (law No. 206/2021). In addition, the rules of the leading Italian arbitral institution, Milan Chamber of Arbitration, grants arbitral tribunals with some precautionary powers, exploiting a loophole in Italian law (*see* R. Oliva, *New Arbitration Rules of Milan Chamber of Arbitration*, in *Spain Arbitration Review*, 2019, p. 38-54. and, in particular, pp. 46-50.).

the scope of the arbitration clause is unclear, the wider construction is to be preferred.

Moreover, this facilitative approach chimes with policy issues. Indeed, the more disputes are settled by arbitration, the less caseload state courts have. The less caseload state courts have, the more is improved their efficiency. Consequently, state courts may hear more cases concerning non-disposable rights (that is to say, disputes that are not capable of arbitration) and deliver their decisions within a reasonable time frame. In other words, if the parties are allowed to have (as they wish) their disputes settled by arbitration, the fulfillment of their wish also advantage the legal system as a whole and the courts system in particular.[5]

In that general framework, it is somewhat surprising to find—as some recent researches found—that in 2016, only 708 administered arbitration proceedings were commenced in Italy.[6] In the same 2016, in contrast, 234,058 civil and commercial lawsuits were brought before Italian Courts of First Instance.[7]

As far as international commercial arbitration is concerned, the reason behind those figures is that, while agreements entered into between Italian and foreign companies usually include an arbitration clause, the usual seats of arbitration are located abroad (mainly in Switzerland, France, and the United Kingdom).

Moreover, only in 2019, the leading Italian arbitration institution adopted specific sets of rules for small claims or fast-track arbitration.[8] Therefore, these claims are mainly dealt with in ad-hoc arbitration proceedings, which do not feature in statistics.

Notwithstanding the above outlined general framework, Italian law does not favor arbitration in insolvency matters, as further elaborated in this chapter.

---

5 Similar considerations drive the Italian Recovery and Resilience Plan, approved in the context of Next Generation EU program, with respect to the relationship between proceedings in a court of law and ADR mechanisms. The text of the Plan is available at https://www.governo.it/sites/governo.it/files/PNRR_0.pdf (last accessed on July 28, 2021).

6 ISDACI, *Decimo rapporto sulla diffusione della giustizia alternative in Italia*, Rome, 2018, available at https://www.camera-arbitrale.it/upload/documenti/centro%20studi%20pubblicazioni/10-decimo-rapporto-giustizia-alternativa.pdf (last accessed on July 28, 2021).

7 According to the data made available by the Ministry of Justice (https://www.giustizia.it/giustizia/it/mg_2_15_7.wp - last accessed on July 28, 2021), and only taking into account disputes on contracts, torts, property rights, leases, corporate and IP matters.

8 *See* R. Oliva, *New Arbitration Rules of Milan Chamber of Arbitration*, in *Spain Arbitration Review*, 2019, pp. 38-54.

Sources of Law

The rules governing the relationship between arbitration and insolvency proceedings in Italy are spread among different statutes and sources of law, namely:

(1) Italian insolvency law;
(2) Italian arbitration law; and
(3) a handful of European Union (EU) and conventional provisions.

As far as insolvency law is concerned, it is worth noting that, in mid-2022, Italian legislative decree 14 of January 12, 2019 ('New Insolvency Code') will enter into force.[9] Its rules concerning the relationship between arbitration and insolvency proceedings are identical to the rules contained in Italian royal decree 267 of March 16, 1942 ('Old Insolvency Code'). Consequently, the repeal of the Old Insolvency Code and the enactment of the New Insolvency Code do not affect the content of the law in force. For these reasons, in this chapter, unless otherwise indicated, all references are made to the Old Insolvency Code.

Relating to Italian arbitration law, it does not exist as a discrete piece of legislation. For the purposes of this chapter, Italian arbitration law is contained in Articles 806-840 of Italian Code of Civil Procedure, bearing in mind that other provisions contained in different acts may be relevant and apply.

As concerns EU and international law, the matter is mainly governed by EU Regulation 848 of May 20, 2015; nonetheless, some international conventions have to be considered, particularly the 1958 New York Convention on the recognition and enforcement of foreign arbitral awards.

Insolvency Proceedings

Old Insolvency Code provides for several proceedings dealing with the insolvency of a debtor.

The main distinction can be drawn between proceedings involving the divestment of the debtor (*'fallimento'* under the Old Insolvency Code and *'liquidazione giudiziale'* under the New Insolvency Code), on the one hand, and proceedings that do not imply such divestment, on the other

9 New Insolvency Code was supposed to entry into force on Aug. 15, 2020; its entry into force was postponed to Sep. 1, 2021 due to Covid-19 pandemic, and further postponed to May 16, 2022.

hand. Moreover, the latter may or may not entail supervision or various checks by the court, depending on the particular proceedings.

This chapter focuses on '*fallimento*' / '*liquidazione giudiziale*' proceedings, which, as said, provide for the divestment of the debtor and the appointment of a receiver dealing with the administration, liquidation, and distribution of the debtor's assets. These proceedings are from now on indicated as 'insolvency proceedings'.

Core Insolvency Functions

Under Italian law, only state courts are allowed to commence, administer, and wind-up insolvency proceedings, including proceedings aimed at liquidating a bankrupt company, assessing its liabilities and distributing pro-rata payments to its creditors (Old Insolvency Code, Article 23).

Under Article 24 of Old Insolvency Code, the court opening insolvency proceedings (the 'Insolvency Court') has exclusive jurisdiction over all the claims resulting from such proceedings, including, among other things, all the claims brought towards a bankrupt defendant concerning its contractual or tort liability.

Moreover, Article 52, paragraph 2, of Old Insolvency Code sets forth that any claim brought against a bankrupt defendant must be assessed according to special procedural rules contained in the same Old Insolvency Code. These rules, in a few words, provide that

(1) the creditors file a petition with the insolvency court (as a matter of fact, with the receiver);
(2) the receiver prepares a draft statement of liabilities, including or excluding the creditors' claims;
(3) the insolvency court (to be more precise, the judge in charge of the insolvency proceedings) upholds or rejects the claims on a summary judgment (based on the receiver's draft and the possible comments on it by the creditors);
(4) the decision issued by the judge in charge of the insolvency proceedings may be appealed before the same insolvency court (three-judge panel).

In other words, the creditors' claims are examined in summary proceedings, where tort claims and, in general, claims without written evidence tend to be rejected. Only after that summary phase, a creditor may have a full trial on its credit: in the appeal proceedings against the summary judgment of the insolvency court.

These insolvency functions, which may be regarded as 'core' functions, are non-arbitrable.

It is likely that the seminal case of that doctrine, that is to say, the first case of the Italian Supreme Court stating that principle, is a decision issued in 1969.[10] In that case, the Italian Supreme Court ruled that all the agreements on jurisdiction—and among them arbitral agreements—are terminated by operation of law due to the insolvency of a party thereto.

In other words: the initial doctrine of the Italian Supreme Court is that policy issues always prevail. No matter if the parties agreed upon an arbitration clause. Their agreement is automatically terminated by operation of law as a direct consequence of the declaration of insolvency of a party thereto. There is no room left for any facilitative approach.

The doctrine mentioned earlier was too rigid since it failed to distinguish between very different cases (that is to say, for instance, the case of a bankrupt claimant and that of a bankrupt respondent).

Nonetheless, that doctrine was not repealed. On the contrary, it was refined by the Italian Supreme Court sitting en banc.[11] The court stated that jurisdiction over a bankrupt defendant could not rest with an arbitral tribunal because, as already mentioned, the jurisdiction over all the claims brought towards a bankrupt defendant only lies with the insolvency court (Old Insolvency Code, Article 24).

After that, several other decisions upheld that refined doctrine.[12]

The latest of such decisions was issued in 2015.[13] Apart from confirming the doctrine at hand, it also distinguished the case of a claim brought towards a bankrupt defendant from the case of a claim brought by a bankrupt claimant. Indeed, arbitral tribunals do not have jurisdiction over the former but have jurisdiction over the latter.

Therefore, the 2015 decision of the Italian Supreme Court distinguished the cases where facilitative approach prevails (the case of a bankrupt claimant, over which arbitral tribunals may have jurisdiction) and the cases where policy issues prevail (the case of a bankrupt defendant, over which the insolvency courts only have jurisdiction).

---

10 Italian Supreme Court, decision June 11, 1969, Number 2064.

11 Italian Supreme Court sitting *en banc*, decision June 6, 2003, Number 9070.

12 *See*, for instance, Italian Supreme Court, decision Feb. 17, 2011, Number 3918.

13 Italian Supreme Court, decision June 24, 2015, Number 13089.

Main Topics

For the sake of clarity, the below discussion will separately consider, with respect to domestic arbitration:

(1) pending arbitrations, that is to say, arbitration proceedings that are pending at the time of the opening of the insolvency proceedings;
(2) new arbitrations, that is to say, arbitration proceedings commenced during the insolvency proceedings based on arbitration agreements entered into before the opening of the said proceedings;
(3) pending awards, that is to say, arbitral awards that have not been complied with at the time of the opening of the insolvency proceedings;
(4) new awards, that is to say, arbitral awards issued after the opening of the insolvency proceedings; and
(5) new arbitration agreements, that is to say, arbitration agreements entered into after the opening of the insolvency proceedings.

In addition, a particular section will discuss the peculiar feature of the relationship between insolvency proceedings and international arbitration, the latter to be intended as overseas-seated arbitration.[14]

Domestic Arbitration

Pending Arbitrations

The sole law provision concerning pending arbitrations is contained in Article 83-bis of Old Insolvency Code, whereby "If a contract containing an arbitration clause is terminated under the provisions of this section, pending arbitration proceedings cannot continue."

The section of Old Insolvency Code containing the said Article concerns the pending contracts, that is to say, the contracts that were not entirely performed at the time of the opening of the insolvency proceedings.

---

14 A number of definitions of 'international arbitration' has been proposed, both from a merely legal or from a sociological point of view, *inter alia* focusing on the parties' nationality, the subject matter of the dispute or the law rules governing the proceedings; in this respect, *see* N. Blackaby et al. (eds.), *International Arbitration*, Oxford, 2015, pp. 7-11.

In a few words, if a contract has not been performed at all, or in any case has not been entirely performed by both parties at the time of the opening of the insolvency proceedings, it is 'suspended'. Italian law vests the insolvency receiver with the power to either:

(1) terminate the pending contract; or
(2) reaffirm it.

In addition, in a few cases, the opening of insolvency proceedings entails the termination of the contracts (such as in the case of bank account contracts, which are terminated on the insolvency of a party thereof, or agency contracts, which are terminated on the insolvency of the agent).

Certain rules are set forth concerning specific contracts (e.g., lease agreements, loans, contracts concerning real estate under construction, etc.). In addition, case law and scholars held discussions on the notion of 'pending contracts', which were not fully solved by enacting the New Insolvency Code. Nonetheless, these rules and discussions are not relevant to the matter outlined in this chapter.

Therefore, the sole express rule in Italian law concerning pending arbitration sets forth that, if the relevant contract is terminated by the insolvency receiver or by operation of law, arbitration proceedings concerning that contract cannot continue.

Italian scholars and case law construe that rule as providing for an exception to separability doctrine. It entails that if the contract is terminated, the arbitration clause is also terminated. As a consequence of the termination of the arbitration clause, arbitration proceedings are stopped, and the award cannot be issued.

On the contrary, if the contract is not terminated, arbitration proceedings may continue, provided that they meet the criteria hereunder discussed with respect to new arbitrations (§ 2.2).

This said concerning arbitral jurisdiction, some procedural issues remain to be discussed.

Italian law provides that, in case a party to proceedings in a court of law goes bankrupt, the proceedings are discontinued, and the interested parties are required to reinstate them within a mandatory term (Old Insolvency Law, Article 43; Italian Code of Civil Procedure, Article 300). The reason is that of allowing the insolvency receiver to receive official notice of the pending proceedings and take his or her choices in the interest of the estate.

The said provisions do not expressly mention arbitration proceedings.

Consequently, some scholars maintain that, in case of insolvency of a party to arbitration proceedings, Article 816-sexies of Italian Code of Civil Procedure would apply. This article concerns the case of death or loss of *locus standi*. It provides that, in those cases, the arbitral tribunal should take all the necessary steps to allow the parties to present their case and could even stay the proceedings.

In case of insolvency, that should imply that, upon request by the arbitral tribunal, the non-bankrupt party:

(1) informs the insolvency receiver of the pending arbitration proceedings; and
(2) invites him or her to appear in those proceedings within a term calculated on the basis of the insolvency procedure timing (taking into account that the receiver has to be authorized by the insolvency court before appearing before the arbitral tribunal).

Some unreported awards were rendered in proceedings where the above construction was followed.

It should be noted, in any case, that other scholars maintain that, also in case of insolvency of a party to arbitration proceedings, the rules concerning proceedings in court would apply. In other words, the arbitral tribunal should discontinue the proceedings that have to be reinstated by the interested party.

There is no clear guidance by Italian case law.[15] Consequently, it cannot be excluded that Italian courts, seized by the award-debtor seeking the award to be set aside, would prefer the latter construction and set aside the award if the arbitration proceedings were not discontinued (and subsequently reinstated) after the insolvency of a party thereof.

New Arbitrations

In case of termination of the main contract by the insolvency receiver or by operation of law, Italian scholars maintain that the parties cannot commence new arbitration proceedings on the basis of the arbitration clause contained therein. It is a further consequence of the rule set forth by Article 83-bis of Old Insolvency Code.

The situation is more complex with respect to non-terminated contracts.

As already noted, the assessment of a bankrupt company liabilities is a 'core' insolvency function reserved to Italian State courts (Old Insolvency Code, Articles 24 and 52, paragraph 2).

15 A sole reported precedent deals with the issue, and it held – although in *obiter* – that arbitration proceedings should be discontinued: Italian Supreme Court sitting *en banc*, July 21, 2015, Number 15200, in *Arbitration in Italy*, 2015, pp. 19-22.

As a consequence of the above, the creditor of a bankrupt entity is not entitled to bring proceedings in ordinary courts or commence arbitration proceedings, for its credit has to be ascertained by the insolvency court. In other words, an arbitration clause cannot be enforced towards insolvency estates, as Italian law does not generally allow a claim to be brought against a bankrupt defendant in arbitration proceedings.

On the other hand, Italian law does not prevent the insolvency receiver from commencing arbitration proceedings. Italian law also provides that, in that case, the possible appointment of the arbitrator is made by the insolvency court (Old Insolvency Code, Article 25).

As a consequence of the above, the general rule is that

(1) if the insolvency receiver is the claimant (the contract-creditor), the arbitration clause is enforceable; on the contrary
(2) if the insolvency receiver is the respondent, the arbitration clause is unenforceable, the insolvency court having exclusive jurisdiction over all the claims vis-à-vis the bankrupt debtor.

The said general rule suffers a number of exceptions. The most notable one concerns the claims towards former directors of a bankrupt company.

The directors' liability towards the company is construed under Italian law as a particular kind of contractual liability. In addition, Italian company law allows non-listed companies to have their disputes (including those between the company and its directors) settled in arbitration.[16] Consequently, if the company's articles of association contain an arbitration clause, the claim raised by the same company against its directors is subject to the jurisdiction of an arbitral tribunal.

Notwithstanding the above, the same claim is subject to the state courts jurisdiction if the insolvency receiver raises it. Indeed, according to Italian case law, in that case, the insolvency receiver:

(1) takes the place of the company in its claim against the director; and
(2) takes the place of the company's creditors in their claim against the director.

The latter claim being, under Italian law, a tortious claim, outside the scope of the arbitration clause contained in the company's articles of association, the jurisdiction over the whole dispute lies with the state courts.[17]

---

16 *See* R. Oliva, *Corporate Arbitration*, in *Arbitration in Italy*, 2020, p. 29-31.

17 *See*, among the more recent decisions, Court of first instance of Turin, March 3, 2021, Number 1126; and Court of first instance of Ancona, May 24, 2021, Number 675.

Pending Awards

As already indicated, the assessment of the bankrupt debtor liabilities is a core function of insolvency proceedings, which is not-arbitrable.

Consequently, the award-creditor shall file a petition with the insolvency court to have its credit inserted in the statement of liabilities. In this perspective, the award constitutes proof of the credit.

The above applies if the arbitration award became final (that is to say, not subject to recourse for setting aside, or in case that recourse was finally rejected) before the declaration of insolvency. Otherwise, the principles laid down in §§ 2.1 and 2.2 apply.

If the insolvency estate is the award-creditor, the receiver is entitled to enforce it, and the relevant proceeds constitute an integral part of the said estate.

New Awards

New awards may only be rendered in proceedings where the insolvency estate is the claimant or with respect to the estate's possible counterclaims if it acted as a respondent. Indeed, concerning claims towards the insolvency estate, the proceedings cannot continue under the principles laid down in §§ 2.1 and 2.2.

New Arbitration Agreements

Italian law expressly provides that the receiver is entitled to enter into new arbitration agreements. These agreements have to be authorized by the insolvency court (Old Insolvency Code, Article 35) and concern disputes where the insolvency receiver acts as the claimant under the principles laid down in §§ 2.1 and 2.2. It should be noted that it is highly unlikely that an insolvency receiver enters into a new arbitration agreement, also in the light of the costs of the arbitration proceedings.

International Arbitration

European Community (EC) Regulation 1346/2000 and EU Regulation 848/2015 on insolvency proceedings could affect the principles laid down in § 1 in the case of insolvency proceedings opened in Italy and arbitration proceedings pending abroad.

According to the Regulations mentioned above, the law of the Member State where insolvency proceedings were opened also determines, among other things, the effects of insolvency proceedings on proceedings brought by individual creditors, except for pending lawsuits. Indeed, the effects upon pending lawsuits are determined by the law of the Member State in which they are pending.

Under EC Regulation 1346/2000, some Member States courts held that a 'pending lawsuit' is only an individual enforcement procedure.[18] On the other hand, other courts held that the relevant provisions on pending lawsuits also apply with respect to proceedings on the merits, including arbitration proceedings.[19]

The latter construction was thereafter upheld by enacting EU Regulation 848/2015, in force starting from June 26, 2017. As a matter of fact, Article 18 of the said regulation expressly provides that "The effects of insolvency proceedings on a pending lawsuit or pending arbitral proceedings concerning an asset or a right which forms part of a debtor's insolvency estate shall be governed solely by the law of the Member State in which that lawsuit is pending or in which the arbitral tribunal has its seat."

The Italian Supreme Court sitting en banc also dealt with the matter in two decisions.[20] A detailed analysis of both these decisions is required, as they are the most authoritative precedents on the relevant points of law.

The latter case heard by the Italian Supreme Court (decision July 21, 2015, Number 15200) concerned an Italian defendant and an Egyptian claimant, which in August 2000 entered into an agreement whereby the claimant leased two hotel premises to the defendant.

In December 2010, a dispute arose between the parties with respect to an alleged breach on the part of the defendant. In the claimant's opinion, such a breach resulted in the termination of the agreement. Therefore, it commenced arbitration proceedings under the ICC Rules, as provided for in the lease agreement.

Pending the arbitration proceedings, at the end of 2011, the defendant went bankrupt.

---

18 The High Court of Ireland so ruled in *Flightlease Ireland Ltd., Re* [2005] IEHC 274: http://www.bailii.org/ie/cases/IEHC/2005/H274.html (last accessed on July 28, 2021).

19 In this respect, *see Syska v. Vivendi Universal SA & Ors* [2008] EWHC 2155 (Comm): http://www.bailii.org/ew/cases/EWHC/Comm/2008/2155.html (last accessed on July 28, 2021), thereafter upheld by *Syska & Anor v. Vivendi Universal S.A. & Ors* (2009) EWCA Civ 677: http://www.bailii.org/ew/cases/EWCA/Civ/2009/677.html (last accessed on July 28, 2021).

20 Italian Supreme Court sitting *en banc*, decision July 21, 2015, Number 15200, and May 26, 2015, Number 10800.

In February 2012, the claimant requested to be admitted to the defendant's statement of liabilities, the insolvency court being the Court of First Instance of Milan. In its application, the claimant noted the pending ICC arbitration proceedings (that is to say, arbitration proceedings governed by French law) and, referring to Article 15 of (at that time, in force) EC Regulation 1346/2000 and the applicable French procedural rules, requested to be admitted to the statement of liabilities on a temporary basis, subject to the outcome of the mentioned arbitration proceedings.

In June 2012, the Court of First Instance of Milan ruled in favor of the claimant and admitted it to the defendant's statement of liabilities on a temporary basis, pursuant to Article 55, paragraph 3, of Old Insolvency Law.[21]

Nonetheless, in October 2012, the claimant appealed the ruling of the Court of First Instance of Milan. In fact, it claimed that the court's decision was partially wrong since it applied the *pari passu* principle to its credit (which it claimed was a preferential credit, that is to say, a credit to which the *pari passu* principle does not apply). The defendant appeared in court opposing the claim and counterclaimed Italian courts' exclusive jurisdiction over the claimant's credit, namely the insolvency court's jurisdiction (preventing the jurisdiction of the ICC arbitral tribunal).

In February 2014, the claimant referred the case to the Italian Supreme Court, so as to have a final decision on jurisdiction (under Italian law, until the Court of First Instance issues the decision on the merits, each party may request the Italian Supreme Court to rule on the jurisdiction over the case).

In the proceedings before the Italian Supreme Court, the claimant asserted that jurisdiction over the dispute was governed by EC Regulation 1346/2000. Under Article 4, paragraph 2, (f) and Article 15 of the said regulation, the opening of insolvency proceedings in a Member State (in this case, in Italy) would not prevent the jurisdiction of another Member State (in this case, France) where a lawsuit was already pending. Indeed, only French law might determine the effects of the opening of insolvency proceedings on French pending lawsuits. According to French law, if the arbitral tribunal has already been appointed at the time of the opening of insolvency proceedings, arbitration proceedings may continue as long as the claimant requests to be admitted to the debtor's statement of liabilities subject to the outcome of arbitration proceedings. All these requirements

---

21 Under Art 55, para. 33, of Old Insolvency Law, contingent claims are admitted to insolvency statement of liabilities on a temporary basis; thereafter, they are finally admitted (or finally not admitted), depending on the occurrence (or non-occurrence) of the event(s) they are conditional upon.

(arbitral tribunal already appointed; request to be admitted to the statement of liability on a temporary basis, that is, subject to the outcome of arbitration proceedings) were fulfilled in the case at hand.

The Italian Supreme Court held that the claimant's request was inadmissible for procedural reasons (in fact, the Court of First Instance of Milan had already issued its decision on the merits). Nonetheless, the Italian Supreme Court also took the chance to indicate its interpretation of Article 15 of EC Regulation 1346/2000 and confirm the exclusive jurisdiction of insolvency courts.

Italian Supreme Court held that the above-mentioned regulation did not apply in the case it heard. In the court's opinion, this is because it only regulates "the relationship arising from insolvency proceedings of parties having their residence or registered office within the European Union" (as already noted, the claimant was an Egyptian company). Moreover, even assuming that EC Regulation 1346/2000 applied, it would only govern "the effects of the opening of insolvency proceedings on pending proceedings, not the effects of pending proceedings on the jurisdiction of insolvency courts. Articles 4 and 15 of the Regulation do not govern the jurisdiction, although these provisions identify the law governing the effects of insolvency proceedings on pending proceedings." The Italian Supreme Court, therefore, concluded that the case at hand (that is to say, the case of arbitration proceedings commenced in France before the opening of insolvency proceedings in Italy) "is not governed by Articles 4, para 2, f) and 15 of EC Regulation 1346/2000."

It seems that the Italian Supreme Court considered that Article 15 of the Regulation then in force only concerns the effects of the opening of insolvency proceedings on a lawsuit pending in another Member State. In other words, that lawsuit may continue if it is so allowed by the law of the Member State where that lawsuit is pending. Nonetheless, the effects on the insolvency statement of liabilities of the decision issued in the pending proceedings are governed by the law of the Member State where the insolvency proceedings were opened. In Italy, such a decision would not have any effect, since—as the Italian Supreme Court noted—"it is settled case law of this court, that the parties are not allowed to bring before an arbitral tribunal claims towards a bankrupt defendant. Indeed, the jurisdiction of an arbitral tribunal is in any case prevented by the exclusive jurisdiction of insolvency courts over such claims."

In other words, the Italian Supreme Court confirms that the policy issues shall prevail in the case of a bankrupt defendant. The scope of the facilitative approach is minimal: arbitration proceedings pending abroad may continue if the foreign law so allows, but they do not affect Italian insolvency proceedings.

In the former case (decision May 26, 2015, Number 10800), a (partial) distinction was made in light of the *Kompetenz-Kompetenz* doctrine.

The case heard by the Supreme Court may be summarized as follows:

In 2007, an airline company and an airport management company entered into a service contract, which contained an arbitration clause. According to this clause, all disputes arising between the parties would have to be referred to arbitration under LCIA Rules.

Once the agreement expired, the airport management company (in the meantime admitted to a pre-insolvency) requested and was granted a European order for payment, issued by an Italian court. However, the air transport company appealed the order. First, it objected to the Italian courts' jurisdiction since the parties had agreed to refer all their disputes to foreign arbitration. During the appeal proceedings, the airport management companies went bankrupt. The proceedings were then reinstated, and, finally, the air transport company referred the case to the Supreme Court to have a final decision on the issue of jurisdiction.

The court analyzed the objection raised by the insolvency receiver, whereby the arbitration clause at hand provided for the referral to an '*arbitrato irrituale*' (i.e., an alternative arbitration procedure which does not result in an enforceable award and does not give rise to jurisdictional issues). To this respect, the Supreme Court held—following its own case law—that "*international arbitration can only be 'arbitrato rituale'*" (i.e., the regular arbitration procedure resulting in an enforceable award), since "the distinction between 'arbitrato rituale' and 'arbitrato irrituale' is well known by the law of the land, but is rarely applied abroad."

Moreover, the Supreme Court used a strict construction of Article 83-bis of Old Insolvency Law. To this respect, the court ruled that:

> […] we cannot draw a general rule, whereby arbitration proceedings cannot continue, from Article 83-bis of Old Insolvency Law. However, the opposite rule may also be drawn. Indeed, the above mentioned Article (…) states that the arbitration clause is terminated in the case governed by it (that of pending arbitration proceedings and the termination of the contract containing the arbitration clause pursuant to Article 72 of Old Insolvency Law). On the basis of the same provision, we must conclude that if the insolvency receiver avails himself of the rights arising out of the contract containing the arbitration clause, this clause is binding on him. Otherwise, the receiver would be allowed to terminate only certain

> clauses of the agreement while claiming the fulfillment of other clauses of the same agreement (…).

The Supreme Court sitting en banc also added that "it does not matter that the agreement had expired and had not been renewed at the time of the appeal of the payment order. Indeed, the purpose of the arbitration clause is to settle the disputes arising out of the agreement, in accordance with the proceeding laid down therein."

The more interesting issue with respect to the subject matter of this chapter is that, in the LCIA arbitration proceedings, the aviation company brought a counterclaim against the bankrupt company. In the opinion of the insolvency receiver, the arbitral tribunal did not have jurisdiction over that counterclaim. The Supreme Court otherwise held, as it stated as follows: "this court is prevented from deciding on the jurisdiction of the arbitral tribunal on the counterclaim (…) concerning the alleged credit towards the bankrupt debtor. Indeed, once excluded the Italian courts' jurisdiction, as a result of the arbitration clause which referred the dispute to a foreign arbitral tribunal, it is on the arbitral tribunal to determine the rules governing the arbitration procedure."

In other words, the Italian Supreme Court applied the *Kompetenz-Kompetenz* doctrine. Based on that doctrine, it concluded that it is not up to Italian courts to determine the effects of Italian insolvency proceedings on arbitration proceedings pending abroad.

Nonetheless, the court did not expressly rule on the vice versa, that is to say, on the effects of an arbitration award issued abroad on insolvency proceedings pending in Italy.

There are no other reported precedents on that very matter.

In the light of the above, it could be concluded that Italian law, as it currently stands, applies with respect to international arbitration proceedings the same principles laid down for domestic arbitration proceedings and their relationship with insolvency proceedings. In addition, Italian courts do not appear to be prepared to recognize arbitral awards issued abroad and allow their enforcement against the insolvency estate.

The construction of the said EC Regulation (and likely similar construction of the above-mentioned EU Regulation) seems to betray their purposes, and Italian scholars criticized the conclusions reached by the Supreme Court.

In addition, further considerations are necessary in light of the obligation the Republic of Italy undertook by entering into the 1958 New York Convention.

Article V, paragraph 1, a) of the said Convention prevents the court of signatory states to refuse recognition and enforcement of awards based on an invalidity/unenforceability of the arbitration agreement on the basis of a law other than those indicated therein.[22] As a consequence, recognition and enforcement of an arbitral award cannot be refused based on the *lex concursus* possibly precluding the enforcement of the arbitration clause, if its enforcement is allowed under the law the parties choose or the law or the country where the award was rendered.

The above implies that a foreign award issued in arbitration proceedings based on an arbitration agreement contained in a contract terminated by operation of law (or by the receiver on the basis of the powers he or she is granted with) might be recognized and enforced in Italy, provided that the receiver acted as the claimant. However, the point is unclear, as there are no reported precedents or Italian scholars' opinions.

On the contrary, if the insolvency estate is the award-debtor, it appears that the award cannot be recognized and enforced in Italy under Article V, paragraph 2, a) of the Convention. Indeed, the said article provides that "Recognition and enforcement of an arbitral award may also be refused if the competent authority in the country where recognition and enforcement are sought finds that: (a) The subject matter of the difference is not capable of settlement by arbitration under the law of that country." And the assessment of the insolvency liabilities is a matter "not capable of settlement by arbitration" under Italian law, as it has exclusively to be made by the insolvency court.

Conclusions

Under Italian law, in insolvency matters, the facilitative approach to arbitration does not always chime with policy issues.

In the case of a bankrupt claimant, the facilitative approach prevails: arbitration proceedings may be commenced or may continue, as the case may be (although it is disputed whether they should be reinstated after the

22 N. Blackaby *et al.* (eds.), *Redfern and Hunter on International Arbitration*, Oxford, 2009, p. 309; P. Nacimiento, *Article V(1)(a)*, in H. Kronke *et al.* (eds.), *Recognition and Enforcement of Foreign Arbitral Awards: Global Commentary on the New York Convention*, Alphen aan den Rijn, 2010, p. 205 e 223; D. Schramm, E. Geisinger, P. Pinsolle, *Article II*, in H. Kronke *et al.* (eds.), *op cit.*, p. 35 e 54; A. van den Berg, *The New York Convention of 1958: Towards a Uniform Judicial Interpretation*, Deventer, 1981, p. 267.

declaration of insolvency). If the arbitrators were appointed before the declaration of insolvency, they would hold their position. The receiver is even entitled to enter into a brand-new arbitration agreement (if duly authorized). Should a dispute arise with respect to a contract containing an arbitration agreement, the receiver is also entitled to commence arbitration proceedings. Eventually, if the bankrupt party to the arbitration proceedings is requested to appoint an arbitrator, the insolvency court shall make the appointment.

In this framework, the facilitative approach does not prevail only in the case provided for by Article 83-bis of Old Insolvency Code: if the insolvency receiver terminates a contract in progress that contains an arbitration clause, arbitration proceedings possibly commenced on the basis of that clause can neither continue, nor be commenced. It is an exception to the separability doctrine—maybe, the only one (and for sure the most relevant one) provided for by Italian law. Nonetheless, the Italian Parliament expressly enacted this exception, so it is not possible to bypass it.

On the contrary, in the case of a bankrupt defendant, policy issues prevail—without any exception (at least, with respect to the relationship between arbitration and insolvency proceedings). Insolvency courts only have jurisdiction over claims against a bankrupt debtor. That jurisdiction excludes any other possible jurisdiction: the jurisdiction of different courts and the jurisdiction of an arbitral tribunal seated in Italy or possibly even abroad.

Several reasons support the exclusive jurisdiction of insolvency courts (and the special procedural rules referred to above), and none of them refers to arbitration. The main reason is that the exclusive jurisdiction of insolvency courts can (at least, theoretically) assure a better fulfillment of the *pari passu* principle and the participation of all the creditors to the collective procedure, which on the contrary is endangered if many courts (and arbitral tribunals) had jurisdiction over the claims against a bankrupt debtor. Therefore, it is clear why the facilitative approach prevails in the case of a bankrupt claimant: in that case, the respect of the *pari passu* principle is not at all endangered.

The relationship between arbitration and insolvency proceedings under Italian law may be summarized as follows:

(1) a bankrupt party may act as a claimant in arbitration proceedings (commenced after or even before the declaration of insolvency), provided that the insolvency receiver has not terminated the agreement containing the arbitration clause—that is to say, in that case, the facilitative approach prevails;

(2) on the contrary, if the agreement containing the arbitration clause was terminated by operation of law or by the receiver, the clause is unenforceable, and arbitration proceedings possibly pending can neither continue nor be commenced—that is to say, this is an exception to the separability doctrine, and policy issues prevail;
(3) the jurisdiction over claims or counterclaims towards a bankrupt party only rests with insolvency courts—that is to say, policy issues prevail;
(4) as far as international arbitration is concerned:
    (a) it appears that, if the receiver acted as the claimant, foreign awards might be recognized and enforced in Italy, even if the relevant contract was terminated by operation of law or by the same receiver—that is to say, in that case, the facilitative approach should prevail;
    (b) if the receiver acted as the respondent, as Italian law currently stands, it appears that foreign awards cannot be recognized and enforced in Italy—that is to say, policy issues should prevail. A possible distinction could be drawn if the arbitration proceedings were pending in a Member State of the EU. Nonetheless, it is worth noting that Italian scholars only made this distinction for the time being, which is denied by case law.

Arbitration and Insolvency: A Conflict of Near Polar Extremes: Contrary Perspective

Bishwajit Dubey
Achromic Point – Dispute Resolution Lawyer of the year 2022
Partner in the Dispute Resolution Practice of Cyril Amarchand Mangaldas 'Top Individual Lawyer' Forbes Legal Powerlist 2021
Radhika Bishwajit Dubey
Advocate Arbitrator and Mediator India
Prafful Goyal
Legal Associate Dispute Resolution Practice of Cyril Amarchand Mangaldas

Introduction

Arbitration and insolvency mechanisms are contrasting in nature and at conflict with each other. Reasons for the conflict are premised on the nature of the proceedings, which are in variance at core. Arbitration as a mechanism advocates for higher party autonomy with minimal to nil involvement of judicial institutions, and there is an aspect of privity, confidentiality, and privacy. Insolvency is a centralised mechanism and requires consolidation of all disputes concerning a debtor before an insolvency court, and it is open and transparent in character.

Practically, however, the conflict is less problematic; and there are possibilities of harmonising the two processes. Recently, scholars have challenged this theoretical conflict and have instead emphasised the increased use of arbitration during insolvency as it may further the objectives of insolvency.[1] It is reasoned that arbitration, as an alternate dispute mechanism, may contribute to insolvency as efficiently as it does to other civil disputes. It would not only reduce the burden on the insolvency courts and allow them to focus on the crucial issues emanating from or in relation to the insolvency process, but also promote party autonomy and re-enforce

1 *See* Paul F. Kirgis, *Arbitration, Bankruptcy and Public Policy: A Contractarian Analysis*, 17 Am. Bankr. Inst. L. Rev. 503 (2009); Stephan Madaus, *The (Underdeveloped) Use of Arbitration in International Insolvency Proceedings*, Maxi Scherer (ed), Journal of International Arbitration (Kluwer Law International 2020, Volume 37 Issue 4) pp. 449—478.

sanctity of commercial contracts by allowing parties to resolve their disputes by and through their preferred mechanism for dispute resolution. We break down the issues and discuss them forthwith.

Understanding 'What' and 'Why' of the Conflict?

The conflict between arbitration and insolvency lies in the tension between the underlying policy objectives of these processes. Insolvency is meant to provide solutions to resolve defaults in ways that command the respect of majority of the debtor's stakeholders[2]. A process that maximises returns for the stakeholders – by maximising the value of the debtor and its assets – and showcases rationality in distribution, by way of ensuring optimum return to all the stakeholders, will best serve insolvency objectives. Such a process would incentivise either voluntary or compulsory collectivisation among the stakeholders. It would encourage stakeholders to recognise the need for a stay on individual enforcement action for the common good, such that not only the returns are maximised but also the interest of those stakeholders who stand lower in the hierarchy vis-à-vis formal creditors is also preserved.[3]

To achieve these objectives, insolvency legislations usually provides for an automatic stay on individual actions,[4] and require all the stakeholders to lodge their respective claims against the debtor in a consolidated process. On submission of claims, the process would be carried out with efforts being made to retrieve maximum value for the debtor and have the same distributed in a rational manner balancing the interest of all stakeholders.[5] In case of dispute during the process, the insolvency law requires it to be addressed exclusively by a specialised court dedicated to oversee such insolvency process. This would lead to consolidation of all disputes, against the debtor, before one forum, and help (a) maintain sanity of the insolvency process, (b) reduce the stress on the debtor, and (c) ensure

---

2 D.R. Korobkin, *Rehabilitating values: A jurisprudence of bankruptcy*, Columbia Law Review (1991), 91, p. 717, Value based theory.

3 Insolvency and Bankruptcy Regime in India —A Narrative, Insolvency and Bankruptcy Board of India, 2020, available at https://vidhilegalpolicy.in/wp-content/uploads/2020/10/2020-10-01-210733-43cms-9224c9b668aac0d6149a5d866bfb4c79-1.pdf.

4 Stay on both institution of new actions and continuations of pending actions so as to provide a 'calming period' to the debtor. *See* Indian Insolvency and Bankruptcy Code, 2016, s. 14; US Bankruptcy Code, 11 U.S.C. § 362(a).

5 *Binani Industries Limited v. Bank of Baroda & Anr.*, NCLAT, Company Appeal (AT) (Insolvency) No. 82 of 2018; *In re Atlantic Computer Systems Plc*, Re (1992) 1 All ER 476, 501-2.

timely completion of the insolvency process. In essence, insolvency law considers it best that the jurisdiction of all other courts and forums remain barred during insolvency, and all matters pending insolvency are heard exclusively by one specialised and centralised forum.

Against this, arbitration law is based on the idea of party autonomy and providing parties a tool of alternate private dispute resolution, which is not only simpler and quicker, but also cost effective in resolving disputes in comparison to statutorily established courts.[6] It aims to give parties the control on their dealings and disputes arising out of it, by limiting the involvement of courts only at the stage of enforcement.[7] The arbitration policy requires that disputes that fall within the scope of the arbitration agreement be referred to arbitration only, and the jurisdiction of courts remains ousted.[8]

This party driven nature of arbitration is also attractive to global corporations as it enables them to move away from the unpredictable and lengthy court processes, and have their dispute resolved by mechanisms/procedures which meet their needs. Economies too, in their bid to come across as business friendly, promote arbitration by providing for robust mechanism of recognition and enforcement of such arbitrations agreements and awards, and minimising judicial intervention. Judiciaries, as part of the larger scheme, also endeavour to enforce the arbitration clauses by referring parties to arbitration, thereby upholding party autonomy, than assuming jurisdiction themselves. This is one of the fundamental aspects of arbitration, and it is even recognised under the United Nations Commission on International Trade Law (UNCITRAL) Model Law on Arbitration which many jurisdictions, including India, has taken into consideration while framing their respective municipal laws. Consequently, the underlying principles of arbitration and the treatment, scope and import of several arbitration related aspects such as arbitration agreements, arbitral awards, among others, are in line with the Model Law.

It is this very principle of party autonomy in choosing the dispute resolution mechanism that conflicts with the insolvency policy objective of

---

6 *See* Christian Buhring-Uhle, *A Survey on Arbitration and Settlement in International Business Disputes: Advantages of Arbitration*, in Towards a Science of Arbitration: Collected Empirical Research, Christopher Drahozal and Richard Naimark eds (Kluwer Law International, 2005), at 38.

7 Alan Redfern and Martin Hunter with Nigel Blackaby and Constantine Partasides, Law and Practice of International Commercial Arbitration (4th Edition, Sweet and Maxwell, 2004), at 1.

8 The Right Hon. Sir Michael Kerr in Ronald Bernstein ed., *Handbook of Arbitration Practice* (Sweet and Maxwell, 1987), at 3.

consolidating all disputes before one court. In essence, it is the conflict of 'choice of forum',[9] wherein although parties have chosen to submit themselves to the jurisdiction of the arbitrator but the compelling interest of insolvency law is forcing them to submit to the jurisdiction of the insolvency court. Thus, in a situation wherein an insolvency proceeding is initiated against a party to the arbitration agreement, a conflict arises that whether the principle of party autonomy to have the dispute resolved through arbitration would subsist, or does it stand frustrated in terms of the bar under the insolvency law – thereby compelling the parties to submit their dispute to the insolvency court[10] – the 'WHAT' of the conflict.

This conflict, at times, is resolved by allowing the policy objectives of insolvency law to overpower the policy objectives of arbitration law, through the moratorium/stay provisions under the insolvency law. In other words, insolvency law is prioritised considering the possible implications that a continued arbitration would have on the recovery to be made by other creditors in the insolvency process. Thus, in case of an intersection between arbitration and insolvency, insolvency process would prevail over arbitration and over-ride the rights of a party claimant/defendant to contest/defend its claims in accordance with the dispute resolution mechanism chosen by, and between, the parties, and compel it to contest/defend the claim before an insolvency court created under the insolvency statute, having no relation to the dispute at hand.[11] In effect, what could otherwise been a private dispute between two parties, merely on acceptance of insolvency application, is transformed into an in rem proceeding – the 'WHY' of the conflict.

Solutions to the Conflict

Since both arbitration and insolvency flow from statute and have equal force of law, letting one overpower the other may not be the best solution to

9 Paul F. Kirgis, *Arbitration, Bankruptcy and Public Policy: A Contractarian Analysi,* 17 AM. BANKR. INST. L. REV. 503 (2009), Available at: http://scholarship.law.umt.edu/faculty_lawreviews/125.

10 In the US, this 'conflict' between the two processes was extensively discussed in *Zimmerman v. Continental Airlines, Inc.*, US Court of Appeals 3rd Circuit, 712 F.2d 55. (3rd Cir. 1983), cert. denied, 464 US 1038, 104 S.Ct. 699, 79 L.Ed.2d 165 (1984). Here, Court concluded that policies of Bankruptcy Code 'impliedly modify' the policies of Arbitration Act and that the enforcement of arbitration agreements in a bankruptcy procedure was to be 'left to the sound discretion of the bankruptcy judge'.

11 *Larsen Oil and Gas Pte Ltd. v. Petropod Ltd.,* Singapore Court of Appeal (2011) 3 SLR 414 at 46.

the conflict.[12] Thus, it merits that efforts be made to find alternatives and to best harmonise the policy objectives of both arbitration and insolvency, so they can subsist together.

Although it is universally uniform that insolvency laws focus on centralisation of disputes upon commencement of insolvency proceedings, there are still some explored deviances, which may provide for a viable alternative to the conflict.

Distinction of 'Core' and 'Non-Core' Matters

Distinction between 'Core' and 'Non-Core' insolvency/bankruptcy[13] matters is prominent in jurisdiction such as the United States of America (US or USA). This distinction proposes to bifurcate between 'core' and 'non-core' insolvency/bankruptcy issues, and permit parties to 'non-core' issues to continue resolution of their disputes before other relevant fora, irrespective of the pendency of insolvency proceedings against the debtor. It considers that 'non-core' matters need not be exclusively adjudicated by bankruptcy courts, as adjudication by an external forum may not necessarily frustrate or jeopardise the bankruptcy process.

The US Court of Appeals in *Hays & Company* affirmed this understanding vis-à-vis arbitration proceedings. It observed that bankruptcy courts are 'to enforce such clause [Arbitration] unless that effect would seriously jeopardize the objectives of the Code [Bankruptcy].'[14]

However, what remained pivotal for this distinction is the US Supreme Court's decision in *Shearson/American Express, Inc. v. McMahon.*[15] In this case, arbitration policy was balanced against the competing interests of other statutes (like bankruptcy) by acknowledging that an exception to arbitration can be made where there exists a 'contrary congressional command' or 'intent'.[16] This test required the party opposing the enforcement of arbitration agreement to satisfy that there exists a contrary congressional command or intent which required creation of an exception to the enforcement of arbitration ('McMahon Test'). The court held that such a command or intent can be evidenced from:

---

12 *Hays & Co. v. Merrill Lynch, Pierce, Fenner & Smith, Inc.*, U.S. Court of Appeals, 885 F.2d 1149, 1161 (3d Cir.1989).

13 The term 'Insolvency' and 'Bankruptcy' is used interchangeably in this part to refer to the collective process.

14 *Hays & Co. v. Merrill Lynch, Pierce, Fenner & Smith, Inc.*, US Court of Appeals, 885 F.2d 1149, 1161 (3d Cir.1989).

15 United States Supreme Court, 482 U.S. 220 (1987).

16 *Ibid.*, at 226.

(a) the relevant statute's text;
(b) the relevant statute's legislative history; or
(c) the existence of an inherent conflict between arbitration and the relevant statute's underlying purposes.[17]

Since, in the US Bankruptcy Code or its legislative history, there is no express or implied exception to arbitration, the McMahon Test narrowed down to the examination of existence of 'inherent conflict' between arbitration and bankruptcy. The conflict, as highlighted above, does exist between the two laws as to whether compelling reference to arbitration of a dispute would jeopardise the underlying purpose of centralising all disputes before a bankruptcy court in the bankruptcy process.[18] Thus, in case the institution or continuation of arbitration would jeopardise the bankruptcy process, there exists an exception, and the dispute cannot be referred to arbitration, while, where it does not jeopardise, then there is no exception, and the parties must be compelled to arbitrate. This notion led to the conception of a distinction between 'core' and 'non-core' bankruptcy matters, with arbitration of 'core' matters being considered to be jeopardising the bankruptcy process,[19] while arbitration of 'non-core' matters not.[20]

However, what constitutes 'core' and 'non-core' remained contentious, since, drawing up an exhaustive list[21] of either of these matters was found

---

17 *Ibid.*, at 227.

18 *MBNA Am. Bank, N.A. v. Hill*, US Court of Appeals 2nd Circuit, 436 F.3d 104, 109 (2d Cir. 2006).

19 *In re White Mountain Mining Co.*, US Court of Appeals 4th Circuit, 403 F.3d 164, 169 (4th Cir. 2005). Here, Court noted that permitting an arbitrator to decide a core issue would jeopardise the bankruptcy process as it would make debtor-creditor rights contingent upon an arbitrator's ruling.

20 *See* Marianne B. Culhane and Michaela M. White, *Enforcing (or not) Arbitration Clauses in Bankruptcy*, 1362 PRAC. L. INSTI. CORP. L. & PRAC. HANDBOOK SERIES 39, 48 (2003).

21 US Bankruptcy Code provides for a non-exhaustive list of 'core' matters under s. 157(b)(2), to include —

(A) matters concerning the administration of the estate;
(B) allowance or disallowance of claims against the estate or exemptions from property of the estate, and estimation of claims or interests for the purposes of confirming a plan under chapter 11, 12, or 13 of title 11 but not the liquidation or estimation of contingent or unliquidated personal injury tort or wrongful death claims against the estate for purposes of distribution in a case under title 11;
(C) counterclaims by the estate against persons filing claims against the estate;
(D) orders in respect to obtaining credit;
(E) orders to turn over property of the estate;
(F) proceedings to determine, avoid, or recover preferences;

difficult. 'Core' matters is broadly understood to be related to those issues that involve substantive rights,[22] arising from and under the Bankruptcy Code, or those that are central to a collective bankruptcy process such as matters related to adjudication of the insolvency itself, verification and priority of creditors' claims,[23] among others. While, 'non-core' matters usually arises outside the bankruptcy law and exist independently in as much as they could be agitated even if there is no bankruptcy processes.[24] They do, however, have an effect on the bankruptcy, for instance, debtor's contractual disputes or tax liability, but they are not central to the process or continuing arbitration in relation to them would not frustrate the bankruptcy process.[25]

Creating this distinction presents a persuasive method to minimise conflict between arbitration and insolvency, as all cases with 'non-core' issues continues to remain arbitrable, and only cases involving 'core' issues, critical to the process, remained under the exclusive jurisdiction of the insolvency court.

(G) motions to terminate, annul, or modify the automatic stay;
(H) proceedings to determine, avoid, or recover fraudulent conveyances;
(I) determinations as to the dischargeability of particular debts;
(J) objections to discharges;
(K) determinations of the validity, extent, or priority of liens;
(L) confirmations of plans;
(M) orders approving the use or lease of property, including the use of cash collateral;
(N) orders approving the sale of property other than property resulting from claims brought by the estate against persons who have not filed claims against the estate;
(O) other proceedings affecting the liquidation of the assets of the estate or the adjustment of the debtor-creditor or the equity security holder relationship, except personal injury tort or wrongful death claims; and
(P) recognition of foreign proceedings and other matters under chapter 15 of title 11.

22 *See Ins. Co. of N. Am. v. NGC Settlement Tr. & Asbestos Claims Mgmt. Corp.* (In re Nat'l Gypsum Co.), United States Court of Appeals, Fifth Circuit, 118 F.3d 1056, 1062 (5th Cir. 1997).

23 *In re Lehman Bros. Holdings Inc.*, U.S. Court of Appeals (2d Cir., 6 Oct. 2016).

24 *Hays & Co. v. Merrill Lynch, Pierce, Fenner & Smith, Inc.*, US Court of Appeals, 885 F.2d 1149, 1161 (3d Cir.1989), at 1156 n.9.

25 France applies similar approach in determining arbitrability of insolvency matters. It provides that issues that '*(a) do not arise from the opening of the insolvency proceedings; (b) which derive from agreements concluded prior to the insolvency; and (c) which would have occurred regardless of the insolvency*', are arbitrable. *See* Veronika Timofeeva and Ketevan Betaneli, *Surviving COVID-19: Arbitrations involving insolvent companies,* FRESHFIELDS Bruckhaus Deringer, 1 April 2021, available at https://www.lexology.com/commentary/arbitration-adr/france/freshfields-bruckhaus-deringer-llp/surviving-covid-19-arbitrations-involving-insolvent-companies.

Distinction of In Rem and In Personam Matters: The *Erga Omnes* Test

Arbitration, being an alternate dispute resolution mechanism, requires voluntary submission. It emanates from the contract between the parties, and is thus, private. It is not to affect the interest of those who are not party to the arbitration agreement as it is mandated to regulate the affairs of only those who submit to its jurisdiction, i.e., *inter partes*.

These characteristics of arbitration indicate that arbitration would not be suitable, or be allowed, for those actions where rights and obligations in contention are owed to the world at large, i.e., in rem.[26] Otherwise, arbitration of such actions would result in unintended implications for the parties not before the arbitration. Due to this, globally, certain types of disputes remain excluded from the list of subject matter capable of arbitration. Insolvency and bankruptcy being an action in rem, requiring consolidation of all claims against the debtor and central adjudication of disputes in the interest of all stakeholders, to remain excluded from scope of arbitration, and lie within the exclusive jurisdiction of bankruptcy courts, whose jurisdiction at its core is in rem.[27]

Arbitration, thus, is primarily meant to adjudicate disputes that are in personam in nature, i.e., where a right is available/enforceable against a specific person or persons.[28] However, whether these in personam disputes would also include subordinate in personam disputes arising out of broader in rem actions remain a point of discussion.

Some jurisdictions, including US,[29] have explored these subordinates in personam disputes in relation to the larger in rem insolvency actions, and observed that subordinate disputes are also arbitrable.[30] In simple words, disputes emanating during the insolvency proceedings but having in personam character continue to remain arbitrable, even though the larger insolvency proceedings itself is non-arbitrable for being in rem. It essentially signifies that actions that would not create effect towards the world, *erga omnes*, will remain arbitrable, irrespective of the fact that it arises out of or during the pendency of insolvency proceedings. Thus, those in

---

26 *Booz Allen & Hamilton Inc. v. SBI Home Finance Ltd. & Ors.*, Supreme Court of India, (2011) 5 SCC 532, at para. 23.

27 *Cent. Va. Cmty. Coll. v. Katz*, US Supreme Court, 546 U.S. 356, 362 (2006).

28 *Booz Allen & Hamilton Inc. v. SBI Home Finance Ltd. & Ors.*, Supreme Court of India, (2011) 5 SCC 532, at paras 22-23.

29 Frank R. Kennedy, *The Automatic Stay in Bankruptcy*, 11 U. MICH.J. L. REFORM 175 (1978).

30 Sir Michael J. Mustill and Stewart Crauford Boyd, *Commercial Arbitration: 2001 Companion Volume to the Second Edition* (Butterworths, 2001).

personam disputes that would have no effect on rights of other stakeholders in the insolvency, or prejudice their legitimate interest under the insolvency process, would continue to be arbitrable during insolvency. Such in personam dispute may include issues related to unsecured claims as they would not operate or create rights against the estate of the debtor.

Distinction Between Beneficial and Prejudicial Disputes

This distinction is in vogue in jurisdictions such as UK,[31] Singapore,[32] and India.[33] Under this distinction, proceedings that are in the interest of the corporate debtor or that may conclude improving the prospects of the corporate debtor are considered to be arbitrable, while those which are prejudicial to the value of the debtor or that may have impact on its estate are considered non-arbitrable.

This distinction upholds the core principle of insolvency law, i.e., to protect and preserve the value of the debtor such that the interest of its stakeholders, who have chosen to participate in a collective process by way of insolvency resolution rather than enforcing their individual actions, can be maximised. Continued adjudication of those disputes that may derive benefits to the debtor is in the interest of the stakeholders. It would help in maximising the value of the debtor that would in turn help in maximising the return to the stakeholders.

On the other hand, disputes that can be perceived to be prejudicial to the debtor's interest or its estate, in particular, for instance, disputes initiated against the debtor at the instance of the more aggressive creditors, would be contrary to this principle as it may cause dismemberment and disappearance of the estate. Continued adjudication of these disputes may expose the debtor to orders which may require payments to be made or assets to be disposed of or transferred to a third party, resulting in dissipating the overall value of the debtor or the asset available under the insolvency process.

---

31 UK Insolvency Act 1986, Schedule 1 ¶ 6, '*Power to refer to arbitration any question affecting the company.*'

32 Insolvency, Restructuring and Dissolution Act 2018, ss 144(1)(e) and 378(b), and para. (e) of the First Schedule to the Insolvency, Restructuring and Dissolution Act 2018.

33 *See Power Grid Corporation of India v. Jyoti Structures Ltd.*, Delhi High Court, (2018) 246 DLT 485; *SSMP Industries Ltd v. Perkan Foods Processors Pvt. Ltd*, Delhi High Court, 2019 SCC Online Del 9339; *Jharkhand Bijli Vitran Nigam Ltd. v. IVRCL Limited & Anr.*, NCLAT, Company Appeal (AT) (Insolvency) No. 285/2018, decided on 3 Aug. 2018.

Thus, in case of any challenge to reference to arbitration of a dispute, the critical determination would be whether the dispute at hand prima facie appears to be beneficial or prejudicial to the interest of the debtor. If it is found beneficial, then the challenge to arbitration would not sustain and the parties would be compelled to arbitrate.

The aforesaid approaches, individually, thus, present a viable alternative to address the conflict between the arbitration and insolvency. However, since, they may overlap at some points, a cumulative application of all on a case-to-case basis may also strengthen the efforts to minimise the conflict and streamline the policy objectives of arbitration and insolvency. However, in order to see how these approaches weigh in vis-à-vis the Indian insolvency regime, it merits that a reference be made to the legislative history of the Indian insolvency law.

Indian Insolvency and Bankruptcy Law: Past and Present

At present, insolvency and bankruptcy in India is regulated through and under the Insolvency and Bankruptcy Code, 2016 (IBC). IBC was promulgated finally in 2016[34] after a long and much-awaited decision that paved the way for a new insolvency paradigm in India. This IBC regime is much more carefully crafted as it is globally more outward looking and in tandem with the key parameters recognised universally to measure efficiency for resolving insolvency, i.e., time, cost, outcome, and recovery rate.[35]

The current Indian insolvency regime (IBC) makes a significant leap forward from the earlier law as it shows substantial improvement on all the aforesaid parameters. As a result, with the introduction of the IBC, India has moved considerably upward in the World Bank Ease of Doing Business Index, which measures a nation's efficiency in 'resolving insolvency' as one of the 12 areas of business regulation that 'encourages efficiency and supports freedom to do business'.[36] As per Doing Business 2020, the recent reforms in India, including the introduction of the IBC,

34 IBC was passed by Lok Sabha on 5 May 2016 and by Rajya Sabha on 11 May 2016. It received the assent of the President of India on 28 May 2016 and was published in the official gazette on 28 May 2016.

35 World Bank. 2020. Doing Business 2020. Washington, DC: World Bank. DOI:10.1596/978-1-4648-1440-2. License: Creative Commons Attribution CC BY 3.0 IGO, page 19.

36 *Ibid.*, p. 3.

have resulted in a significant move upwards for India as being ranked from 130th in 2016 to 63rd in 2020.[37]

Failure of Pre-existing Legislations

The erstwhile insolvency and bankruptcy regime in India was severely plagued with inordinate delays and unintended outcomes. It failed to stand tall at any of the aforesaid parameters of time, cost, outcome, and recovery rate. It was characterised as a complex system with fragmented laws accompanied by an inadequate institutional set-up.[38]

Earlier insolvency regime was scattered under many laws. Personal insolvency was, and is to some extent even now, governed by and under the archaic Presidency Towns Insolvency Act, 1909 and the Provincial Insolvency Act, 1920. The 26th Law Commission had suggested amendments in the year 1964, however, till date, even after a period of hundred years, nothing has changed in this space.[39]

For corporates, there was no law specifically dealing with insolvency and bankruptcy till 1985. Tiwari Committee (1981) acknowledged the vacuum in this area and recommended a legislative tool, namely, Sick Industrial Companies Act, 1985 (SICA). SICA was meant to identify the stress and then employ measures, including providing for stay on all proceedings against the industry, to revive them. However, SICA failed as (a) it allowed the debtor to be in control of the corporate even after it being adjudicated sick, (b) endeavoured to rehabilitate the sick corporate in all situations, even when there were negligible possibilities of revival, and (c) the tribunal set up to support SICA could not match with the increasing number of cases.[40]

---

37 *Ibid.*

38 Rajeswari Sengupta, Anjali Sharma, and Susan Thomas, *Evolution of the insolvency framework for non-financial firms in India*, Indira Gandhi Institute of Development Research, Mumbai June 2016, available at http://www.igidr.ac.in/pdf/publication/WP-2016-018.pdf.

39 Government of India, Notification dated 15 Nov. 2019, notifying provisions of Part III of the IBC so far as they relate to 'personal guarantors to corporate debtors'.

40 *See Madras Petrochem Ltd. and Anr. v. Board for Industrial and Financial Reconstruction and Ors.*, Supreme Court of India, (2016) 4 SCC 1. In this case, Supreme Court of India referred to Eradi Committee report wherein it was observed that out of 3068 cases referred to BIFR between 1987 and 2000, 2006 cases have been disposed of, out of which 264 cases were revived, 375 cases were under negotiation for revival process, 741 cases were recommended for winding up, and 626 cases were dismissed as not maintainable. These facts and figures speak for themselves and place a big question mark on the utility of the Sick Industrial Companies (Special Provisions) Act, 1985.

Thereafter, the Recovery of Debts Due to Banks and Financial Institutions Act, 1993 (RDDB')[41] and the Securitisation and Reconstruction of Financial Assets and Enforcement of Securities Interest Act, 2002 ('SARFAESI')[42] were enacted on recommendations of Narasimham Committee I[43] and II[44] respectively. However, severe difficulties existed even in these legislations[45] as instead of having one single statute consolidating all aspects of insolvency and bankruptcy of corporates, it provided for four different laws, namely, SICA, RDDB, SARFAESI, and Companies Act, 2013 governing different, though inter-related, aspects of the insolvency and bankruptcy of corporates. Each of these statutes further provided for creation of multiple fora such as Board of Industrial and Financial Reconstruction ('BIFR'), Debts Recovery Tribunal ('DRT'), and National Company Law Tribunal ('NCLT') and their respective Appellate Tribunals, including National Company Law Appellate Tribunal ('NCLAT'). This multiplicity of statute and fora led to a framework which was inadequate and ineffective, and resulted in undue delay.[46]

The Report of Bankruptcy Law Reform Committee (BLRC Report),[47] which paved the way for present IBC, also noted these shortcomings and observed that the existing law is a highly fragmented framework with powers of creditors and debtors under insolvency being provided for under different statutes. Existence of multiple forums to decide inter-related issues causes grave prejudice to the resolution framework and results primarily in two types of problems, namely:

---

41 RDDB provided for setting up of the Debt Recovery Tribunals (DRT) and the Debt Recovery Appellate Tribunals (DRAT). These tribunals were intended to be specialised tribunals facilitating expeditious recovery of debt from the defaulters by banks and a defined set of financial institutions.

42 SARFAESI provided sweeping powers to the banks and financial institutions to recover against non-performing secured loans. Since the DRTs had not proved to be as effective in enabling recovery as expected, the SARFAESI provided an alternative route for recovery. SARFAESI allowed banks and FIs to take possession of the collateral security without court intervention.

43 Reserve Bank of India's Committee on the Financial System, under the chairmanship of M Narasimham, 1991.

44 *Ibid.*, 1998.

45 The Supreme Court of India, in *ArcelorMittal India Private Limited v. Satish Kumar Gupta and Ors.*, Supreme Court of India, Civil Appeal Nos. 9402-9405/2018 (decided on 4 Oct. 2018) ('***ArcelorMittal***'), observed that SICA and RDDB Act have completely failed, and that even though SARFAESI Act has recorded improvement in the amounts recovered as compared to other two enactments, yet it is inadequate.

46 Statement of Objects and Reasons leading up to the enactment to the IBC.

47 The Report of Bankruptcy Law Reform Committee Vol I: Rational and Design, Ministry of Finance, (Nov. 2015).

(a) Where one forum decides on the issue relating to creditor in an insolvency, while the other forum decides on the issue relating to the debtor; such decisions are usually challenged and often stayed or set aside by the appellate court causing a significant delay in arriving at the outcome. If this concern is to be remedied, it is best suited that the rights and liabilities of debtor and creditor are both adjudicated before one single forum, who may after considering both sides of the argument render a reasoned judgment expeditiously.

(b) Multiple fora under different statutes often expose the issues to be adjudicated by a forum which may not have adequate commercial or business expertise, knowledge, or experience to decide issues relating to insolvency and bankruptcy. This leads to delay and inconsistency in the decisions and increases the vulnerability of challenge to such decisions.

The BLRC further records that due to this uncertainty in judicial and legislative environment on insolvency and bankruptcy, the outcome of insolvency in India is very poor. It notes that, in 2014, India took 4 years to resolve insolvency, while Singapore took 0.8 year and UK took 1 year.[48] Supreme Court of India also emphasised on this in *Innoventive Industries Ltd. v. ICICI Bank and Anr.*[49] It noted that in the World Bank's Ease of Doing Business Index, 2015, India was ranked 135th out of 190 countries on the ease of resolving insolvency. Post IBC, however, the rankings have significantly improved as India in 2020 was ranked 52nd.[50]

Transition to IBC

Introduction of the IBC, as stated above, was not a sudden measure but a gradual outcome of detailed deliberations by various committees constituted. It was noticed by each of these committees that the existence of numerous laws governing different aspects of the same process and each law providing jurisdiction to different fora in case of disputes, has frustrated the overall objective of the mechanism instituted for resolving insolvency.

---

48 Ref. World Bank, Doing Business Project, Time to resolve insolvency (years) – India, 2014, available at https://data.worldbank.org/indicator/IC.ISV.DURS?most_recent_year_desc=true&locations=IN.

49 Supreme Court of India (2018) 1 SCC 407 ('*Innoventive*').

50 World Bank, 2020. Doing Business 2020. Washington, DC: World Bank. DOI:10.1596/978-1-4648-1440-2. License: Creative Commons Attribution CC BY 3.0 IGO, p. 3.

As a consequence, in 1999, Justice Eradi Committee[51] recommended significant amendments to the Companies Act and proposed repeal of SICA. Report noted that

> … there is a need for establishing a National Tribunal as a specialized agency to deal with matters relating to rehabilitation, revival and winding up of companies. With a view to avoiding multiplicity of fora, the National Tribunal should be conferred with jurisdiction and powers to deal with matters under Companies Act, 1956 presently exercised by the Company Law Board; jurisdiction, power and authority relating to winding up of companies vested with High Courts and power to consider rehabilitation and revival of companies presently vested in the BIFR.

This was the first time that a tribunal with power and jurisdiction to decide all issues of insolvency, bankruptcy, and liquidation/winding up was conceptualised for Indian corporates, as it exists now under the IBC. Although the committee's recommendation did translate into amendment to Companies Act in 2002,[52] it remained dormant until 2016, i.e., till the time the IBC got promulgated.

Subsequently, in 2001, N.L. Mitra Committee recommended a new comprehensive Bankruptcy Code. However, this Committee report was not acted upon directly. In 2005, the JJ Irani Committee relied heavily on N.L. Mitra Committee Report and suggested transition from 'inability to pay' to 'failure to pay' threshold under Indian law. The current Indian Companies Act, 2013 is based on the recommendations of the JJ Irani Committee Report. The Companies Act 2013 provided for setting up of NCLT and NCLAT as the dedicated tribunals for dealing with matters involving corporates, particularly winding up and liquidation of companies. Although, Companies Act, 2013 in itself was a major break-away from the earlier laws, it still lacked a mechanism for effective reorganisation of insolvency and bankruptcy of corporates, as SICA, RDDB, and SARFAESI continue to govern these limited aspects.

Consequently, in 2014, the Ministry of Finance set up the BLRC to formulate a consolidated and comprehensive insolvency and bankruptcy regime for India. BLRC was mandated to draw up a system that would

---

51 The High Level Committee on Law relating to Insolvency and Winding Up of Companies, chaired by Justice V. Balakrishna Eradi (31 July 2000).

52 Company (Second Amendment) Act, 2002 was passed providing for establishment of NCLT and NCLAT to take-over the functions which are being performed by CLB, BIFR, AAIFR and the High Courts.

replace the erstwhile mechanism and consolidate all the different processes and subjects under one law. In 2015, BLRC submitted its report recommending enactment of the IBC, as it stands today. IBC stands at a great departure from the erstwhile regime under SICA, RDDB, and SARFAESI as it addresses all the shortcoming of the erstwhile laws by:

(a) Providing a common insolvency and bankruptcy framework for all type of corporates and individuals.
(b) Uniformising the trigger for initiating insolvency and bankruptcy proceedings against a debtor.
(c) Separating the debtor from its promoters and shifting from debtor-in-possession to creditor-in-possession framework.
(d) Providing rights to all types of creditors, financial or operational, to initiate insolvency against a debtor.
(e) Providing for an automatic moratorium on all actions pending or to be instituted against the debtor during the insolvency resolution period.
(f) Providing for a specified and condensed timeline for completion of the insolvency resolution process.
(g) Providing for exclusive jurisdiction to NCLT and NCLAT for adjudicating disputes 'arising out of' or 'in relation to' the insolvency and bankruptcy of the debtor.
(h) Setting up of multiple benches of the adjudicatory forum (NCLT) to enable effective dealing of the rising cases of insolvency.
(i) Conceptualising and providing for mechanisms/protection to the interim-financing of the debtor during insolvency resolution.
(j) Providing for clear classes of creditors and the specified hierarchy of their claims against the debtor's estate.
(k) Providing primacy to IBC over other laws inconsistent with IBC thereby leading to minimisation of conflicts between different statutes.

IBC Affirms and Upholds Each of the Parameters of Effectively Resolving Insolvency

As stated above, IBC is a well-thought out and comprehensive economic legislation. In wake of the growing menace of loan defaults with which most of the banks were, and are, swamped with, it had long been felt to have a disciplined legislation like IBC to address this issue.

The preamble to the IBC sets out the objects as follows:

> An Act to consolidate and amend the laws relating to reorganisation and insolvency resolution of corporate persons, partnership firms and individuals in a time bound manner for maximisation of value of assets of such persons, to promote entrepreneurship, availability of credit and balance the interests of all the stakeholders including alteration in the order of priority of payment of Government dues and to establish an Insolvency and Bankruptcy Board of India, and for matters connected therewith or incidental thereto.

The Preamble gives a clear indication of the objectives that IBC seeks to achieve. The stated objects of the IBC are two-fold: first, consisting of the scope of the laws – (i) reorganisation of corporate persons, which will include reorganising the capital of the corporate person in terms of IBC; (ii) insolvency resolution of corporate persons; (iii) undertaking the first two in a time-bound manner; and second, setting of the overall objectives of the law; (iv) maximisation of value of the assets of the corporate debtor; (v) promotion of entrepreneurship; (vi) promotion of availability of credit; and (vii) balancing the interests of the stakeholders.

Each of these objects, taken individually and cumulatively, puts India's IBC along-side the most developed insolvency regimes in the world. Further, it suggests that India, being an active member of international community, is striving towards laws which are more outward looking and that fits well with the idea of promoting entrepreneurship and ease of doing business. Furthermore, these objects, directly or indirectly, also further India's position on the parameters of time, cost, outcome, and recovery rate, which are relevant to measure efficiency of a law in resolving insolvency, as detailed hereinafter. Individually taken, these parameters suggest the fundamentals of any robust insolvency law.

Speed Is of the Essence: 'Time'

'Time' as a parameter identifies and measures the period taken between the default by the debtor and the payments of the debt owed to the lender. It also considers the time consumed in contesting proceedings, legitimate or frivolous, extensions in time sought to complete proceedings, the inter-se dispute between the lender and the debtor, among others.

BLRC Report notes that 'speed is of essence for the working of the bankruptcy code'.[53] Consequently, IBC, through its overall scheme and in its objects, emphasises on the vital role of a time-bound insolvency resolution process. The Preamble states that time-bound reorganisation and insolvency resolution is essential for value maximisation. It acknowledges that better realisation is obtained when a corporate is sold off as a 'going concern', rather by way of a piecemeal sale in liquidation, which results in retrieval of lesser value to the creditors. Hence, when delays bring liquidation, there is value destruction. Further, even during liquidation, the value tends to reduce in cases of delay as assets usually suffer depreciation. Thus, for maximising the value, it is pertinent that the causes of delays are eliminated, and the process is strengthened.

The provisions of the IBC individually, and its scheme in general, address this problem. IBC provides for a self-contained mechanism whereby the legislative policy is reflected to place an ailing cooperate debtor to the process of insolvency resolution at the earliest and not wait till the fiscal stability of the corporate debtor becomes so vulnerable that either insolvency resolution process becomes difficult or liquidation becomes inevitable.[54] IBC, on the one hand, provides for moratorium that ensures a 'calming period' for the corporate debtor as during this time it remains stress-free and afloat, while simultaneously appoints a qualified insolvency professional at the helm of the debtor's management, who take ownership and control of the ailing debtor and make important decisions to maintain the corporate debtor a 'going concern'. This insolvency professional is tasked to conduct the insolvency resolution process of the corporate debtor in a time-bound manner, i.e., within 180 days (extendable to the maximum of 330 days),[55] while protecting and preserving the value of the debtor.

The results that ensued from these provisions in the decrease in time consumed in resolving insolvency is astounding. IBBI data as of March 2021 provides that the 348 cases (out of 2,653 closed till March 2021), which have been resolved by way of reorganisation, took on average of 406

53 BLRC, p. 14.

54 The emphasis on early recognition and admission of a company into the protective framework of the CIR Process is also demonstrated by explanation to s. 7(1) of the IBC which enables a financial creditor to seek admission of the corporate debtor even in case of a default with respect to debts owed to a different financial creditor as any default of financial debt is an indication of insolvency, and its resolution rather than rights of any party is the intended objective of the IBC.

55 Insolvency and Bankruptcy Code 2016, s. 12.

days (excluding the time consumed on account of litigation and COVID-19) to conclude. While, the 1,277 cases that ended in liquidation, took on average of 351 days to conclude.

This is a significant jump from the time taken in earlier insolvency regime. As per the World Bank Data of 2016, India took 4.3 years to resolve insolvency under the earlier mechanisms,[56] while as per the World Bank Data of 2020 (benchmarked as on data received by May 2019), India now takes 1.6 years to resolve insolvency on an average.[57]

Promoting Entrepreneurship and Availability of Credit: 'Cost'

'Cost' measures the amount of money spent for carrying on the proceedings for resolving insolvency qua the total value of insolvent debtor's estate. This includes cost incurred towards court fees, taxes, fees of personnel engaged to manage the insolvency estate during the process, lawyers, and other professionals and advisors.

Cost of reorganisation and bankruptcy procedures is inversely associated with growth of entrepreneurship and availability of credit in the economy. Economies compete and endeavour to become business friendly. India is a young republic and has a dynamic pool of young entrepreneurs who are risk-taking and competition-loving. They are the growth drivers for the times to come. However, they stand dissuaded from contributing to their full potential due to red-tapism and the general legal and regulatory environment that leads to excessive delays and increased cost in resolving issues concerning repayment and availability of credit. For a country like the size of India, the availability of credit to new and existing viable businesses is so staggered, as a large portion of money remains held up in non-performing accounts due to defaults in repayments and delay in recovery, that many businesses close before they even start.

The World Bank in its Report on Principles and Guidelines for Effective Insolvency and Creditor Rights, April 2001 also highlights the relationship between the cost and flow of credit. At Para 8, it observed role of enforcement systems as follows:

> [A] modern, credit-based economy requires predictable, transparent and affordable enforcement of both unsecured and secured credit

56 Doing Business 2016 (13th edn.), World Bank Group Flagship Report, Measuring Regulatory Quality and Efficiency, Economy Profile 2016, India, p. 126.

57 World Bank Group (2020). Economy profile India: Doing Business 2020. World Bank. https://www.doingbusiness.org/content/dam/doingBusiness/country/i/india/IND.pdf.

claims by efficient mechanisms outside of insolvency, as well as a sound insolvency system. These systems must be designed to work in harmony. Commerce is a system of commercial relationships predicated on express or implied contractual agreements between an enterprise and a wide range of creditors and constituencies. Although commercial transactions have become increasingly complex as more sophisticated techniques are developed for pricing and managing risks, the basic rights governing these relationships and the procedures for enforcing these rights have not changed much. These rights enable parties to rely on contractual agreements, fostering confidence that fuels investment, lending and commerce. Conversely, uncertainty about the enforceability of contractual rights increases the cost of credit to compensate for the increased risk of non-performance or, in severe cases, leads to credit tightening.

An insolvency regime with lower insolvency cost and a transparent process is likely to encourage more, and timely, insolvency filings[58] leading to improved chances of revival of viable businesses and a quicker liquidation of unviable businesses, preventing burning of further cash.[59] Thus, practically, variation in the insolvency cost will influence an individual's or enterprise's reaction towards entrepreneurial entry, success or failure. In other words, promotion of entrepreneurship will take place when there is assurance of easy exit in case of failure, and lower costs being a crucial factor in the regard, would promote creation of new firms and promote healthy competition in the economy.[60]

The cost of insolvency proceedings is also directly proportionate to the length of the process. The lengthier the process to resolve insolvency or effectuate liquidation, the higher the cost to recover the credit. The reasons for the same are two-fold: (a) the corporate debtor would remain in stress during this process, and would be required to be managed by insolvency professionals and its advisors, whose fees would form part of insolvency costs and would be adjusted against the value available to the creditors on

58 Jason Allen and Kiana Basiri (2016). *The impact of bankruptcy reform on insolvency choice and consumer credit*, Bank of Canada Staff Working Paper, Number 2016-26, Bank of Canada, Ottawa.

59 Potential economic gains from reforming insolvency law in Europe, AFME Finance for Europe, Feb. 2016.

60 *See* Elena Cirmizi and Leora F. Klapper, and Mahesh Uttamchandani, *The Challenges of Bankruptcy Reform* (1 Oct. 2010), World Bank Policy Research Working Paper No. 5448.

completion of the process, and (b) during the process, the debtor would not operate at its full potential due to its inability to raise adequate finances, which it may otherwise raise if operating outside the rigour of insolvency process. A quicker recovery would also lead to availability of better credit in the market, which can be channelled back to the same debtor, from whom it is recovered, on fresh terms. This importance of quicker recovery of credit was also recognised by Gujarat High Court in *Alka Ceramics v. Gujarat State Financial Corporation and Ors*[61] – 'If quick recovery is not ensured, the credit would be slow in giving and would thus hinder the industrial growth.'

IBC addresses these concerns by (a) providing for clear trigger thresholds of default and setting up of information utilities for recording defaults, thereby minimalising the requirement of adjudication; (b) streamlining the process with no ambiguity on the rights and powers of the stakeholders leading to lesser chances of conflicts and disputes, saving time and cost; (c) providing for a time-bound process to conduct reorganisation; (d) envisaging the need of interim finances to keep viable businesses alive during reorganisation process; (e) stipulating limits on the fees of the professionals appointed to conduct the process; and (f) providing for separate and priority treatment of cost incurred during the process.

As per the data released by IBBI as of March 2021, under the IBC, the average cost for resolution is approximately 0.49% of the resolution value, while it is 0.92% in cases of liquidation. The increased cost in liquidation is understandable as (a) under IBC, liquidation of the corporate debtor is treated as the last resort and is only preferred in case the resolution fails, and therefore, the cost calculation accounts for costs incurred for both resolution and liquidation, and (b) liquidation value is usually lesser than the resolution value for a stressed debtor, and thus, a percentage increase in cost during liquidation. Despite this, there is a significant reduction in costs under the IBC as compared to the erstwhile insolvency regime.

Revival of the Debtor: 'Outcome'

'Outcome' is a crucial parameter as it measures the success of the insolvency resolution process. Proceedings that lead to revival or reorganisation of the debtor and ensure preservation of the value of the debtor is regarded as a better outcome[62] as compared to those that leads to liquidation. It is

---

61 Gujarat High Court, AIR 1990 Guj 105.

62 *Orderly & Effective Insolvency Procedures: Key Issues*, Legal Department, International Monetary Fund 1999, available at https://www.imf.org/external/pubs/ft/orderly/.

primarily for the reason that liquidation leads to a lower recovery as compared to reorganisation, as in cases of piecemeal sale of the debtor, the debtor is bound to recover a lesser value as compared to what it can generate as a 'going concern'. Moreover, reorganisation ensures that the debtor does not die and continue to support its stakeholders by generating revenue.

IBC's primary focus, by the above stated aims of 're-organization and insolvency resolution', is to ensure the revival and continuation of the corporate debtor, which it seeks to achieve by protecting the corporate debtor, at the first instance from its various interested parties, such as the creditors, and its own management and shareholders; and in the second instance, from a corporate death by liquidation.[63] IBC intends and places the interests of the corporate debtor on a higher pedestal than the interests of any other party. This is based on the rationale that the continuation of a viable economic enterprise will have the potential to return more value than any other form of distribution, or management.

In this regard, IBC framework is a departure from the erstwhile insolvency regime as it does not attach any stigma to corporate insolvency resolution process and in fact encourages companies which need insolvency resolution to be admitted immediately into such a protective process. Therefore, by design and in light of its objects, the IBC is a beneficial legislation for corporate debtors and not a recovery legislation for the creditors.

The data available as of March 2021 also amply indicates that IBC has been a relative success as compared to its predecessors in this regard. Figure 7.1 shows the data in relation to 2,653 closed cases since 2016.[64]

63 *Swiss Ribbons Pvt. Ltd. v. Union of India*, Supreme Court of India, Writ Petition (Civil) No. 99 of 2018, decided on 25 Jan. 2019.

64 *Insolvency Reform Developing Metrics, Tracking Outcomes*, Insolvency and Bankruptcy News, January-March 2021, Vol. 18, available at https://ibbi.gov.in/uploads/publication/2021-05-29-204331-atxcy-3363461de858b06bfa1afdbf13151b90.pdf.

Figure 7.1 Status of 2,653 cases closed under IBC since 2016

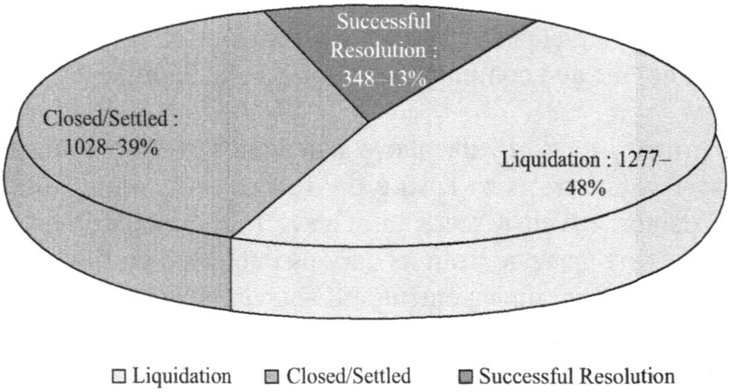

Thus, as evident, out of total 2,653 closed cases, 348 cases have resulted in approval of resolution plan, while 1,277 have ended in liquidation, and another 1,028 have either been closed as withdrawn or settled or on appeal or review. Further, a major chunk of the 1,277 that ended in liquidation, i.e., 946 cases to be precise, belonged to and transferred from the BIFR or were already defunct before IBC was enacted.[65] These 946 cases had assets with average value of 5% of the outstanding debt owed by them.

Further, another crucial figure in this regard is that the 348 corporate debtors who were rescued by way of approval of resolution plan had a total asset valuation of INR 1.11 lakh crore (USD 14.88 billion approx.), while the 1,277 cases that ended in liquidation had a total asset value of INR 0.46 lakh crore (USD 6.16 billion approx.) as on the date of admission into insolvency process. This data suggest that in monetary terms almost 70% of the distressed assets are rescued under the IBC.

Cumulative Impact of Improvement in Time, Cost, and Outcome on 'Recovery Rate'

'Recovery Rate' is at the centre of the whole resolving insolvency matrix, as it ranks a system the highest which maximises the value of the debtor and ensures maximum return on the lender's debt. It is measured based on

65 *Insolvency Reform Developing Metrics, Tracking Outcomes*, Insolvency and Bankruptcy News, January-March 2021, Vol. 18, available at https://ibbi.gov.in/uploads/publication/2021-05-29-204331-atxcy-3363461de858b06bfa1afdbf13151b90.pdf.

the cumulative effect of the other three parameters, i.e., time, cost, and outcome. For its calculation, 'outcome' provides the data as to whether the debtor is reorganised and is continuing as a 'going concern' or that the debtor's estate is sold off and liquidated. 'Cost' provides the data as to how much money is spent in recovery of a penny of the debt owed. 'Time' provides the data as to the loss of value, including on account of depreciation, during the time the process to resolve insolvency was on-going and the loss of interest as the money owed by the debtor remained tied up with the proceedings.

The improvement in performance in each of these three parameters has a cumulative effect on the overall recovery rate under the IBC. As stated above, the 348 debtors rescued had a total asset value of INR 1.11 lakh crore, while they had a total creditor claim of INR 5.67 lakh crore against them. Under IBC, reorganisation of the 348 debtors led to recovery of INR 2.09 lakh crore for the creditors; which is approximately 189% of the total asset value of these debtors. In other words, resolution has fetched an excess of 89% to the creditors, in comparison to the recovery that would have been possible under liquidation or any other process, including the erstwhile insolvency regime. Further, this recovery is exclusive to the process initiated for the corporate debtor and the recovery to be made from guarantors, corporate or personal, and from the avoidance/preferential transactions would be over and above this.

This exponential increase in recovery rate from the distressed assets under the IBC is also evident from the data released by Reserve Bank of India in its Report on Trend and Progress of Banking in India 2019-2020.[66] Report indicates that the recovery from IBC was 61% of the total amount recovered by banks through 'all' means in 2019-2020. It is a further increase of 5% from the recovery made in 2018-2019 through IBC. Further, in 2019-2020, the recovery made under IBC was 45.5% of the total amount involved in cases before IBC, while only 26.1% and 4.1% of the total amount involved was recovered under SARFAESI and RDDB respectively during the same period. Thus, the improvement in comparison to previous insolvency regime is evident.

The aforesaid improvements have also resulted in global acknowledgment of Indian efforts in changing landscape of doing business in India, and specifically in the index of 'resolving insolvency'. As per the World

---

66 Reserve Bank of India, *Report on Trend and Progress of Banking in India 2019-2020*, 29 Dec. 2020, available at https://rbidocs.rbi.org.in/rdocs/Publications/PDFs/0RTP2020_F3D078985540A4179B62B7734C7B445C9.PDF.

Bank Resolving Insolvency Index, India is now ranked 52nd among 190 countries, which is the best ever ranking in this Index for India and a huge move upward from being ranked 136th in 2016.[67] Similarly, the Global Innovation Index, 2020 edition,[68] has ranked India as 47th in 'Ease of Resolving Insolvency'. The World Bank, in a press release, also applauded India's effort and noted that under the IBC regime, 'the overall recovery rate for creditors has jumped from 26.5 to 71.6 cents on the dollar. India now is by far the best performer in South Asia on this component and does better than the average for OECD high-income economies.'[69]

Scheme of IBC

The improvement in rankings evidences that IBC has transformed India's insolvency regime. How it does so is evident from its scheme. IBC, as a consolidating statue, provides for a detailed and streamlined process focussed primarily on insolvency resolution, and in case, the resolution is not possible or feasible, then liquidation. It also envisages creation of multiple bodies to support the process, including and not limited to, the 'Insolvency and Bankruptcy Board of India',[70] which is tasked to frame detailed guidelines in the form of Rules to supplement the IBC provisions and have overall regulatory oversight over the process, and the 'Information Utilities'[71] which is to collect, collate, authenticate, and disseminate financial information on debt and default such that delays and disputes can be eliminated, when a default takes place. Further, IBC provides for insolvency professionals, who act as dedicated officials of the court and oversee the smooth conduct of the insolvency resolution process of a debtor.

67 Doing Business 2016, Measuring Regulatory Quality and Efficiency, 13th Edition, World Bank Group, —World Bank. 2016. Doing Business 2016: Measuring Regulatory Quality and Efficiency. Washington, DC: World Bank. DOI: 10.1596/978-1-4648-0667-4. License: Creative Commons Attribution CC BY 3.0 IGO.

68 Cornell University, INSEAD, and WIPO (2020). The Global Innovation Index 2020: Who Will Finance Innovation? Ithaca, Fontainebleau, and Geneva, available at https://www.insead.edu/sites/default/files/assets/dept/globalindices/docs/GII-2020-report.pdf.

69 Doing Business 2020: Reforms Boost India's Business Climate Rankings; Among Top Ten Improvers for Third Straight Year, 24 Oct. 2019, https://www.worldbank.org/en/news/press-release/2019/10/24/doing-business-india-top-10-improver-business-climate-ranking.

70 Insolvency and Bankruptcy Code 2016, s. 188.

71 Insolvency and Bankruptcy Code 2016, s. 196.

Under IBC, once the corporate debtor is admitted into insolvency process, an insolvency professional is appointed as the resolution professional and is required to take control and custody of the debtor. On appointment, the resolution professional is to make a public announcement declaring the initiation of insolvency process against the debtor and inviting claims, due and outstanding as on insolvency commencement date ('ICD'). The creditors to the debtor are required to submit their claims to the resolution professional, along with sufficient proofs, as specified in regulations framed under the IBC.

Once the claims are submitted, the resolution professional prepares a list of creditors which forms part of Information Memorandum (IM) and is disclosed to public at large. Simultaneously, the resolution professional invite expression of interests from prospective resolution applicants who may express interest in submitting a revival proposal for the corporate debtor, known as 'resolution plan' under IBC.

The claims submitted by the creditors are subject to their treatment under the resolution plan, as may be approved by committee of creditors (consisting of financial creditors) of corporate debtor in their commercial wisdom, and subsequently by NCLT. Under IBC, these claims are to be only resolved as per the resolution plan and the timelines stated therein. They cannot be enforced in preference to other creditors as enforcement of all claims against the corporate debtor is stayed in light of the protection of moratorium under section 14(1) of IBC.[72] Further, all claims, filed or unfiled, stand frozen on the date of NCLT order approving the resolution plan, such that the successful resolution applicant starts with a 'clean slate' and is not flung with any surprise claims.

If, in case, however, there is no resolution plan approved by the committee of creditors within the timelines prescribed under the IBC, the insolvency process would stand terminated and the liquidation process would begin.

---

72 During insolvency process, Resolution Professional is however allowed to make the payment of insolvency resolution process costs from cash flows of corporate debtor, and in case not paid from cash flows, then in priority to other dues under the approved resolution plan. These costs include the costs incurred by Resolution Professional in running the business of the corporate debtor as a going concern during insolvency process.

Scheme of IBC Vis-à-Vis Arbitration

IBC strives to provide a stressed and an ailing debtor a 'calming period' by staying actions already initiated and pending or yet to be initiated against the debtor, including legal and regulatory proceedings, execution and enforcement actions, etc. Termed in India as 'moratorium' period ensures that a corporate debtor does not create further stress on its estate and is relieved from contesting or participating in these actions, and focus on its revival.

The provision for moratorium is widely worded and provides for stay on all type of proceedings against corporate debtor, including (a) institution of fresh proceedings, (b) continuation of pending proceedings, and (c) execution of any judgment, decree, or order of a court, tribunal, arbitral panel, or any authority. Since, the provision mentions both suits and proceedings and covers order from arbitration panels, it does not remain ambiguous that arbitration proceedings are included within the scope of the moratorium. Thus, institution, continuation, enforcement/execution (as the case maybe) of arbitration proceedings and awards shall also remain prohibited during the moratorium period. Reading other clauses of the section 14 in conjunction with the aforesaid provision would fully illustrate the scope and basis of the moratorium, i.e., (a) ensuring maximisation of value of assets of the corporate debtor by staying all actions against them, and (b) protecting and preserving the assets of the corporate debtor by staying all recoveries that may prejudicially affect the estate of the debtor, or may allow a particular creditor to prioritise its claims and derive repayment in preference to other creditors participating in the process.

Judicial pronouncements have, time and again, affirmed these principles and used them as the thresholds for determining whether a particular action is hit by a moratorium or not. Since, section 14 does not provide a list of proceedings covering all type of eventualities that may attract moratorium, these judicial pronouncements occupy a crucial position in determining the true stance of Indian IBC vis-à-vis the scope of moratorium. For instance, Supreme Court of India in *Alchemist Asset Reconstruction Company v. Hotel Gaudayan Pvt Ltd.*, has held that the commencement of arbitrations or related proceedings post initiation of insolvency process is *non-est* in law.[73] This position, however, subsequently has undergone change by way of creation of certain exceptions to this general rule through

73 *Alchemist Asset Reconstruction Company Ltd. v. Hotel Gaudayan Pvt Ltd.*, Supreme Court of India, AIR 2017 SC 5124.

judgments of the Indian Courts, including the Supreme Court of India and the high courts of various Indian states.

Impact of Moratorium on Arbitrations During, Pre- and Post-Initiation of Insolvency Process: The Indian Status Quo

Arbitrations are dealt under IBC only in the context of the moratorium provision, namely, section 14. Since, section 14 refers to stay on arbitration and other proceedings in a general sense, the peculiarities of different scenarios of arbitration and the applicability of moratorium over them are not detailed therein. Consequently, courts in India took upon themselves the duty to interpret the provision on a case-to-case basis. While the moratorium provision in itself is straightforward, the courts could not prevent themselves into exploring, or to say narrowing the scope of moratorium on arbitrations in certain eventualities as detailed below.

For ease in understanding all the scenarios possible, the arbitration proceedings are analysed herein within four timelines:

(a) Pre-Insolvency Process Stage – Arbitration(s) involving a corporate debtor commenced prior to commencement of insolvency proceedings against the debtor.
(b) Pre and During Insolvency Process Stage – Arbitration agreement(s) entered into prior to commencement of insolvency, but arbitration commenced post-insolvency.
(c) During Insolvency Process Stage – Arbitration agreement(s) entered into during insolvency.
(d) Post Insolvency Process Stage – Continuation/validity of arbitration clause and pending disputes post conclusion of insolvency proceedings.

Although, the underlying rationale in treatment of all these scenarios remain the same as highlighted in portions above, the contextual application of them varies on certain parameters as indicated in the following texts.

Scenario (A): Pre-insolvency Process Stage

Claims being contested in arbitrations unrelated to an insolvency process are categorised as claims with a 'pre-existing dispute'[74] under IBC. Such a claimant creditor is not permitted under IBC to initiate insolvency proceedings against a debtor basis claims. Any attempts to initiate insolvency process by a creditor on the ground of existing disputes are often looked at by tribunals and courts as malicious; as – unless there are admitted debts – they amount to misuse the process under IBC to arm-twist a faster recovery of the claim.

However, there is a possibility that the pre-insolvency process arbitration is initiated at the instance of the debtor, i.e., debtor being the claimant in such proceedings. Although, a moratorium may impede continuation of all pending suits or proceedings, section 14 categorically outlines that in context of proceedings against the corporate debtor. The provision at no place creates a bar on proceedings instated by the corporate debtor, as ultimately, they may lead to maximisation of asset value. Moreover, the resolution professional is required by section 25 to continue with such proceedings (in this context arbitration) which are for the benefit of the corporate debtor. Courts in India were quick to affirm this understanding. Proceedings, conclusion of which would not endanger, diminish, dissipate, or affect the assets of the corporate debtor in any manner whatsoever, would be in sync with the purpose of moratorium and would not attract the bar under moratorium.[75] Therefore, continuation of certain arbitrations which are not prejudicial to the insolvency process of the corporate debtor can validly continue. Any recovery through a money claim or affirmation of right to an asset from such arbitrations would strengthen the financial position of the corporate debtor and improve the prospects for reorganisation.

However, there are further aspects to such arbitrations as well. There is a possibility that in an arbitration where the claimant is the corporate debtor, the opposite party has a counter-claim, or a vice versa, i.e., claim by the opposite party and a counter-claim by the corporate debtor. This

74 *K. Kishan v. M/s Vijay Nirman Company Pvt. Ltd.*, Supreme Court of India, 2018 SCC OnLine SC 1013.

75 *See Power Grid Corporation of India v. Jyoti Structures Ltd.*, Delhi High Court (2018) 246 DLT 485; *SSMP Industries Ltd v. Perkan Foods Processors Pvt. Ltd*, Delhi High Court, 2019 SCC Online Del 9339; *Jharkhand Bijli Vitran Nigam Ltd. v. IVRCL Limited & Anr.*, NCLAT, Company Appeal (AT) (Insolvency) No. 285/2018, decided on 3 Aug. 2018.

scenario has been a little contentious, as initially, the NCLAT[76] had stayed such arbitrations for being barred under section 14. The reasons for the same can be attributed to an existence of a counter-claim, which may result in an award in favour of the opposite party requiring the corporate debtor to pay under an award, and thus causing an impact on the assets of the debtor's estate, which are now under the control and custody of the resolution professional for the benefit of all the creditors.

However, lately, the position in this regard has also evolved with NCLAT decision in the case of *Jharkhand Bijli Vitran Nigam Ltd. v. IVRCL Limited & Anr.* In this case, it was held that both claim and counter-claim can continue to be arbitrated even during moratorium period,[77] but only in scenarios that an award requires payment to be made to the corporate debtor (on set off), that it would be enforced and recovery be made. However, if on final award, the claim (counter-claim, as the case maybe) of the opposite party exceeds the claim of the corporate debtor and corporate debtor is required to pay any amount, such award would not be enforceable and the award holder would not be able to recover, but be only able to file its claim with the resolution professional.

Post-arbitral Proceedings

Commencement or continuation of post-arbitral proceedings involving challenges to or execution of an award, that aid the corporate debtor, will also likely be permissible under the scheme of IBC. The impact of a moratorium would narrow down to simple assessment of whether the arbitral award is in favour of the corporate debtor, in favour of the opposite party, or is partly in favour of corporate debtor and partly in favour of the opposite party. If an arbitral award is in favour of the corporate debtor, a resolution professional may continue seeking enforcement of an award. However, a scenario arises when an award-debtor (the opposite party) challenges an award. In such a situation, the question arises as to whether such challenge would be hit by moratorium provision or not.

In *Power Grid Corporation of India v. Jyoti Structures Ltd.*, Delhi High Court considered this question and observed that as long as any proceeding does not violate the prime objects that moratorium seeks to uphold, i.e., preventing any action that may prejudicially impact the assets and overall

76 *K.S. Oils Ltd.* vs *State Trade Corporation of India*, NCLAT, Company Appeal (AT) (Insolvency) No. 284 of 2017.

77 *See also SSMP Industries Ltd. v. Perkan Food Processors Pvt. Ltd.*, Delhi High Court, 2019 SCC Online Del 9339.

estate of the debtor, such proceedings may continue. High court emphasised that it is the 'debt recovery action' that is critical to insolvency process, and not any other proceedings that precedes such action.[78] Court observed:

> … In the light of above purpose or object behind the moratorium, Section 14 of the Code would not apply to the proceedings which are in the benefit of the corporate debtor, like the one before this court in as much these proceedings are not a 'debt recovery action' and its conclusion would not endanger, diminish, dissipate or impact the assets of the corporate debtor in any manner whatsoever and hence shall be in sync with the purpose of moratorium which includes keeping the corporate debtor's assets together during the insolvency resolution process and facilitating orderly completion of the process envisaged during the insolvency resolution process and ensuring the company may continue as a going concern.

Courts in India have found it appropriate to allow proceedings challenging awards issued in favour of a corporate debtor even during moratorium period. However, in the event, an award-debtor succeeds in such challenge, the award is set aside and an order is passed against the corporate debtor, enforcement of such order shall be hit by the moratorium.[79]On the other hand, if an award is in favour of the opposite party and a challenge is pending on behalf of the corporate debtor, such award is not actionable as the pending section 34 challenge would qualify as an existence of a 'pre-existing dispute' under the IBC.[80] Until the challenge is decided, the claim of the opposite party would remain 'contingent' against the corporate debtor. In this regard, the another high court in *Sirpur Paper Mills Limited v. I.K. Merchants Pvt. Ltd.*,[81] recently held that the opposite party in such cases shall submit its claim to the resolution professional, based on

---

78 *See P. Mohanraj & Ors. v. M/s Shah Brothers Ispat Pvt. Ltd.*, Supreme Court of India, Civil Appeal No. 10355 of 2018. Here, Supreme Court, while dealing with an appeal in another matter, considered *Power Grid* (*supra*) in brief and observed that it does not state the law correctly as proceedings seeking setting aside of an arbitral award may result in an arbitral award against the corporate debtor being upheld, as a result of which, monies would then be payable by the corporate debtor, and that therefore, such proceedings would be covered under moratorium. The Supreme Court, however, does not reason nor considers the detailed reasoning of the *Power Grid* (*supra*).

79 *Power Grid Corporation of India v. Jyoti Structures Ltd.*, Delhi High Court, (2018) 246 DLT 485.

80 *K. Kishan v. M/s Vijay Nirman Company Pvt. Ltd.*, Supreme Court of India, 2018 SCC OnLine SC 1013.

81 Calcutta High Court, A.P. 550 of 2008, decided on 7 May 2021.

the award in its favour, and the resolution professional shall consider the same. Although, the treatment of such claim would depend on the terms of the resolution plan, which may provide that such contingent claims, once crystallised, may be paid in a certain fashion. If the opposite party feels aggrieved by such treatment, it may approach the NCLT seeking relief.

An alternative may exist even in this situation which allows section 34 challenge by a corporate debtor to be continued during moratorium. Since, it is preferred by the corporate debtor, it is not prejudicial to its interest. However, at present, barring the passing observation of the Supreme Court in *P. Mohanraj* (*supra*), there is no precedent in our knowledge that analyses this situation further. Nonetheless, if seen in light of the underlying rationale proposed in the *Power Grid* (*supra*), it could be argued that there appears to be no bar on such proceedings from being continued. To illustrate, in the event, the section 34 challenge is decided in favour of the corporate debtor and the award is set aside, the order passed under section 34 shall not be hit by moratorium and would be enforceable by the corporate debtor against the opposite party. While, in the event, the section 34 challenge is rejected and the award in favour of the opposite party is upheld, then the action for enforcement and execution of such award under section 36 shall be hit by moratorium, and the award holder would only be entitled to file its claim before the resolution professional, but as a crystallised claim at this point of time.

In cases of arbitral award which are a mix of both, i.e., award partly in favour of corporate debtor and partly in favour of the opposite party, the part of the award that is in favour of corporate debtor ideally be made enforceable while the part of award in favour of the opposite party shall be hit by moratorium. However, it remains to be seen if such a segregation of award is even feasible while enforcing, and that whether such question of segregation is to be decided by the executing court under arbitration law or the insolvency tribunal.

Another variation that exists in relation to application of IBC moratorium on arbitration is vis-à-vis the foreign seated arbitrations.[82] A foreign seated arbitration can include arbitrations of two types: (a) foreign seated

---

82 International arbitrations seated in India would attract similar treatment as any domestic arbitration seated in India for the reason that the IBC provides for territorial and not subject matter jurisdiction.

arbitration between an Indian and a foreign party,[83] and (b) foreign seated arbitration between two Indian parties.[84]

Foreign Seated International Arbitration

Continuation of Pending Foreign Seated International Arbitration

IBC section 1 stipulates that the provisions of IBC, including the moratorium, extend to the whole of India. Hence, there is no extra-territorial enforceability of such moratorium on proceedings outside India. The provisions of IBC that deals with extra-territorial enforceability and recognises cross-border insolvency are IBC sections 234 and 235, but the same has not yet been notified as law.[85] Hence, the provisions of IBC, including moratorium, are not applicable and enforceable to proceedings against corporate debtor outside India, including the continuation of foreign seated international arbitrations.[86]

Enforcement of Foreign Seated International Arbitration Awards

As IBC does not have extra-territorial applicability, there is no restriction on foreign arbitral award holder to have the same enforced against the corporate debtor's assets located abroad, unless there is a reciprocal arrangement between India and the government of the country where the assets are located.

However, enforcement and execution of such awards in India and against the assets located in India, is directly barred by the moratorium

83 Arbitration Act, 1996, s. 2(1)(f).

84 *PASL Wind Solutions Private Ltd. v. GE Power Conversion India Pvt. Ltd.*, Supreme Court of India, Civil Appeal No. 1647 of 2021 arising out of SLP (Civil) No. 3936 of 2021. Supreme Court of India, in this case, has held that two companies incorporated in India can validly designate a foreign seat for arbitration of their disputes.

85 Insolvency and Bankruptcy Code 2016, s. 234. This provision empowers the Central Government to enter into reciprocal agreements with other countries to enforce the provisions of the Code and s. 235 envisages a 'Letter of Request' by the liquidator to the authority of a country with which a reciprocal agreement has been made under s. 234 of IBC for action on the assets of the company situated in such country.

86 *Ashapura Minechem Ltd. v. Armada (Singapore) Pte. Ltd. & Ors.*, Bombay High Court, Arb. Petition No. 1359 of 2010. This was a case under s. 22 of the SICA (which is similar to s. 14 (Moratorium) of IBC). Here, Court held that since the provisions of SICA, including s. 22 thereof, extended to only the territory of India, it does not have any application to proceedings outside India. Applying the same rationale, it can be safely implied that even moratorium under IBC s. 14 would not apply to any proceedings outside India.

provision.[87] The only remedy available to such an award holder is to submit a claim to the resolution professional based on such foreign arbitral award. However, since a foreign arbitral award is not directly recognisable and enforceable under Indian Arbitration Act, unless it passes through the test of sections 47 and 48, namely, the two-fold test of recognition and enforcement under Part II of the Arbitration Act, such an award is not treated as a valid proof of claim under the IBC.[88] This is unlike the position of a domestic award, which is equivalent to a decree of a court,[89] and directly admissible as a proof of claim, provided the period to file a challenge against it under section 34 has expired.

Foreign Seated Arbitration Between Two Indian Parties

Until April 2021, the position on the legality of two Indian parties choosing a foreign seat of arbitration was not sufficiently clear. Although neither the Arbitration Act nor the Indian Contract Act, 1872 ever prohibited two Indian parties from resolving their disputes in a country other than India, the Supreme Court of India decision in *PASL Wind Solutions Private Limited v GE Power Conversion India Private Limited*,[90] has made it clear that two Indian parties can very well choose a foreign seat of arbitration. Supreme Court has also clarified that award of such an arbitration would be a 'foreign award' and shall be enforceable in accordance with Part II of the Act.

With such an arbitration being judicially recognised, it is essential that we analyse this vis-à-vis the moratorium provision under IBC as well to provide an exhaustive outlook for all type of arbitrations under this chapter. However, this being a nascent development, there is no existing judicial data that may set out the position of law in this regard conclusively.

Continuation of Foreign Seated Arbitration Between Two Indian Parties

Regarding the impact on continuation of such arbitration during insolvency process, it remains an open question as to whether the claimant

87 *Vitol S.A. v. Asian Natural Resources 9India) Ltd. & Ors*, NCLT, Ahmedabad Bench in (2018) 145 SCL 30.
88 *Adityaa Energy Resource Pte Ltd. v. Simhapuri Energy Ltd.*, NCLT Hyderabad Bench, CP(IB) No. 389/9/HDB/2018.
89 Arbitration Act, 1996, s. 36.
90 Supreme Court of India, Civil Appeal No. 1647 of 2021 arising out of SLP (Civil) Number 3936 of 2021.

Indian party to the arbitration can be made subject to the moratorium under IBC, without the moratorium provision having any force of law at the foreign seat of arbitration. In this regard, guidance may be drawn from the position under Singapore law[91] which permits courts to restrict continuation of arbitration seated outside Singapore, as long as the claimant to such arbitration proceedings is subject to the Singapore's jurisdiction.

Enforcement of Award Passed in Foreign Seated Arbitration Between Two Indian Parties

As stated above, Supreme Court in *PASL Wind* (*supra*) has unequivocally observed that if an arbitration is seated outside India, irrespective of the nationality of parties, such award will be a 'foreign award'.[92] Thus, such arbitrations would attract a similar treatment as accorded to an award of an otherwise foreign seated arbitration, i.e., it would not be directly recognisable and enforceable in India, unless it passes through the two-fold test of Part II.

Scenario (B): Pre and During Insolvency Process Stage

In the event a fresh arbitration is allowed to be initiated against the corporate debtor during the insolvency process, all the eventualities considered in scenario (A) above shall be equally applicable.[93] However, what remains a crucial issue in this scenario is whether an agreement entered into prior to commencement of insolvency would retain its validity during the insolvency process. The question of commencing a fresh arbitration during insolvency process, thus, becomes a secondary issue, as the validity of the agreement containing arbitration assumes the primacy in this regard.

---

91 Companies Act, 1967, s. 211B; Insolvency, Restructuring and Dissolution Act 2018, s. 64.

92 Supreme Court of India, Civil Appeal Number 1647 of 2021 arising out of SLP (Civil) No. 3936 of 2021, at para. 57. *See* also *Bharat Aluminium Co. v. Kaiser Aluminium Technical Services Inc.*, Supreme Court of India (2012) 9 SCC 552. In this case, it was held that 'Foreign award' is an award in any arbitration whose juridical seat is outside India, which would be enforceable in India, if at all, under Part II and only to the extent provided therein.

93 Although Alchemist case held that all arbitrations commenced post initiation of insolvency process is non-est in law, the exceptions drawn by the courts subsequently (as highlighted in scenario (a)) continue to remain applicable even in scenario (b) as once arbitration is commenced, there remains no distinction between scenario (a) and scenario (b).

As identified above, the resolution professional under the IBC is tasked to protect and preserve the assets of the corporate debtor and continue business operations of the corporate debtor on a 'going concern' basis.[94] To do so, IBC provides the resolution professional with the authority to take all actions as are necessary to keep the corporate debtor a going concern. One such authority is 'to enter into contracts on behalf of the corporate debtor or to amend or modify the contracts or transactions which were entered into before the commencement of corporate insolvency resolution process'.[95]

The resolution professional thus can not only enter into fresh contracts, but also continue to act under the existing contracts entered by the corporate debtor prior to the initiation of insolvency process and amend and modify the same. This also clarifies that initiation of insolvency proceedings against a corporate debtor would not lead to any 'legal incapacity', which is a ground for setting aside of arbitral award under Indian Arbitration Act[96] as well as under the Model Law[97] and United Nations Convention on the Recognition and Enforcement of Foreign Arbitral Awards.[98] The corporate debtor, thus, remains competent during insolvency process to enter into contracts, including arbitration, and act by and through the resolution professional.

Further, this authority to modify or amend the contracts would not have been envisaged, if in case the IBC considered termination of all existing contracts *ipso facto* on account of the initiation of the insolvency process.

Similarly, the IBC does not bar termination of contracts by the counter party[99] or termination of the burdensome contract by the resolution professional during the insolvency process, in accordance with the terms of the agreement. In the event, however, the termination by the counter party is impacting the 'going concern' status of the corporate debtor or violating the objects of the moratorium, such termination can be challenged by the

---

94 Insolvency and Bankruptcy Code 2016, s. 25.

95 Insolvency and Bankruptcy Code 2016, s. 20(2) (b).

96 Indian Arbitration Act, 1996. s. 34(2)(a)(i) & 48(1)(a).

97 UNCITRAL Model Law on International Commercial Arbitration in 1985, Arts 34 and 36.

98 United Nations Convention on the Recognition and Enforcement of Foreign Arbitral Awards (New York, 10 June 1958), Art. V.

99 *Gujrat NRE Coke Limited.*, CP (IB) No 326/KB/2017 (NCLT Kolkata, 22 Aug. 2017). NCLT allowed the termination of a contract for maintenance of certain windmills during the moratorium, due to failure of the corporate debtor to pay outstanding dues under the contract.

resolution professional before the adjudicating authority under the IBC.[100] In a nutshell, the pre-insolvency process agreements remain in force even post initiation of insolvency process and the parties continue to remain bound by the terms of such agreements, except where the adjudicating authority may suspend rights of an opposite party to terminate a contract.

This position is further strengthened from the fact that the IBC casts a duty on the resolution professional, under section 25(2)(b), to 'represent and act on behalf of the corporate debtor with third parties, exercise rights for the benefit of the corporate debtor in judicial, quasi-judicial or arbitration proceedings'. This implies that the legal capacity of the corporate debtor under the contracts entered by it does not undergo any change on initiation of insolvency process, and it is only the resolution professional, who supersedes the board of the corporate debtor, who will now act as the official representative of the corporate debtor relating to all such contracts. Thus, if an agreement of the corporate debtor provides for dispute resolution by way of arbitration, and if a dispute arises under it, irrespective prior or during the insolvency process, the parties to agreement are free to commence and continue arbitration[101] within the permissible contours highlighted in scenario (A).

Scenario (C): During Insolvency Process Stage

As stated in scenario (B), the resolution professional has an authority under the IBC to enter into contracts on behalf of the corporate debtor,[102] in line with the larger object of continuing the business of the corporate debtor as a going concern; with the objective to preserve, protect, and maximise the value of its assets. To effectively discharge such duties and smoothly conduct the insolvency process of the corporate debtor, it is essential that the resolution professional is given a free hand in this regard. For instance, resolution professional would need to negotiate and arrange for interim-financing of the corporate debtor, and to do so, he or she would be required to enter into contractual obligations with the financer. Similarly, in order to continue receiving supplies to carry on the production activities or providing services, as the case maybe, and to continue to generate revenue as a

---

100 *Pepsico India Holdings Pvt Ltd. v. Mr V Nagarajan*, CP/564 (IB)/CB/2017 (NCLT Chennai, 28 May 2019); *SREI Infrastructure Finance Ltd. v. Sundresh Bhatt*, Company Appeal (AT) (Insolvency) Number 781 of 2018 (NCLAT, 31 July 2019).

101 France and Netherlands provide for similar position that arbitration agreement remain binding even post initiation of insolvency process.

102 Insolvency and Bankruptcy Code, 2016, s. 20(2)(b).

going concern, the resolution professional would have to arrive at fresh commercial understandings with the supplier and with its customers during the insolvency process as well. These commercial understandings may be contained in a completely fresh agreement or may be incorporated in the existing agreements by way of modification/amendment. Further, these agreements may provide for any type of dispute resolution mechanism, including by way of arbitration, as there is no embargo under the IBC expressly providing exclusive jurisdiction to the NCLTs over disputes under agreements entered during the insolvency process.

Although the agreements entered during the insolvency process, and supplies made thereunder, would be covered as the insolvency resolution costs under the IBC, and any payment required to be made to a supplier by the corporate debtor would be required to be paid in priority in both resolution and liquidation, there may be situations where the parties see a roadblock and a dispute arises. In any such situations, the dispute resolution clauses may be referred and if it provides for arbitration, then appropriate arbitration proceedings may be commenced and continued during the insolvency process again within the permissible cont.

Scenario (D): Post-Insolvency Process Stage

Post insolvency process stage encompasses within itself two possibilities, i.e., (a) successful resolution of the corporate debtor by way of approval of a resolution plan of a resolution applicant who would now take over the ailing corporate debtor and turn it around into a viable running business, and (b) initiation of liquidation proceedings due to failure to resolve the insolvency by way of a revival plan. In both these possibilities, the impact on arbitration is different.

Successful Revival by Way of Approval of Resolution Plan

If the insolvency process results in a successful resolution/reorganisation of the corporate debtor, the corporate debtor will likely be taken over by a new management subject to the arrangement approved as regards the successful resolution applicant. This applicant is obligated to revive the corporate debtor in terms of the approved resolution plan. However, in order to do so, it is recognised that certain protections to the assets of the corporate debtor and its actions (independent of its earlier management), post resolution, are necessary.[103]

One such protection is the certainty and predictability of the pending claims against the corporate debtor. The IBC provides for a time frame within which claimants can file their claims. Based on the filed claims, a resolution professional is obligated to prepare an Information Memorandum, and disclose it to the prospective resolution applicants, who may take cognisance of all such claims, and accordingly prepare a resolution plan providing for treatment of each of such claims. However, in case a claim, not submitted during insolvency process, is raised post resolution, it would frustrate the resolution plan and the commercial planning of the successful resolution applicant who had, in terms of the information shared by the resolution professional, submitted a plan considering such list of claims against the corporate debtor to be exhaustive.

This eventuality has been considered in a number of cases, and it has been held that no such claims survives post resolution under IBC.[104] For instance, in *Ghanashyam Mishra and Sons Private Limited v. Edelweiss Asset Reconstruction Company Limited*,[105] the Supreme Court of India held as follows:

> 86. … The legislative intent behind this is, to freeze all the claims so that the resolution applicant starts on a clean slate and is not flung with any surprise claims. If that is permitted, the very calculations on the basis of which the resolution applicant submits its plans, would go haywire and the plan would be unworkable.
>
> … 95. In the result, we answer the questions framed by us as under:
>
> (i) That once a resolution plan is duly approved by the Adjudicating Authority under sub section (1) of Section 31, the claims as provided in the resolution plan shall stand frozen and will be binding on the Corporate Debtor and its employees, members, creditors, including the Central Government, any State Government or any local authority, guarantors and other stakeholders. On the date of approval of resolution plan by the Adjudicating Authority, all such claims, which are not a part of resolution plan, shall stand extinguished and no

103 Insolvency and Bankruptcy Code, 2016, s. 32A.

104 *Committee of Creditors of Essar Steel v. Satish Kumar Gupta & Ors.*, Supreme Court of India, (Civil Appeal No. 8766-67 of 2019), para. 67.

105 Supreme Court of India, Civil Appeal No. 8129 of 2019.

person will be entitled to initiate or continue any proceedings in respect to a claim, which is not part of the resolution plan;

Thus, no claim for the pre and during insolvency process period can be continued post approval of a resolution plan. This also answers the issue of validity of the arbitration clauses under the agreements entered pre and during insolvency process period. If the agreement pertains to a claim which is provided treatment for under the resolution plan, then such resolution plan will bind the parties to the agreement, and depending on the terms of the resolution plan, such agreement would either remain in force or terminate. For example, if the claim is fully settled under the plan, then the agreement would subside, while if the claim is considered to be 'contingent' and the plan requires such claims to be continued, then the agreement will remain in force and continue to govern the acts of the parties in that regard, including dispute resolution by way of arbitration.

However, lately, majority of the resolution applicants submit resolution plans containing a standard clause providing for extinguishment of all pending and contingent claims. These clauses are widely worded so as to cover all eventualities and prevent the successful resolution applicant from any unforeseen liability. These clauses sit well with the principle of providing a 'fresh plate' to the resolution application and preventing the 'hydra head' from popping up post resolution. A sample clause, in this regard, may look like as below:

> All liabilities in relation to any period prior to the resolution plan approval date, whether due or contingent, asserted or unasserted, crystallized or uncrystallised, known or unknown, secured or unsecured, disputed or undisputed, present or future, whether or not set out in the Information Memorandum, the balance sheets or the profit and loss account statement or the list of creditors, will be settled at NIL value and shall be deemed to be permanently extinguished by virtue of the resolution plan approval order.

'Settled at NIL' implies that claims, whether in knowledge or not, will deemed to be settled against the new management, thus, providing a fresh start to the new corporate.

(ii) Liquidation on failure to approve resolution plan

Thrust of moratorium is lesser in liquidation as compared to insolvency resolution. As stated above, insolvency resolution process prohibits institution and continuation of all suits or proceedings, as well as all actions of enforcement and execution of any judgment, decree, or order against the corporate debtor. On the other hand, liquidation process merely stipulates that 'no suit or other legal proceeding shall be instituted by or against the corporate debtor.'[106] In comparison to insolvency resolution, liquidation does not stay (a) continuation of pending suits or proceedings, and (b) enforcement and execution of the judgment, decree, or order. But, unlike insolvency process, liquidation does stay suits or proceedings by the corporate debtor. However, the proviso to section 33(5) provides an exception and allows a liquidator to initiate suits or proceedings on behalf of the corporate debtor with the prior permission of the NCLT. This proviso makes IBC consistent and in line with the section 41[107] of the Arbitration Act.

The aforesaid understanding also reflects under IBC section 35(1)(k), which considers it a duty/power of the liquidator 'to institute or defend any suit, prosecution or other legal proceedings, civil or criminal, in the name of on behalf of the corporate debtor'. This suggests that the liquidator in the name of corporate debtor can (a) institute suit, prosecution or other legal proceedings, civil or criminal, and (b) defend suit, prosecution, or other legal proceedings, civil or criminal, as may be pending against the corporate debtor.

The aspect of instituting and continuing proceedings by the liquidator that are in the interest of the corporate debtor is in line with the understanding and scope of moratorium applicable under insolvency process. But the aspect of continuation of proceedings pending against the corporate debtor and actions for execution/enforcement proceedings against the corporate debtor during liquidation is a significant departure from the moratorium during insolvency process.[108] One reason for such a departure can may be the nature of liquidation process itself, i.e., the process requiring the assets

---

106 Insolvency and Bankruptcy Code 2016, s. 33(5).

107 Arbitration Act, 1996, s. 41. '*Provisions in case of insolvency.— ... (2) Where a person who has been adjudged an insolvent had, before the commencement of the insolvency proceedings, become a party to an arbitration agreement, and any matter to which the agreement applies is required to be determined in connection with, or for the purposes of, the insolvency proceedings, then, if the case is one to which sub-section (1) does not apply, any other party or the receiver may apply to the judicial authority having jurisdiction in the insolvency proceedings for an order directing that the matter in question shall be submitted to arbitration in accordance with the arbitration agreement, and the judicial authority may, if it is of opinion that, having regard to all the circumstances of the case, the matter ought to be determined by arbitration, make an order accordingly.*'

108 Report of the Insolvency Law Committee, Ministry of Corporate Affairs, Government of India, February 2020. Report records that this departure is possibly an 'error' and

to be sold off and payment being made to the creditor, in the order of priority of their rights.[109] Thus, if these legal rights in contention are determined by way of continuing the pending proceedings, then the proceeds from assets can be allocated to the creditors in accordance to their rights, without further dispute.

This divergence would also affect those proceedings (including arbitration), which got stayed on initiation of insolvency process, as highlighted under scenario (a) above, as they can be re-commenced during liquidation on account of the narrower moratorium provision.[110]

Indian Status Vis-a-Vis Global Approach Towards Reference to Arbitration During Insolvency: An Attempt to Reconcile

As dealt in above, the collision between arbitration and insolvency has been globally recognised. This explains why some jurisdictions such as US and UK, are much more settled in this regard as they have adopted interpretations/mechanisms that minimises the impact of this collision, or to say, have found solutions to prevent the collision by harmonising the policy objectives of insolvency and arbitration. Since, prior to IBC, there was no full-fledged statutory insolvency process in India that could compare with the insolvency regime of the developed jurisdictions, this conflict of arbitration and insolvency remain insignificant in India. However, since 2016, India too has witnessed these concerns requiring balance the conflicting interests of arbitration and insolvency. Therefore, it merits that a comparison be made of these globally recognised approaches in the Indian context.

As highlighted in the portions above, the most common methods adopted globally for minimising the effect of this collision is based on the idea of segregating disputes which lie exclusively in the domain of an insolvency court, from the disputes which may continue to be adjudicated

---

suggests that the Indian legislature amend section 33(5) for it to include continuation of pending proceedings within its cover. However, till date, no such amendment has been made.

109 Insolvency and Bankruptcy Code 2016, s. 35(1)(j). Section 35(1)(j) —'*to invite and settle claims of creditors and claimants and distribute proceeds in accordance with the provisions of this Code.*'

110 Report of the Insolvency Law Committee, Ministry of Corporate Affairs, Government of India, March 2018, at para. 5.4.

by the relevant forum during the insolvency process. The approaches can broadly be classified as follows:

(a) Creating a distinction between 'core' and 'non-core' insolvency dispute, and reserving only a core matter for insolvency court;[111]
(b) Analysing a dispute based on its in rem and in personam character, and reserving only such disputes for insolvency courts which have *erga omnes* effect;[112] and
(c) Analysing a dispute based on its impact on the debtor, i.e., disputes being either beneficial or prejudicial to the debtor, and reserving only such disputes for insolvency courts that are prejudicial to the interest of the insolvent debtor, or that have the effect of dissipating the estate of the debtor to the detriment of the creditors.[113]

Although statutorily none of the above approaches has been referred in the IBC expressly or impliedly, the method (c) was first to find its way in by way of the purposive interpretation undertaken by the Indian judiciary in numerous decisions as indicated above. Indian courts have, time and again, affirmed that the proceedings which are not prejudicial to the corporate debtor or has the potential of diminishing the value of the estate of the corporate debtor, but are beneficial and in the interest of the corporate debtor, are not barred under the IBC during moratorium. These proceedings can continue to be adjudicated or enforced or executed, as the case maybe, before the relevant forum having jurisdiction. Courts have acknowledged that proceedings, outcome of which might improve the prospects of the corporate debtor being resolved, are not critical to the interest of creditors of the corporate debtor in the insolvency process per se and their continuing adjudication would not act to their detriment or reduce the estate of the corporate debtor, available to be resolved for their collective benefit in the insolvency process.

The method (a) and (b), on the other hand, have not been talked about or analysed in the context of IBC by the courts directly yet. However, their glimpse, although couched in different terms, in the judicial pronouncements is evident, as detailed below.

111 For instance, US and France.
112 For instance, US.
113 For instance, UK, Singapore, and India.

Method (A): Core and Non-core Distinction

As stated earlier, 'core' and 'non-core' distinction is pretty elaborate and of wide judicial discourse in jurisdiction such as US. In US, although there exist judgments which list down the issues that qualify as 'core', yet there is a lot of inconsistency in the decisions of different courts. In India, the closest courts came to acknowledging this distinction is in a recent judgment of the Supreme Court of India in *Gujarat Urja Vikas Nigam Limited v. Amit Gupta & Ors.*[114] wherein it was held that[115]

> ... NCLT has jurisdiction to adjudicate disputes, which arise solely from or which relate to the insolvency of the Corporate Debtor. However, in doing do, we issue a note of caution to the NCLT and NCLAT to ensure that they do not usurp the legitimate jurisdiction of other courts, tribunals and fora when the dispute is one which does not arise solely from or relate to the insolvency of the Corporate Debtor. The nexus with the insolvency of the Corporate Debtor must exist.

Here, the point in contention was termination of a power purchase agreement (PPA) by Gujarat Urja Vikas Nigam Ltd. (GUVNL) entered into and with Astonfield Solar (Gujarat) Private Limited, the corporate debtor. GUVNL was corporate debtor's sole client and the PPA was the only agreement that was keeping the corporate debtor afloat.[116] The ground for termination of the PPA was the initiation of insolvency proceedings against Astonfield (*ipso facto* clause). The resolution professional of Astonfield challenged the termination before the NCLT, who upheld the challenge and rejected the termination. GUVNL assailed the NCLT decision before the NCLAT, but NCLAT too rejected the termination of the PPA. Finally, an appeal was preferred to the Supreme Court of India, the apex authority. Before the Supreme Court, GUVNL, *inter alia*, contended that PPA being a contractual arrangement between the parties is not subject to the jurisdiction of the NCLT under the IBC, but to the authority[117] set up under Indian Electricity Act, 2003.

The Supreme Court analysed the issue in the context of IBC section 60(5) which provides for the wide jurisdiction to NCLT. Section 60(5)(c)

---

114 *Gujarat Urja Vikas Nigam Limited v. Amit Gupta & Ors.*, Supreme Court of India, Civil Appeal Number 9241 of 2019. ('*Gujarat Urja*').

115 Gujarat Urja, at para. 67.

116 Gujarat Urja, at para. 165.

117 Gujarat Electricity Regulatory Commission.

particularly reads that NCLT shall have jurisdiction to entertain or dispose of 'any question of priorities or any question of law or facts, arising out of or in relation to the insolvency resolution or liquidation proceedings of the corporate debtor or corporate person under this Code.' The Supreme Court held that section 60(5)(c) is a 'residuary jurisdiction' provision as it provides wide jurisdiction to NCLT to adjudicate all questions of law or facts *arising from* or *in relation to* the insolvency resolution process.[118] Court further held that this provision is not confined to the contours of section 14 moratorium, as otherwise it would be rendered otiose in relation to cases, which may not fall foul of section 14,[119] but still involve the issue of preserving the value of corporate debtor or its status as 'going concern',[120] such as the instant fact scenario.

In the instant case, if the PPA was allowed to be terminated, no resolution applicant would have shown interest in submitting a resolution plan, and the corporate debtor would have headed towards liquidation, i.e., corporate death. Since IBC strives for resolution and liquidation[121] is the last resort,[122] the Supreme Court of India deemed it fit, in the peculiar facts of this case, i.e., centrality of the PPA to the insolvency process and termination being made on the sole ground of initiation of insolvency proceedings, that the NCLT rightly assumed jurisdiction and decided upon the validity of the termination of PPA by GUVNL.[123]

However, while doing so, the Supreme Court emphasised that they are not laying down a general principle of law on the contours of NCLT

---

118 Gujarat Urja, at para. 87.

119 For instance, termination of PPA where corporate debtor is to supply power to third party to generate revenue and not the other way round, i.e., corporate debtor receiving the supply, termination of which is expressly restricted under s. 14. Also *see GRIDCO Limited v. Surya Kanta Satapathy and Ors.*, NCLAT, CA (AT) (INS) Number 1271 of 2019 (decision dated 14 July 2020).

120 *See*, for e.g., *Pepsico India Holdings Pvt Ltd v. V Nagarajan, Resolution Professional of Oceanic Tropical Fruits Pvt. Ltd.*, NCLAT, CA (AT) Insolvency No. 686 of 2019 (decision dated 13 Nov. 2019); *Tata Consultancy Services v. Vishal Ghisulal Jain*, NCLAT, CA (AT) Insolvency No. 237 of 2020 (decision dated 24 June 2020).

121 Even in case of liquidation, NCLAT has set aside the termination of PPA. *See Gujarat Urja Vikas Nigam Ltd. v. Yes Bank Limited*, NCLAT, CA (AT) (Insolvency) Number 601 of 2020 (decision dated 20 Oct. 2020). However, an appeal (bearing Civil Appeal No. 3965 of 2020) is pending adjudication before Supreme Court against the NCLAT decision.

122 *Swiss Ribbons Pvt. Ltd. v. Union of India*, Supreme Court of India, Writ Petition (Civil) Number 99 of 2018, decided on 25 Jan. 2019.

123 Gujarat Urja, at para. 165.

jurisdiction, and that the NCLT do not have jurisdiction over matters that are dehors the IBC.[124] The Supreme Court observed that

> [T]he jurisdiction of the NCLT under Section 60(5)(c) of the IBC cannot be invoked in matters where a **termination may take place on grounds unrelated to the insolvency of the corporate debtor**. Even more crucially, it cannot even be invoked in the event of a legitimate termination of a contract based on an ipso facto clause like Article 9.2.1(e) herein, **if such termination will not have the effect of making certain the death of the corporate debtor**. As such, in all future cases, NCLT would have to be wary of setting aside valid contractual terminations which would **merely dilute the value of the corporate debtor, and not push it to its corporate death by virtue of it being the corporate debtor's sole contract** (as was the case in this matter's unique factual matrix).[125]

By way of these observations, the Supreme Court essentially identified and distinguished the matters that are 'core' and 'non-core' to the insolvency and held that the insolvency court (NCLT) would not assume or usurp the legitimate jurisdiction of other courts when the matter pertains to a 'non-core' issue. As per the above quoted portion of the judgment, 'Core' matters may be where the preservation of the value of corporate debtor or maintaining its 'going concern' status is so threatened by an action that if not prevented the corporate debtor would be pushed into liquidation. While, 'non-core' may be those where either the subject action is unrelated to the insolvency or the action is not likely to cause liquidation of the corporate debtor, or at most, merely dilute the value of the corporate debtor.[126] Inclusion of the latter in the 'non-core' list is significant as it indicates that NCLT's jurisdiction can be excluded even in matters that may affect the value of the corporate debtor. This essentially broadens the scope of this distinction and renders much more disputes amenable to adjudication by forums (including arbitration) having original jurisdiction over the matter. For instance, in a subsequent Supreme Court judgment in *Tata Consultancy Services Limited v. Vishal Ghisulal Jain*,[127] the challenge to termination of a contract was held to be not maintainable before the insolvency court 'for want of jurisdiction' as there was no analysis as to

124 Gujarat Urja, at para. 87.
125 Gujarat Urja, at para. 165.
126 *See MF Global Holdings Ltd. et al. v. Allied World Assurance Co. Ltd. et al.*, No. 1:16-ap-01251 (Bankr. S.D.N.Y. 24 Aug. 2017).
127 Supreme Court of India, Civil Appeal Number 3045 of 2020.

how the termination 'would put the survival of the Corporate Debtor in jeopardy'.

However, considering that the judgment in *Gujarat Urja* is recent, it is yet to be conclusively seen that how far this distinction between 'core' and 'non-core' matters is observed and followed by the courts in India. In any case, it is significant step ahead in putting the Indian insolvency regime (IBC) in tandem with the global practises.

Method (B): Disputes of In Personam Nature and Not Having *Ergo Omnes* Effect

It is not disputed that certain types of disputes are non-arbitrable in light of the underlying nature of arbitration proceedings. Supreme Court of India[128] has identified these non-arbitrable disputes to, *inter alia*, include matters pertaining to insolvency. This is considering the fact that the insolvency proceedings are of *in rem* nature, i.e., proceedings against the world at large. An insolvency proceeding requires a collective action in resolving the stress faced by the debtor. It is a proceeding conducted in the interest of all the creditors who have submitted their claims against the debtor in a consolidated insolvency resolution process, rather than initiating individual actions against the debtor. Therefore, these proceedings are not to be arbitrated but dealt exclusively by a centralised forum, i.e., the NCLT herein, which is a specialised tribunal constituted for this purpose, and is expected to be more efficient and have full jurisdiction to dispose of the entire matter efficaciously.[129]

Thus, the question with respect of non-arbitrability of the dispute requiring determination of insolvency has been settled conclusively. However, the question that whether all disputes pertaining to such insolvency proceedings are non-arbitrable, for being *in rem* in nature, remains inconclusive. This being a question of law and fact requires analysis that whether those disputes which although arises from an *in rem* insolvency proceeding but themselves are of in personam nature can be arbitrated or not.

In this regard, it has been time and again held that the disputes whose subject matter and cause of action relates to rights *in rem* are not arbitrable,[130] with the exception of those subordinate disputes that arise from

---

128 *Booz Allen and Hamilton Inc. v. SBI Home Finance Ltd.*, Supreme Court of India, (2011) 5 SCC 532.

129 *Vidya Drolia v. Durga Trading Corpn.*, Supreme Court of India, (2021) 2 SCC 1, at para. 77.

130 *Vidya Drolia v. Durga Trading Corpn.*, Supreme Court of India, (2021) 2 SCC 1.

the rights/actions *in rem* but pertains to rights in personam.[131] For instance,[132] Bombay High Court in *Eros International v. Telemax Links India Pvt. Ltd.*,[133] held that although a copyright is a right *in rem* and exercisable against the world at large, a copyright infringement action under a contract is a dispute vis-à-vis the other party to the contract, i.e., an in personam action against an individual and the determination of this action would not have any effect on any third party unrelated to the contract. Accordingly, this dispute was held to be in personam and arbitrable.[134]

The above-mentioned line of distinction of arbitrability between an in rem action and the subordinate in personam matters arising from such in rem action, can be suitably applied to matters relating to in rem insolvency proceedings. For an in rem insolvency proceeding, a subordinate in personam matter may include, for instance, a dispute between the debtor and the supplier under a contract on account of the supply of defective goods by the supplier and the consequent non-payment by the debtor. Here, the supplier as a claimant may institute arbitration and seek payments for the supply of goods made. If seen in the context of the *Telemax* case, the dispute is arbitrable as it arises out of a contract between two parties and any determination made, by way of an arbitral award, would only relate to the rights of the debtor and supplier to pay for or receive payments for the goods supplied. It is only if the determination is in favour of the supplier, i.e., requiring the debtor to make payments, and that the supplier files for the enforcement/execution of such an award, that it would possibly affect the other creditors involved in the insolvency proceedings, as it may then amount to prioritising the payments to the supplier at the cost of other creditors.

In the insolvency context, essentially, till the time, a proceeding merely assess or determine liability, it is in personam in nature, but the time it becomes a proceeding to recover the assessed or determined liability, the nature of proceeding transforms into an in rem action as it stands to impact the interest of all the other creditors in an insolvency proceeding. Since, arbitration, as a proceeding, is required merely to assess and determine the liability, while the underlying action to enforce such determination lies

131 *See also Booz Allen and Hamilton Inc. v. SBI Home Finance Ltd.*, Supreme Court of India, (2011) 5 SCC 532.

132 *See HDFC v. Satpal Singh*, Delhi High Court (2012) 193 DLT 203, at paras 10 and 12.

133 Supreme Court of India, 2016 SCC Online Bom 2179.

134 *See also Hindustan Petroleum Corpn. Ltd. v. Pinkcity Midway Petroleums*, Supreme Court of India, (2003) 6 SCC 503; *Olympus Superstructures (P) Ltd. v.* Meena Vijay Khetan, Supreme Court of India, (1999) 5 SCC 651.

before an executing court, it can be argued that the subordinate in personam disputes is arbitrable and can continue to be referred to arbitration even post-initiation of the insolvency proceeding.

This argument also sits well with the *erga omnes* principle. Similar to the exception of in rem actions, disputes having *erga omnes effect*, i.e., affecting third-party rights and liabilities even though they are not bound by the arbitration agreement, are also considered non-arbitrable.[135] If, however, we consider the above distinction between the proceedings that merely determine the dispute and the proceedings that enforces/execute such determination, i.e., the step succeeding the determination, then the former stage of proceedings will appear to have no *erga omnes* effect, and therefore, remain arbitrable.[136] While, the latter stage of proceedings will have *erga omnes* effect, and therefore, becomes non-arbitrable. In other words, proceedings at any stage preceding the enforcement/execution action are arbitrable under law for having no *erga omnes* effect.

In the context of IBC, the Delhi High Court judgment in *Power Grid* (*supra*) may act as a pivotal point for this approach.[137] In *Power Grid* (*supra*), Delhi High Court affirmed this understanding and observed that it is the 'debt recovery action' that is critical to insolvency process, and not any other proceedings that precedes such action. In other words, it is when the execution proceeding to recover the debt is initiated that the moratorium kicks in, as it is only such debt recovery action that has the effect of diminishing or dissipating the assets of the corporate debtor and affecting the third-party rights of the other creditors. Apart from such debt recovery proceedings, the moratorium provision does not bar or restricts institution or continuation of any other proceedings (including arbitration).

From the judgments discussed earlier, it can be deduced that the Indian judiciary is already on the path to explore and reconcile these globally tried and accepted methods of harmonising and preventing collision between arbitration and insolvency in the context of the IBC. There is no doubt that in the times to come we may see more direct application of these global approaches by the Indian courts, and India contributing to the global jurisprudence in this regard.

---

135 *Vidya Drolia v. Durga Trading Corpn.*, Supreme Court of India, (2021) 2 SCC 1.

136 *See* France Supreme Court's decision in *Jean X. v. International Company for Commercial Exchanges (Income)*, 6 May 2009, Case Number 08-10281. This case applies similar principle and held that an arbitral tribunal may only render a decision deciding the amounts owed by the insolvent party, but not order the insolvent to pay any amount.

137 *See supra* n. 81.

Plausible Drawbacks of Applying These Approaches under IBC

The current Indian insolvency regime under IBC is a big leap upward from the erstwhile severely plagued and scattered insolvency regime. IBC has been identified as an overhauling legislation which has cemented India's outlook towards promoting business and commerce globally. Global publications hail IBC as a momentous step by the Indian legislature to put India on the map of an attractive business destination.[138] It has improved India's position on various fronts, including the ease of doing business[139] and resolving insolvency.

IBC has contributed significantly to the Indian economy in its original form and is considered a success in terms of (a) substantially increasing the recovery rate for lenders, (b) reducing the time consumed to resolve insolvency, (c) reducing the cost for resolving insolvency, and (d) ensuring better outcomes in terms of increased chances of revival than liquidation. Further, the overall scheme of the IBC to promote, protect, and preserve the value of the debtor, and take steps that leads to value maximisation is progressive and in line with global aspirations.

In this backdrop, it becomes essential to analyse, in the Indian context, that whether adopting the approaches that promote increased use of arbitration during the pendency of the insolvency proceedings would have any downsides or drawbacks? Whether it may faulter with the IBC's overall efficiency and acuity in producing results as it does presently? If yes, does it merit adopting these changes or is India better served with the present status quo? The best way to answer these would be to analyse the effect of these approaches on the very four parameters of time, cost, outcome, and recovery rate, that any insolvency regime is measured upon globally.

Impact on 'Time' Taken to Resolve Insolvency

There are no two thoughts that moving away from or narrowing the exclusive jurisdiction of the insolvency court over insolvency matters would have significant impact on the efficiency and time-bound nature of

---

138 Sui-Jim Ho and Surya Kiran Banerjee, *Indian Bankruptcy Code—How Does It Compare?*, Emerging Markets Restructuring Journal, Issue Number 8 — Winter 2018–2019.

139 MS Sahoo, Moving up in 'ease of resolving insolvency', The Hindu Business Line, updated on 5 March 2020, available at https://www.thehindubusinessline.com/opinion/moving-up-in-ease-of-resolving-insolvency/article30992998.ece.

the process. The impact would be visible for, *inter alia*, the following reasons:

(a) No control of insolvency court over other court or tribunal: In India, insolvency tribunal is statutorily not given precedence over any other court or tribunal (including arbitration). If a dispute is allowed to be continued or instituted during the insolvency process before any other forum, then the insolvency courts would not be able to dictate or seek disposal of the dispute within the timeline specified under the IBC. To illustrate, if an arbitration is allowed to be instituted at the later stages of the insolvency process or if the section 34 challenge is pending before the court, then the insolvency court would not be in a position to direct such proceedings to be concluded within the time prescribed under IBC to conclude the insolvency process. In such a case, either the timeline under IBC would stand frustrated or the claims pending adjudication as on the insolvency completion date would stand extinguished on successful resolution under IBC, thereby frustrating the institution or continuation of such proceeding at the first place.
(b) IBC process and process of other courts and tribunals are at variance: IBC provides for a faster redressal of disputes through dedicated and specialised tribunals. Further, IBC appeal provisions are limited and can be availed only in observance of strict timelines. Other courts and tribunals may not provide for similar provisions. This exposes a possibility where the disputes allowed to be adjudicated during insolvency process may lie before forums (including arbitration) which have relaxed timelines or provide for broader and increased appeal avenues.

Thus, possibly, adopting these approaches that advocates for increased use of arbitration during insolvency may delay the timely completion of the insolvency process.

Impact on 'Cost' Incurred to Resolve Insolvency

Cost is directly connected with the time to resolve insolvency. Thus, increase in time will automatically increase the process cost. However, cost for the extended time is only a part of the concern, as an increased reference to these approaches would also mean that the corporate debtor will see more proceedings during the insolvency process, as compared to the present status quo. This would imply that the corporate debtor would be required to participate and represent its interest at various forums (not required earlier) thereby requiring the assistance of more human and other resources. The employment of additional resources would involve significant cost towards litigation and management that will add to the stress faced by the debtor, which will ultimately reflect by way of deduction in value retrieved by the creditors on completion of the process. In other words, the recovery made would be lesser on a cent.

Impact on 'Outcome' of the Insolvency Proceedings

IBC aims and strives for resolution/revival of the ailing debtor. Successful resolution is contingent on the fact that the business is seen viable to a resolution applicant. A business is viable if its value is preserved during the insolvency process. Value is preserved when the assets are managed properly, and business is continued on a 'going concern' basis. However, if the resolution professional, who is designated as the official to oversee these aspects, is occupied primarily in defending the suits or proceedings, then the duty to maintain the corporate debtor as a going concern and protect and preserve its value would become secondary and may even be neglected.

Further, the increase in time in completing the insolvency process may also dissuade potential resolution applicants from continuing to express their interest in submitting the resolution plan for a stressed debtor. Since preparation of resolution plan and conducting due diligence in itself a costly affair, any delay in the prescribed timeline under the IBC may discourage the resolution applicant, leading to withdrawal from the process. This would affect the prospects of successful resolution of the debtor and may push the debtor into liquidation.

Impact on 'Recovery Rate' Under the Process

Negative impact on time, cost, and outcome is bound to have negative effect on the recovery rate. With the increase in time, the recovery rate would be less as during the time the insolvency process is on-going, the corporate debtor would not operate to its full potential, and accordingly, would not retrieve a value that justifies its full potential. Further, with increase in time, the value lost on account of depreciation would also increase. This will lead to a further reduction in the recovery made on completion of the process.

With increase in costs, the recovery rate is bound to go low as well. Every extra penny spent as insolvency process cost would factor in the value received by the creditors on completion of the process. Similarly, the diminishing probabilities of successful resolution and increasing chances of liquidation, would further affect the recovery rate. As stated earlier, liquidation is expected to retrieve a lesser value for the creditors as compared to a value that a successful resolution may attract. Thus, overall, the recovery rate under the insolvency process may fall if these approaches are to be considered and applied under the IBC.

The question, therefore, arises that whether does it merit for India to adopt these globally applied approaches of reconciling the conflict between arbitration and insolvency or is India better served with the status quo.

Conclusion

As stated earlier, US,[140] UK,[141] and other European nations[142] apply several approaches under their respective insolvency and arbitration laws to prevent collision between the policy objectives of arbitration and insolvency and perform much better than India on the index of 'resolving insolvency'. However, there is an inherent distinction between India and these jurisdictions which makes such comparison unviable, which is, these jurisdictions are comparatively advanced and a quicker legal system in place overall, than the legal regime of India.

Further, the parameters to measure the score for resolving insolvency is based on a composite metric of time, cost, outcome, and recovery rate, which although is broad and cover a lot of aspects, but still has its own limitations. For instance, these parameters are made to be applicable to around 200 jurisdictions, and thus, are required to be focussing on broader issues that are common and prevalent than those that are particular or

140 Ranked 2, World Bank. 2020. Doing Business 2020. Washington, DC: World Bank. DOI:10.1596/978-1-4648-1440-2. License: Creative Commons Attribution CC BY 3.0 IGO.

141 Ranked 14, World Bank. 2020. Doing Business 2020. Washington, DC: World Bank. DOI:10.1596/978-1-4648-1440-2. License: Creative Commons Attribution CC BY 3.0 IGO.

142 Germany – Ranked 4; France – Ranked 26, World Bank. 2020. Doing Business 2020. Washington, DC: World Bank. DOI:10.1596/978-1-4648-1440-2. License: Creative Commons Attribution CC BY 3.0 IGO.

unique to some jurisdictions. Since each jurisdiction would have their own unique experiences in dealing with insolvencies and their outcome, one parameter of measuring the efficiency of insolvency law may not fit all. For instance, there are several social and economic aspects that are unique to India and bear significant effect on how the stress is seen and credit is made available. Similarly, India has its own legal peculiarities, such as having no settled hierarchy among courts, tribunals, and forum other than the Supreme Court of India or availability of multiple avenues to challenge one order, which may not get measured under these parameters but remain critical to determine the true state of IBC and its impact.

Hence, considering India's unique circumstances and acknowledging existence of a vibrant legal space that is outward looking and observant of the global developments, it may be prudent that India adopts a more careful and calculated approach in this regard. For instance, courts may allow all beneficial actions to a corporate debtor and subordinate in personam disputes to continue while applying other global recognised methods contextually on a case-to-case basis.[143] It would enable courts to further the prospects of the IBC and the objects it seeks to achieve, rather than being bogged down under global peer pressure by following them indiscriminately, upsetting the progress made so far under the IBC.

143 For instance, as done in the jurisdictions like UK and Singapore wherein courts have devised broad principles to assess whether a case is to be allowed to be arbitrated or to be adjudicated by the bankruptcy court.

Effectiveness of Corporate Insolvency Proceedings and Commercial Arbitration

Vigintas Višinskis
Professor at Vilnius University Faculty of Law, Department of Civil Procedure
Remigijus Jokubauskas
Leader of company Justitia, UAB. Vilnius
Mykolas Kirkutis
Assistant to the Supreme Court of Lithuania and lecturer and researcher at Mykolas Romeris University

Introduction

Corporate insolvency proceedings shall be effective.[1] To achieve this purpose, the legislators often establish a special procedure for submission and confirmation of creditors' claims in insolvency proceedings, whereby all creditors' claims shall be heard in the insolvency court. This coordination of creditors' claims is an essential feature of insolvency proceedings. The dilemma arises when creditors have an arbitration agreement with the debtor and the insolvency proceedings of the debtor are commenced. Creditors have a right to challenge claims of other creditors, challenge transactions of an insolvent company, and coordinate other common defense strategies. The arbitral award which confirms the creditor's claim should be submitted to the insolvency court which should confirm the creditors' claim according to such decision. However, in such cases other creditors which are not parties to the arbitration agreement do not have right to challenge arbitral award. The autonomy of parties to an arbitration agreement and the principle of *pacta sunt servanda* are fundamental rules, and parties are bound by an arbitration agreement unless they decide otherwise. Nevertheless, in such a case, other creditors are deprived of their individual right to contest the validity of such a claim.

1 Instrument of the European Law Institute, Rescue of Business in Insolvency Law, 2017.

This chapter focuses on the major problems of how to ensure that arbitration proceedings of an insolvent entity are compatible with the effectiveness of insolvency proceedings and the equality of creditors (*pari passu*). For this analysis the authors focus on the legal regulation of Lithuania and Lithuanian case law, but also consider foreign legal systems. Also, this chapter deals with the question whether an arbitration agreement remains binding when one of the parties (or all) become insolvent. In some jurisdictions, an insolvency administrator has the right to terminate all debtor's contracts which had been concluded before commencement of insolvency proceedings. The authors raise the question whether an insolvency administrator is entitled to terminate an arbitration agreement when the insolvency proceedings of the debtor are commenced. What aspects should be considered in this case? Also, what disputes during insolvency proceedings can be submitted to the arbitral court? Different jurisdictions deal with these questions differently. For instance, the courts of the United States allow litigation of "non-core" issues of a bankrupt company in arbitration, but "core" issues shall be heard only by the bankruptcy court. Various countries in Europe do not prohibit arbitration of an insolvent company, but often grant the right to the court to suspend the validity of an arbitration agreement if it negatively affects efficiency of insolvency proceedings. Thus, the chapter focuses on the current approach of different jurisdictions on how they reach a proper balance between the autonomy of parties to an arbitration agreement, the principle of *pacta sunt servanda* and effectiveness of insolvency proceedings.

The problems of compatibility of effectiveness of insolvency proceedings and arbitration also raise with the directive on restructuring and insolvency (hereinafter—the directive)[2] which came into force on 17 July 2021. The major question is whether arbitration agreements of insolvency companies are compatible with the new regulation of the European Union in the area of insolvency. The directive is silent whether an arbitration agreement remains in force when one of the parties (or all) become insolvent or find themselves likely to become insolvent soon. Nevertheless, it establishes the requirement that insolvency proceedings shall be effective and regulates the performance of executory contracts which are essential for continuation of company's activities and confirmation of the

2 Directive (EU) 2019/1023 of the European Parliament and of the Council of June 20, 2019 on preventive restructuring frameworks, on discharge of debt and disqualifications, and on measures to increase the efficiency of procedures concerning restructuring, insolvency and discharge of debt, and amending Directive (EU) 2017/1132 (Directive on restructuring and insolvency) OJ L 172.

restructuring plan. Thus, the chapter covers the issues of compatibility of the application of the directive and arbitration agreements.

This chapter initially analyses the collective nature of insolvency proceedings and the settlement of creditors' claims in these proceedings. Then, it presents and assesses the regulation of the laws on insolvency and arbitration of the Republic of Lithuania. The problems of enforcing arbitration agreements when insolvency proceedings are commenced against one of the parties to the agreement are analyzed. Finally, it deals with the settlement of disputes in arbitration and the application of the directive, and whether the goal of effectiveness of insolvency (restructuring) proceedings can be reached in this case.

The Collective Nature of Insolvency Proceedings

The collective nature of insolvency proceedings is a fundamental aspect of these proceedings. It also has great importance for the analysis of arbitration proceedings when one of the parties to the arbitration agreement becomes insolvent. The collective nature of insolvency proceedings is mentioned in various international legal instruments and national laws.[3] These proceedings are the only remaining way for creditors to collect on their debt which is why insolvency proceedings are viewed as a collective debt collection procedure.[4] In insolvency proceedings all debtor's creditors (or creditors affected by the restructuring plan) have their financial interests, and they have to coordinate defense mechanisms of their rights. In other words, debtors' creditors should participate in these proceedings as a group and give up individual enforcement rights. This problem of insolvency proceedings is referred to as "grab law" which reflects first-come first-served[5] enforcement, meaning that creditors who are aware of debtor's financial difficulties may quickly enforce their claims and a debtor may remain assetless.

3 UNCITRAL Legislative Guide on Insolvency Law, 2004; Art. 1(1) of the Regulation (EU) 2015/848 of the European Parliament and of the Council of 20 May 2015 on insolvency proceedings; Art. 1 of the Insolvency Code of Germany; 3(1)(a) of the Law on Insolvency of the Czech Republic.

4 Stephan Madaus, "Leaving the Shadows of US Bankruptcy Law: A Proposal to Divide the Realms of Insolvency and Restructuring Law," *European Business Organization Law Review* 19 (2018).

5 Jackson, H. T. (1986), "The Logic and Limits of Bankruptcy Law." Harvard University Press, p. 9.

One of the aspects of collective nature of insolvency proceedings is that creditors lose their individual rights to enforce claims and have to submit financial claims against the debtor to the single insolvency court which, after examination of the validity of the claim, can either approve or not approve the claim. Such examination of the validity of the creditors' claims may not be needed when the claim had been already confirmed by the court or another institution which has an authority to render binding decisions. After confirmation of the claim, a creditor acquires all individual and collective rights in insolvency proceedings. This acquisition of creditor's rights in insolvency proceedings is particularly relevant since one of the individual rights which each creditor has is the right to contest the validity (or amount) of claims of other creditors. The right of creditors to challenge other creditors' claims is embedded in the nature of collective insolvency proceedings since the larger amount of approved creditors' financial claims means that all creditors get the smaller piece of the debtor's assets (proceeds after its realization in case of liquidation proceedings). Thus, insolvency proceedings often establish a particular dispute resolution mechanism for challenges of the creditors' claims.

The said peculiarities of the collectivism of insolvency proceedings may not be compatible with the *individual* dispute settlement in arbitration. Some authors rightly pointed out that insolvency and arbitration are two different types of procedures, each having its own purpose, objectives, and underlying policy.[6] Since arbitration is based on the arbitration agreement which is binding only upon the parties who signed it (with some notable exceptions), other persons are not allowed to participate in arbitration proceedings. Exceptions can be when arbitration rule provide for participation of third parties or consolidation of different proceedings. This leads to the problem when the creditor's claim is satisfied by the arbitration court and such arbitral award is submitted to the insolvency court. In general insolvency proceedings are based upon the principle of *vis attractiva concursus* meaning that all financial claims against the debtor should be concentrated in the insolvency court. However, if the valid arbitration agreement exists, the validity of the creditor's claim is examined in arbitration court, meaning that accumulation of the claims against the debtor cannot be reached in insolvency court. The arbitral award is final and binding, and it shall be challenged neither by the insolvency court nor by the creditors, save in limited circumstances. Thus, when the creditor submits the claim to the insolvency court which is based on the arbitral

6 Vesna Lazic, Arbitration and Insolvency Proceedings: Claims of Ordinary Bankruptcy Creditors, ECJL, 3(3), 1999.

award, all other creditors are deprived of their right to challenge such claim. The same situation appears when an insolvency administrator challenges a creditor's claim in arbitration, but the claim is dismissed. This situation contradicts one of the core elements of collectivism of insolvency proceedings. Such conclusion leads to the need to weight the balance between the individual right to a creditor to enforce the arbitration agreement (to settle the dispute against the debtor in arbitration) and the nature of collective insolvency proceedings (accumulation of creditors' claim in the insolvency court).

The problems of the creditors' right to challenge other creditors' claims should also be analyzed from the perspective of human right, first of all, the right to a fair trial (access to court). Article 6(1) of the European Convention on Human Rights (hereinafter—Convention) establishes the right to a fair trial. It is also applicable in arbitration proceedings.[7] One of the main elements of this right is access to the court which in this case is the right to effectively challenge the creditors' claim in the insolvency court. But due to autonomy of an arbitration agreement only the parties to this agreement can exercise this right with respect to a specific dispute subject to arbitration agreement. This is another issue which should be considered when analyzing the compatibility of arbitration and insolvency proceedings. In the sense of the Convention, conclusion of arbitration agreement is deemed as a "waiver" of the rights of the Convention, namely the right to access to the court.[8] Article 6 of the Convention does not therefore preclude the setting up of arbitration tribunals in order to settle certain disputes.[9] The European Court on Human Rights (thereinafter – ECHR) has interpreted that neither the letter nor the spirit of Article 6 prevents a person from waiving them of his or her own free will, either expressly or tacitly. However, such waiver must, if it is to be effective for Convention purposes, be established in an unequivocal manner and be attended by minimum safeguards commensurate with its importance.[10] According to the ECHR, in the contracting states' domestic legal systems a waiver of this kind is

7 Dalia Višinskytė, Mykolas Kirkutis, Remigijus Jokubauskas, Vigintas Višinskis, "Application of Article 6 of the European Convention of Human Rights in Enforcement Proceedings," LeXonomica, 13(1), 2021.

8 Dalia Višinskytė, Remigijus Jokubauskas, Mykolas Kirkutis, "Arbitration Agreements and Protection of the Right to a Fair Trial," Baltic Journal of Law & Politics; Warsaw 13(2), 2020.

9 Judgment of the ECHR of December 16, 2003 in case *Transado-Transportes Fluviais Do Sado, S.A., v. Portugal*, petition, Number 35943/02.

10 Judgment of the ECHR of Sep. 17, 2010 in case *Scoppola v. Italy (Number 2)*, petition Number 10249/03, para. 135.

frequently encountered both in civil matters, notably in the shape of arbitration clauses in contracts, and in criminal matters in the shape, *inter alia*, of fines paid by way of composition. The waiver, which has undeniable advantages for the individual concerned as well as for the administration of justice, does not in principle offend the Convention.[11] Pursuant to the case law of the ECHR, the waiver of rights guaranteed by the Convention—in so far as it is permissible—must be established in an unequivocal manner.[12] In other words, a person can waive the right to access to the court, but such waiver shall be clearly expressed.

Another significant procedural issue is that the waiver of rights shall affect only a person who expressed the waiver and it shall not affect other persons.[13] In case *Suda v. the Czech Republic*, the applicant was a minor shareholder in an enterprise in the Czech Republic. The shareholder meeting of the enterprise decided (the applicant voted against) to wind up the enterprise and sell all shares to the major shareholder. The agreement to sell all shares of the enterprise to the major shareholder was concluded between the enterprise and the major shareholder and established that the price of the sale can be challenged in two months in arbitration. The applicant filed an action to the court challenging the sale agreement, but the domestic courts declared the action inadmissible since the arbitration clause was included in the sale agreement. Therefore, in this case it was not the applicant who signed an arbitration clause, and the ECHR considered whether such arbitration clause fulfills the requirements set out in Article 6 of the Convention since the applicant was forced to settle the dispute in an arbitration though had not signed an arbitration clause. The court found that since the domestic law established a mechanism to force the minor shareholders to sell their shares to the major shareholder, appropriate means of defense should be granted for the minor shareholder. This incompatibility of the waiver of the right to access to the court and arbitration agreements is another question regarding not only effectiveness of insolvency proceedings, but also protection of the fundamental human rights (the right to a fair trial).

The problem of collectivism of insolvency proceedings and individual creditor's right to challenge creditors' claims is not a mere theoretical

11 Judgment of the ECHR of Feb. 27, 1980 in case *Deweer v. Belgium*, petition Number 6903/75.

12 Judgment of the ECHR of Feb. 23, 1999 in case *Suovaniemi and others v. Finland*, petition Number 31737/96.

13 Judgment of the ECHR of Oct. 28, 2010 in case *Suda v. Czech Republic*, petition Number 1643/06.

problem. This problem of compatibility of different interests has also been analyzed in the case law. For instance, in one case the Supreme Court of Lithuania had to deal with the balance of these interests.[14] We believe this case is an ample example of the collision between the collectivism of insolvency proceedings and arbitration proceedings.

In this case, bankruptcy proceedings against the defendant were commenced in 2014. The appellant had entered into a legal services agreement with the defendant, according to which all disputes relating to the agreement would be settled by an arbitral tribunal. Subsequently, the parties entered into an additional agreement on the provision and payment for further legal services. There was no dispute as to the validity of the arbitration clause.

It was established that the creditor of the defendant exercised the right established in Article 26(6) of the Law on Bankruptcy of Enterprises of the Republic of Lithuania (existing at that time) and contested the financial claim of the other creditor (appellant) in the bankruptcy court. It was only after the court of first instance had examined the dispute and that creditor had appealed to the appellate court, the insolvency administrator exercised his right to challenge the same transaction on the same grounds and essentially identical arguments as the creditor in arbitration. The creditor applied to the arbitral tribunal to involve him as a third party, but the request was rejected because the creditor was not a party to the arbitration agreement. The case raised the question of how to deal with the situation when a claim concerning the validity of a creditor's claim has already been submitted by another creditor, who is not a party to the arbitration agreement.

The Supreme Court of Lithuania found that when a dispute under one creditor's claim as to the validity and amount of another creditor's claim has already been instituted in the bankruptcy court and the dispute is based on a possibly null and void of the contract from which the claim derives (the legality of which must be examined ex officio), the conclusions reached by the arbitral tribunal are not binding on the bankruptcy court and are not binding and the court has the right and obligation to resolve the dispute within the limits of the claim.[15] Thus, the court decided that the

14 Judgment of the Supreme Court of Lithuania of April 3, 2017 in case Number 3K-7-74-313/2017.

15 Judgment of the Supreme Court of Lithuania of April 3, 2017 in case Number 3K-7-74-313/2017.

individual right of a creditor to challenge other creditor's claims in insolvency proceedings has great importance, and this right should be implemented by the bankruptcy court. The court did not explain whether the conclusion would be different if the arbitration proceedings had been instituted before the commencement of court proceedings regarding the validity of the creditor's claim in the bankruptcy court. However, it seems that according to the existed legal regulation at that time (according to which commencement of insolvency proceedings does not affect validity of arbitration agreements) in such case the arbitration proceedings should have continued.

What is also debatable regarding the mentioned judgment is the conclusion that the binding arbitral award of the arbitral tribunal has no legal force. In other words, though the national law establishes that the final decision of the arbitral tribunal is binding, such legal force was simply not recognized due to the collective nature of insolvency proceedings. This conclusion not only creates more legal riddles regarding the final and binding nature of the arbitral award, but also makes an arbitration agreement forceless since it may not be respected by the court in insolvency proceedings. This situation is a concrete example when the regulation on arbitration and insolvency proceedings is not harmonized, and significant legal problems arise.

The problems of compatibility of insolvency proceedings and arbitration have also been noticed by other national courts. For instance, Spanish case law also recognizes the problem of arbitration in insolvency proceedings. In one case heard in 2019, the Commercial Court of Santander found that the parties (a company incorporated in Spain and persons operating in England) had entered into an agreement that all disputes arising out of the contract should be submitted to arbitration in London.[16] A company registered in Spain has opened insolvency proceedings in Spain. No arbitration proceedings were instituted at the time the insolvency commenced. Under Spanish law (Article 52.1 of the Spanish Insolvency Law), the opening of insolvency proceedings does not affect the arbitration agreement, but the court may suspend enforcement of such agreement (*suspensión de sus efectos*), subject to the requirement of the effectiveness of the insolvency proceedings. The court applied this exception, and gave priority to efficiency of the insolvency proceedings, and found that arbitration proceedings would lead to new costs for the debtor, thus reducing the creditors' claims even more. Nevertheless, the question arises what

16 Judgment of Sep. 30, 2019 of *Juzgado de lo Mercantil*, SJM S 1003/2019 - ECLI: ES:JMS:2019:1003.

practical relevance would such decision have to the arbitral tribunal seated in another state and whether the international arbitration shall declare lack of jurisdiction to hear the dispute only because of such decision in another state? However, when comparing this case in Spain and the one in Lithuania, the principal difference seems to be embedded in the national regulation. Since the court in Spain had the right to suspend proceedings, this means that the court has discretion to decide which interest is more important in a particular case. The gap in national legislation on the issue (such as in Lithuania) leaves riddles and does not solve the delicate problem of the possibility to arbitrate in insolvency proceedings.

Another significant aspect of insolvency proceedings is the procedure of confirmation of creditors' claims. In general insolvency proceedings shall regulate how disputes regarding the creditor's claim should be solved. In Lithuania, there are a number of peculiarities of such proceedings. First, the Law on Insolvency of Enterprises of the Republic of Lithuania (thereinafter—LIE) establishes a two-step confirmation procedure of a creditor's claim: first, the claim is submitted to the insolvency administrator; second, the insolvency administrator has to send the claim to the court irrespective of their position to the validity of the claim. Each creditor has the right to challenge the validity (or amount) of the claim in the court. This is an accelerated procedure which aims to deal with the question of the validity of creditors' claim as soon as possible. The collectivism of insolvency proceedings is one of the major reasons why the problems of compatibility of arbitration and insolvency proceedings arise. The collective nature of insolvency proceedings has certain peculiarities, and it basically requires a collective dispute settlement of creditors' claims.

Application of Arbitration Agreement in Case of Insolvency of One of the Parties

The crucial question regarding arbitration in insolvency is application of the arbitration agreement. The problem of validity and application of an arbitration agreement when one of the parties of the agreement becomes insolvent is regulated by the national law. In some states, commencement of insolvency proceedings does not affect validity of an arbitration agreement. For instance, according to Article 49(7) of the Law on Commercial Arbitration of the Republic of Lithuania (hereinafter—LCA), opening of insolvency (bankruptcy) proceedings against a party to an arbitration agreement or application of another insolvency procedure to a party to an arbitration agreement shall not affect the arbitration proceedings, the validity and application of the arbitration agreement, the possibility of arbitration, and the jurisdiction of the arbitral tribunal. The LIE lacks any regulation on arbitration during insolvency proceedings and only makes a reference to the said provision of the LCA. Similarly, in Germany, opening of insolvency proceedings does not affect the arbitrability of a dispute. There is no specific legal provision which would regulate the validity of an arbitration agreement in case of insolvency. However, pursuant to the general rule of the competence of the arbitration tribunal any claim under property law may become the subject matter of an arbitration agreement. An arbitration agreement regarding non-pecuniary claims has legal effect insofar as the parties to the dispute are entitled to conclude a settlement regarding the subject matter of the dispute.[17] Also, there is no provision that arbitration proceedings shall be stayed following the commencement of an insolvency.

The second approach is restriction of arbitration proceedings when insolvency proceedings are commenced. The example of such legal regulation can be found in the United Kingdom. Under the 1986 English Insolvency Act, once a company enters administration, arbitration may not be commenced or continued against the company without the consent of the administrator or the permission of the court. If the proceedings are unlikely to impede the achievement of the purpose of the administration, leave may be granted. Another example of prioritization of insolvency proceedings is Latvia. Pursuant to Article 5(8) of the Arbitration Law of the Republic of Latvia, an arbitration court shall resolve any civil legal disputes, provided that the parties have voluntarily agreed upon and concluded an arbitration agreement, except for the disputes regarding the rights and obligations of persons who have entered into insolvency procedures.

A third could be regarded as a "hybrid approach" since commencement of arbitration proceedings does not lead to automatic invalidity of an arbitration agreement, but rather gives authority to the insolvency court to decide whether arbitration proceedings would be compatible with the arbitration. Such approach can be found in the US insolvency law. In the US insolvency law, any proceedings (including arbitrations) brought against an insolvent party or the property of the estate shall be stayed, with leave for a party to apply for relief from a stay. In such case the court has to decide whether arbitration proceedings shall be continued or the

17 The German Code of Civil Proceedings, Art. 1030(1).

collectivism of insolvency proceedings should be prioritized. The case law of the US courts has formed an important division between core and con-core issues. Courts have wide discretion to decide whether arbitration proceedings should be permitted or not.[18] US case law also recognizes the wide discretion of courts in deciding whether a particular arbitration agreement may violate the purposes of bankruptcy proceedings. The court is therefore entitled to decide whether the execution of the arbitration agreement may adversely affect the administration of the insolvency proceedings.[19]

The problem of compatibility between arbitration and insolvency disputes is also recognized in the case law of Singapore. In the Larsen Oil case, the Singapore Court of Appeal acknowledged that, on the one hand, arbitration is characterized by the principle of party autonomy and the decentralization of private dispute resolution. Insolvency proceedings, on the other hand, are collective proceedings in which public centralization of disputes is carried out in order to achieve economic efficiency and optimal satisfaction of creditors' claims. In this case, the court found that the purpose of insolvency proceedings to facilitate the resolution of a company's creditors' disputes against the company takes precedence over the company's right to agree before insolvency proceedings where the disputes are to be heard.[20]

Another hybrid approach can be found in France, in which the arbitrability of a claim is determined by the nature of the dispute. Similarly as in the US legal system, "core" insolvency issues are deemed non-arbitrable whereas contractual matters remain arbitrable. However, even if the arbitration court has jurisdiction over a claim, it has to respect the fundamental principles of insolvency law.

The contractual nature of an arbitration agreement is recognized in Lithuania. In essence, an arbitration agreement is a contract and the rules of contract law for its application and interpretation are applicable. Pursuant to Article 3(5) of the LCA, an arbitration agreement is defined as an agreement between two or more parties to submit to arbitration all or certain disputes which have arisen or which may arise between them in connection with any specific contractual or other legal relationship which

18 Decision of United States Court of Appeals, Eleventh Circuit of Feb. 23, 2007 *In re* Electric Machinery Enterprises, 479 F.3d 79147 Bankr. Ct. Dec. 234.

19 Decision of United States Bankruptcy Court, E.D. Pennsylvania of Aug. 8, 2007 *In re* Herrington, 374 B.R. 133.

20 Decision of Court of Appeal of 11 May 2011 in case *Larsen Oil and Gas Pte Ltd v. Petroprod Ltd*, 2011, SGCA21.

may be the subject of arbitration. An essential condition for establishing the existence of an arbitration agreement is the will of the parties to submit disputes to arbitration. The main requirement for the content of an arbitration agreement is that it must express the will of the parties to resolve disputes not in any other way (state court, mediation, etc.), but in arbitration.[21]

In insolvency proceedings, the performance and termination of contracts of the insolvent company are often specifically regulated in the law. Treatment of contracts is of overriding importance to insolvency proceedings.[22] Insolvency law should assist in the separation of prospectively profitable contracts which are necessary for business from burdensome and loss-bearing contracts that would only add to the debt pile.[23] International standards also suggest considering specific legislation for executory contracts that are essential for continuing the business of the debtor— such as, for instance, real estate leases, energy supply contracts, intellectual property and domain services, or license agreements.[24] Also, it is suggested that treatment of contracts in insolvency proceedings shall focus on maximizing debtors' assets. In achieving the objectives of maximizing the value of the estate and reducing liabilities and, in reorganization, enabling the debtor to survive and continue its affairs to the maximum extent possible in an uninterrupted manner may involve taking advantage of those contracts which are beneficial and contribute value to the estate (including contracts that will enable the continued use of crucial property that may be owned by a third party) and rejecting those which are burdensome or those where the ongoing costs of performance exceed the benefit to be derived from the contract.[25]

Nevertheless, despite the importance and relevance of arbitration agreements, international standards and legal doctrine do not pay attention to the treatment of arbitration agreements in insolvency proceedings. Since arbitration agreements are in essence contracts, the question arises, whether the same goals and rules on treatment of contracts should be applicable to the treatment of arbitration agreement? Does an insolvency administrator have the right to terminate unilaterally the arbitration agreement relying on the general rules of treatment of contracts in insolvency proceedings?

---

21 The decision of the Supreme Court of Lithuania of Nov. 14, 2019 in case Number e3K-3-343-916/2019.

22 UNCITRAL, Legislative Guide on Insolvency Law, 2004, p. 119.

23 Reinhard Bork, "Corporate insolvency law," IntersentiaBork, 2020, p. 181.

24 European Law Institute, Rescue of business, 2017, pp. 238–239.

25 *Supra* n. 29, p. 120.

Pursuant to Article 61 of the LIE, from the date of entry into force of a court decision to open bankruptcy proceedings, all legal person's obligations shall be deemed to have expired, unless (1) the insolvency administrator, taking into account the economic benefit of the obligation to the legal person and its creditors, within 30 days from the date of entry into force notify the other party to the obligation that it will perform the obligation; (2) the obligations arise from the continuing economic and commercial activity, which the insolvency administrator, taking into account the economic benefit of its continuation to the legal person and its creditors, decides to perform before the first creditors' meeting. Since there are no indications that these rules are not applicable to an arbitration agreement, it can be argued that an insolvency administrator can decide to terminate an arbitration agreement simply by analyzing the economic benefit of such contract to the creditors and the company itself. It could be debatable how an insolvency administrator could assess the economic benefit of an arbitration agreement. However, in case the company clearly lacks funding to participate in the arbitration proceedings, it may be regarded as an option to terminate arbitration agreements. Nevertheless, there is still lack of Lithuanian case-law in this regard.

To sum up, the national regulation of validity of an arbitration agreement in insolvency proceedings varies greatly between the countries. At least three different models which address this question can be established. Also, it is debatable, whether the general rules on treatment of contracts in insolvency proceedings are applicable also to the arbitration agreement or not. Since an insolvency administrator has the right to decide which contractual relations (contracts) should be continued in insolvency proceedings, this discretion may also encompass arbitration agreements. Nevertheless, it seems that such decision requires careful balance between the autonomy of the parties to arbitration agreement and their lawful expectations and the effectiveness of insolvency proceedings

Compatibility of Arbitration and Insolvency Proceedings in Lithuania

In Lithuania arbitration has been recognized as a valid commercial dispute settlement mechanism since the adoption of the LCA in 1996. Article 8 of the LCA establishes the principles of commercial arbitration, such as independence of arbitration, equality of parties. Also, this article establishes that arbitration process shall be conducted in accordance with the principles of party autonomy, adversarial proceedings, economy, coopera tion, and expediency. According to Article 12 of the LCA, all disputes may be settled by arbitration, except as provided in this article. However, there are no indications in this article that the disputes involving an insolvent party cannot be settled in arbitration.

The problems of compatibility of arbitration and insolvency proceedings in Lithuania are addressed in the LIE. The LIE does not regulate the arbitration proceedings of an insolvent enterprise, instead it only refers to the LAC. Article 49(7-9) of the LCA regulates the compatibility of arbitration and bankruptcy proceedings. Noteworthy, the LCA deals only with bankruptcy, but not restructuring proceedings. The LIE, in turn, regulates insolvency proceedings which may be bankruptcy or restructuring. This gap in the law leads to the dilemma, whether the same rules on compatibility of arbitration and bankruptcy proceedings should be also applicable to restructuring proceedings as well.

First, it should be noted that commencement of bankruptcy proceedings does not affect arbitration agreements of the insolvent company. Pursuant to Article 49(7) of the LCA, opening of insolvency proceedings against a party to an arbitration agreement or application of another insolvency procedure to a party to an arbitration agreement shall not affect the arbitration proceedings, validity and application of the arbitration agreement, the possibility of arbitration and jurisdiction of the arbitral tribunal, except as provided in paragraphs 8 and 9 of this article. The Court of Appeal of Lithuania has found that bankruptcy proceedings and arbitration are compatible, and the opening of insolvency proceedings does not remove the binding nature of the arbitration agreement.[26] In other words, the opening of insolvency proceedings does not in itself affect the validity of the arbitration agreement and does not allow the conclusion that the dispute is not arbitrable.[27] However, such examples of the case law do not provide answers to more delicate and relevant issues regarding the compatibility of arbitration and insolvency proceedings and merely restate the national regulation.

However, in practice, there are problems in dealing with the compatibility of insolvency and arbitration proceedings. In one case Lithuanian courts had to decide on the procedure for resolving the issue of approving a creditor's financial claim when the dispute over the validity of the

---

26 Judgment of the Court of Appeal of Lithuania of March 20, 2017 in case Number 2A-440-464/2017.

27 Judgment of the Court of Appeal of Lithuania of Dec. 1, 2016 in case Number 2-1987-370/2016.

financial claim is pending before the arbitral tribunal. The creditor filed a claim against defendant in the International Court of Commercial Arbitration at the Chamber of Commerce of the Russian Federation regarding the repayment of the debt. During the pendency of the dispute before the arbitration tribunal, the bankruptcy proceedings were commenced against the defendant in Lithuania. Pending a decision of the arbitral tribunal, the creditor applied to the insolvency court for confirmation of his financial claim which validity was being decided by an international arbitral tribunal. The first instance court suspended the civil proceedings for confirmation of creditor's financial claim until the arbitral award of the International Court of Commercial Arbitration at the Chamber of Commerce of the Russian Federation enters into force. Since the arbitral tribunal was international, its awards had to be recognized in accordance with the United Nations Convention on the Recognition and Enforcement of Foreign Arbitral Awards (1958). The Court of Appeal of Lithuanian confirmed this decision noting that according to the settled case law, if another case is previously filed regarding an identical claim, the issue of approval of the financial claim is not examined separately in the bankruptcy case.[28] Nevertheless, the court did not address the right to a creditor to submit a claim to the bankruptcy court while the arbitration proceedings were pending and only focused on the need to wait for the judgment of the foreign arbitration and its recognition in Lithuania. Such decision could restrict the rights of potential creditors to participate and vote in insolvency proceedings since a creditor acquire all rights and duties in insolvency proceeding after confirmation of the claim. Another peculiarity of the case was that the creditor's claim was heard by the foreign arbitration which would also require recognition of the arbitral award in Lithuania. Such recognition procedure would also prolong confirmation of the creditor's claim in the bankruptcy, and the creditor even with a significant claim would not have a right to participate in the bankruptcy proceedings.

Second, the law regulates the right of a company to conclude an arbitration agreement after bankruptcy proceedings are commenced. According to Article 49(8) of the LCA, a company that has been declared bankrupt cannot enter into a new arbitration agreement. Thus, from the moment when a judgment to commence bankruptcy proceedings becomes binding, conclusion of the arbitration agreement is prohibited. However, the law also establishes a possibility to refuse to settle the dispute in arbitration. Property claims of a party to an arbitration agreement against

28 Judgment of the Court of Appeal of July 27, 2020 in case Number e2-1266-881/2020.

which bankruptcy proceedings have been instituted shall be heard in the court which opened the bankruptcy proceedings at the request of all the parties to the arbitration agreement who have not been declared bankrupt (Article 49(8) of the LCA). It means that the parties to the arbitration agreement may decide to withdraw from the arbitration agreement and instead file the claim before the bankruptcy court. Nevertheless, this is the only option for the parties, and they may not be willing to use it.

Third, the law regulates how an insolvency administrator should participate in the arbitration proceedings when the proceedings had begun before commencement of bankruptcy proceedings. According to Article 49(9) of the LCA, if the property claims of the party to the arbitration agreement relating to which the insolvency proceedings have been instituted are subject to arbitration, the arbitral tribunal shall allow the insolvency administrator a reasonable time to familiarize with the case and prepare for the arbitration proceedings, and the claimant shall notify the insolvency court and provide a description of the evidence. The arbitral tribunal shall determine the amount of the claims between the parties. Following the award of the arbitral tribunal, the insolvency court shall confirm the claims between the parties established by the award of the arbitral tribunal.

The systematic analysis of the mentioned provisions of the LCA reveals that arbitration and insolvency proceedings are in essence compatible. However, as it was showed with the analysis of some relevant cases, such compatibility is still very debatable and complicated. Noteworthy, the mentioned provisions of the LCA were adopted when the previous regulation of bankruptcy proceedings of corporate entities was in force. The LIA was adopted in 2019 and amended the concept of insolvency proceedings of corporate entities in Lithuania by emphasizing the effectiveness of insolvency proceedings as the principal goal of these proceedings. However, there new regulation does not establish any rules regarding compatibility of insolvency proceedings and arbitration. Nevertheless, according to the existing legal regulation, it can be concluded that commencement of insolvency proceedings does not affect the arbitration agreement concluded prior such proceedings. However, the law allows the parties to withdraw from the arbitration agreement, and the creditor can submit the claim to the bankruptcy court. Though the existing legal regulation is in favor of arbitration, it does not harmonize insolvency proceedings and arbitration in practice. The case law of Lithuanian courts reveals that this compatibility of different interests is very hard to reach and since the legislator has not properly addressed this issue, courts encounter difficulties in trying to solve what is essentially a regulation problem.

Application of the Directive on Restructuring and Insolvency and Dispute Settlement in Arbitration

The directive is primarily aimed at effective insolvency (restructuring proceedings). Though the term "effectiveness" is not defined in the directive, it makes various references to this goal. For instance, it establishes that viable enterprises and entrepreneurs that are in financial difficulties should have access to effective national preventive restructuring frameworks which enable them to continue operating.[29] This requirement of effective insolvency proceedings means that the national regulation, case law, and insolvency administration shall aim to achieve this goal. This is the first attempt in the European Union law to regulate certain material aspects of corporate restructuring proceeding, and it only regulates certain elements of insolvency proceedings which shall allow for increase effectiveness.

The directive does not regulate arbitration proceedings of insolvency companies. This is understandable since insolvency cases can be heard only in the state courts. Nevertheless, the question arises whether the commencement of insolvency proceedings would be compatible with the ongoing arbitration proceedings and what impact it should have on arbitration agreements under the directive. Also, does the regulation of the directive make any effect on validity of arbitration agreements? Though the insolvency proceedings regulated in the directive are also collective, it should be emphasized that they result in a different form of insolvency collectivism.[30] This is because according to the directive, the restructuring proceedings involve only the creditors affected by the restructuring plan. In other words, during restructuring proceedings, all debtor's creditors can be divided into two groups: creditors affected by the restructuring plan and creditors not affected by the restructuring plan. This is an important distinction which means that the creditors which are not affected by the restructuring plan will not be impacted by it and the debtor shall exercise all contractual obligations and all contracts remain in force, including arbitration agreements.

Since the directive establishes that insolvency proceedings shall be effective, the question arises whether this goal is compatible with arbitration proceedings of the debtor. Obviously, the term "court" in the directive refers only to the state court and not an arbitration. However, what impact has commencement of insolvency proceedings on validity of arbitration

29 Recital 1 of the Directive.
30 Recitals 43 and 44 of the Directive.

agreements? It seems that since no reference to the validity of arbitration agreement is made in the directive, the respective national laws should be applicable. Noteworthy, the directive give significant discretion to the Member States (the principle of subsidiary) and its implementation may vary in each state.

Another relevant issue for consideration is whether the notion of an essential contract also could encompass an arbitration agreement? Pursuant to Article 2(5) of the directive, an executory contract means a contract between a debtor and one or more creditors under which the parties still have obligations to perform at the time the stay of individual enforcement actions is granted or applied. The performance of executory contracts should be ensured by the national laws. According to Article 7(4) of the directive, Member States shall provide for rules preventing creditors to which the stay applies from withholding performance or terminating, accelerating or, in any other way, modifying essential executory contracts to the detriment of the debtor, for debts that came into existence prior to the stay, solely by virtue of the fact that they were not paid by the debtor. "Essential executory contracts" shall be understood to mean executory contracts which are necessary for the continuation of the day-to-day operations of the business, including contracts concerning supplies, the suspension of which would lead to the debtor's activities coming to a standstill.

Though the directive's aim of ensuring continuity in the performance of essential executory contracts in restructuring proceedings is economically reasonable, it may cause some difficulties. First, it may engender additional disputes between a debtor and creditors as to whether a certain contract is essential or not for day-to-day business. Second, a debtor may be willing to abuse their contractual rights and justify the non-performance of contractual obligations.[31] The question arises whether the rules on the treatment of essential executory contracts are applicable to arbitration agreements as well? It seems that since the directive deliberately avoids regulation of application of arbitration agreements in insolvency proceedings. However, an arbitration agreement according to its nature (agreement to settle a dispute in arbitration) does not fall under the notion of an executory contract since it would hardly be important to ensure continuation of the day-to-day operations of the business itself. Thus, an arbitration

---

31 Remigijus Jokubauskas, Marek Świerczyński, and Audronė Balsiukienė, A Stay of Individual Enforcement Actions as a Basis for Effective Restructuring Proceedings, International Comparative Jurisprudence, 7(1), 2021.

agreement itself should not be regarded as an executory contract under the directive.

Conclusions

The collective nature of insolvency proceedings is an essential aspect of these proceedings meaning that all creditors shall submit their claims in insolvency court and each creditor has the right to challenge the claims submitted by other creditors. However, if the dispute between a creditor and an insolvent company is heard before the arbitral tribunal, other creditors are deprived of this right. The analyzed national case-law shows that this problem is particularly relevant. Also, the authors found that this problem also raises the dilemma of the application of the right to a fair trial guaranteed by Article 6(1) of the Convention. Since other creditors are deprived on the challenge of the creditor's claim in the insolvent court according to the specific rules on insolvency proceedings, it is regarded as waiver of the right to a fair trial. However, pursuant to the case law of the ECHR, such waiver shall be unequivocal and clearly expressed. Since such waiver is not provided, it raises the question whether the right to other creditors to challenge claims in insolvency court is not disproportionally restricted.

It was also found that the national regulation of validity of an arbitration agreement in insolvency proceedings varies greatly between the countries. It is debatable, whether the general rules on treatment of contracts in insolvency proceedings are also applicable to the arbitration agreement or not. The international standards and legal doctrine do not address the treatment of arbitration agreements in insolvency proceedings. Since arbitration agreements are in essence contracts, the question arises, whether the same goals and rules on treatment of contracts should be applicable to the treatment of arbitration agreement? It seems that since an arbitration agreement is a contract, the rules on treatment of contracts in insolvency proceedings should also be applied, unless other rules are specified in the national law.

The regulation of arbitration and insolvency proceedings of the Republic of Lithuania is not harmonized. Though there is no indication in the LCA that insolvency disputes cannot be heard in arbitration courts, the national regulation fails to regulate how both proceedings should be compatible. The analysis of the case law of Lithuanian courts reveals that this compatibility of different interests is hard to reach and since the legislator has not properly addressed this issue, courts encounter difficult riddles as to how to solve regulation problem.

The directive establishes the general requirement for insolvency proceedings to be effective. However, there are no indications in the directive regarding the treatment of an arbitration agreement and the possibility to settle the dispute before the arbitral tribunal. Also, it seems that the rules on treatment of essential executory contracts are also not applicable to arbitration agreements.

COVID-19 and Arbitrability of Insolvency: Cross-Country Comparative Analysis in MENA Region

Amir Khalil
Assistant Professor at the Faculty of Law and Public Administration
amkhalil@birzeit.edu
Nawal Hend
Jindal Global University—Law School nawalhend@gmail.com
Mohammed Alqaisi
Assistant Professor at the Faculty of Law and Public Administration
mqaisi@birzeit.edu

Introduction

The outbreak of COVID-19[1] has caused severe economic recessions worldwide, leading to a market crash,[2] business shutdowns, oil wars,[3] cessation of international investment, and high unemployment and poverty rates. As a result, businesses have suffered from a high rate of insolvencies and bankruptcies, leading in its turn to a sharp increase of insolvency disputes.

Due to the novel COVID-19 recession, businesses have faced severe devitalization and insolvencies in developed economic countries, as well as in low- and middle-income countries (LMICs) in the Middle East and North Africa (MENA) Region. This substantial decline in domestic and international business has led to a rapid increase of insolvency disputes where most were left unadjudicated due to the following reasons:

(1) the non-arbitrability of insolvency per most MENA region arbitration legislations; and
(2) the dysfunction of judicial platforms due to continuous lockdowns.

---

1 World Health Organization, "An infectious disease caused by a newly discovered coronavirus." Health Topics, Coronavirus.
2 International Monetary Fund, World Economic Outlook Update, A Crisis Like No Other, an Uncertain Recovery, June 2020.
3 Russia and Saudi Arabia Oil War.

Arbitration was further implemented amid the COVID-19 crisis, where case pendency was witnessed before courts in most jurisdictions due to state emergency regulations and lockdowns. This led to suspension of the judicial adjudication process, issuance of verdicts, and most importantly enforceability of arbitral awards. Due to the accumulation and increase of insolvency disputes, most businesses opted for arbitration as per their contractual clauses and agreements, owing to the efficiency of arbitration as a commercial adjudication mechanism, and to the de facto judicial paralyzation. However, businesses in the MENA region were faced by further difficulties, other than pendency and physical restraints on judicial and arbitral platforms, when opting for arbitration. Some of the main difficulties manifested in delays and pendency of enforcing arbitral awards before judicial courts and non-arbitrability of insolvency in most jurisdictions due to its collision with states' territorial sovereignty and of public policy. This has caused a dilemma for businesses opting out of courts into arbitration during the COVID-19 pandemic.

Deriving from the judicial depletion of the adjudication systems and increase of insolvencies in the MENA region due to the COVID-19 recession, in addition to the non-arbitrability of insolvency, the eminent need in both advanced and LMICs[4] for a binding dispute resolution mechanism adequate for adjudicating and enforcing insolvency related disputes, has emerged.

This chapter examines the arbitrability of insolvency during the COVID-19 in the following MENA region jurisdictions: Palestine as a captive economic country, Egypt as a low- and middle-income country, and the United Arab Emirates as a flourishing international arbitration seat. This examination of the arbitrability of insolvency focuses on the validity of the arbitration agreement, parties' capacity to arbitrate their disputes, arbitrability of the subject matter in dispute, and subsequent recognition and enforcement of the awards by national courts. As an effort to propose adequate legislative amendments to domestic arbitration and insolvency legislations in the targeted jurisdictions, this takes an analytical and comparative approach in addressing the intersection between insolvency and arbitration under these jurisdictions, during COVID-19 recession.

---

4 LMICs: World Bank abbreviation for Low and Middle Income Countries.

An Overview of the Regulatory Framework Governing Arbitration and Insolvency in the Relevant Countries

Different MENA countries regulate arbitration as a dispute settlement mechanism in their domestic laws to establish the legal framework for arbitration as well as to guarantee the effectiveness of arbitration as an alternative dispute resolution method for commercial disputes. The following texts highlight the regulatory framework governing arbitration and insolvency in each of the relevant countries.

Palestine

Arbitration

The legal framework of arbitration in Palestine goes back to *Al-Majalla*,[5] the Ottoman Civil Code, where arbitration has been regulated in volume 16 titled "the Administration of Justice by the court," mainly in chapter 4 under Articles 1841-1851. Arbitration has been defined in Article 1790 as:

> arbitration consists of the parties to a contractual relationship in agreement to select a third party to settle the question at issue, called an arbitrator.

Moreover, *Al-Majalla* has addressed the arbitrability of subject matters under Article 1841 "actions relating to rights concerning property may be settled by arbitration."[6] Further, it addressed the appointment of the arbitral tribunal and its role,[7] the arbitral award,[8] and the arbitration award enforcement.[9] Later on, during the British Mandate rule over Palestine, several arbitration acts were enacted, mainly the Arbitration Act of 1926, the Foreign Arbitration Awards Act of 1930, and the arbitration procedure of 1935. In addition, during the Jordanian rule over the West Bank, the Foreign Arbitration Awards Act of 1952 and the Jordanian Arbitration Law

5 Al-Majallah al-Ahkam al-Adaliyyah (Aref Ramadan's Collection, the Ottoman Empire), Number (0) of 1876.
6 The Palestinian Court of Cassation held in Ramallah, Number 1177/2017, date Jan. 28, 2018.
7 Arts. 1843-1847 of Al-Majalla.
8 Art. 1842 of Al-Majalla.
9 Arts. 1848-1851 of Al-Majalla.

of 1953 have been in force until the establishment of the Palestinian Authority in 1993.

The promulgation of the Arbitration Act in 2000 was a milestone in providing a comprehensive legal framework for the arbitration process in Palestine.[10] This arbitration law is still applied in both the West Bank and the Gaza Strip. The current legal framework of commercial arbitration in Palestine is the Arbitration Law Number (3) of 2000,[11] and the Ministerial Council Decision Number (39) of 2004 regarding the implementation regulations of Arbitration Law Number (3) of 2003.[12] The arbitration law establishes the legal framework for commercial arbitration in Palestine,[13] and it regulates arbitration in 6 main chapters that are divided into 58 articles. Chapter 1 merely provides definitions and general provisions of the law, where the arbitration is defined as a:

> means for dispute settlement between the parties to the dispute by presenting the issue in conflict before an arbitration panel to make a decision thereon.

Moreover, the law specifies the competent courts, depending on the type of arbitration. For instance, in cases of local arbitration the competent court is the court that is originally authorized to review the dispute submitted to the arbitration panel, and in cases of an international arbitration taking place in Palestine, the competent court shall be the first instance court within the geographic limits this court is entitled to cover. In case of foreign arbitration, the competent court in registration and implementation of the decisions of arbitration shall be the first instance court in Jerusalem, or in temporary premises: Gaza.

Moreover, the Arbitration Law under Article 2 clarifies the legal capacity of arbitration where it stipulates that:

> without jeopardizing the provisions of Article 4 of this law, the provisions of this law shall apply in arbitration between natural or

---

10 Palestinian Arbitration Law Number (3) of 2000, published under the *Palestinian Official Gazette*, Number 33, June 30, 2000.

11 *Ibid.*

12 Ministerial Council Decision Number (39) of 2004 regarding the implementation regulations of Arbitration Law Number (3) of 2003, published under the *Palestinian Official Gazette*, Number 50, Aug. 29, 2004.

13 Lubna Katbeh and Jenan Qados, An Assessment of Alternative Dispute Resolution Mechanisms in Palestine, working paper developed by Equity Legal Group with the support of the UNDP, UN Women and UNICEF Joint Programme (Sawasya II: Promoting Rule of Law in the State of Palestine), 2019, p. 7.

> legal persons who enjoy legal capacity to hold rights regardless of the nature of the legal relation subject of the conflict … ..

In addition, the arbitration law specifies arbitration types and differentiates between local, international, foreign arbitration, ad hoc and institutional arbitration as per Article 3. In Article 4, the arbitration law indicates subject matters that are non-arbitrable, mainly, issues related to public order in Palestine, issues that cannot be solved by conciliation by law, and disputes related to personal status. Chapter 2 tackles the arbitration agreement, where it specifies the arbitration clause and the scope of arbitration. Article 5 defines the arbitration agreement which is:

> an agreement between two or more parties stipulating for referral of all or some of the conflicts that emanated or may emanated from a specific legal relation whether contractual or not contractual.[14]

It further stipulates that the arbitration agreement shall be in writing[15] whether it is a form of arbitration clause in a contract between the parties or in a separate agreement. Furthermore, the arbitration agreement may not be revised without the approval of the parties or by the competent court.[16] Moreover, Article 5.4 refers to the submission agreement in case an agreement is made pursuant to the emergence of the conflict, and therefore it must include the issue of the conflict or it would be void. Article 5.5 refers to the principle of separability of the arbitration clause where it states, "the arbitration clause shall not be void upon breach, annulment or termination of the contract." Article 6 of the arbitration law clarifies that the arbitration agreement shall not end with the death of any of the arbitration agreement parties unless the dispute is related to the person of the deceased party. Further, the Palestinian legislature under Article 7 has clarified the matter of the substantive claim before the court by one of the arbitration agreement parties. Chapter 3 regulates the arbitration panel and it describes the composition of the arbitral tribunal,[17] the condition of arbitrator,[18] the institutional arbitration,[19] the role of the competent court

---

14 Art. 5.1 of the Palestinian Arbitration Law.
15 Art. 5.2 of the Palestinian Arbitration Law.
16 Art. 5.6 of the Palestinian Arbitration Law.
17 Art. 8 of the Palestinian Arbitration Law.
18 Art. 9 of the Palestinian Arbitration Law.
19 Art. 10 of the Palestinian Arbitration Law.

in appointing the arbitral tribunal,[20] arbitrator's acceptance of his appointment,[21] grounds for arbitrator and arbitral procedures' challenge,[22] competence of arbitral tribunal,[23] and determination of rules of procedure.[24] Chapter 4 details the arbitration procedures in Articles 20 to 34. It should be noted that these procedures are based on the United Nations Commission on International Trade Law (UNCITRAL) Model Law on International Commercial Arbitration of 1985 and its amendment of 2006.[25] Lastly, Chapter 5 regulates the arbitral award and the annulment of arbitration awards, as well as the recognition and enforcement of arbitral awards in Articles 35 to 53.

Insolvency

Insolvency and bankruptcy disputes in Palestine are regulated by several pieces of legislation. In south of the Palestine mainly in Gaza Strip the Bankruptcy Ordinance, 1936[26] and the amending Bankruptcy Ordinance, 1942[27] regulate such matters. However, the mentioned legislations have been annulled in the North of Palestine, namely; the West Bank by the issuance of trade law[28] by the Jordanian Parliament in 1966, during the rule of Jordan over the West Bank. The trade law regulates insolvency issues under Chapter 5 as a main part regulating commercial transactions, contracts, and merchants.

---

20 Art. 11 of the Palestinian Arbitration Law.
21 Art. 12 of the Palestinian Arbitration Law.
22 Arts. 13,14, and 15 of the Palestinian Arbitration Law.
23 Art. 16 of the Palestinian Arbitration Law.
24 Arts. 18 and 19 of the Palestinian Arbitration Law.
25 United Nations Commission on International Trade Law (UNCITRAL) Model Law on International Commercial Arbitration of 1985, its amendment of 2006. Available online at UNCITRAL Model Law on International Commercial Arbitration 1985, with amendments as adopted in 2006, access on May 27, 2021.
26 Bankruptcy Ordinance of 1936, *Palestine Gazette* (British Mandate), Issue Number 566, Jan. 24, 1936.
27 Bankruptcy Ordinance of 1942, *Palestine Gazette* (British Mandate), Issue Number 1168, Feb. 13, 1942.
28 Trade Law (Number 12) of 1966, *Jordan Gazette* (Jordanian Rule), Issue Number 1910, March 30, 1966.

Egypt

Arbitration

Arbitration in Egypt has become an increasingly important means for settling investment and commercial disputes. The current legal framework of arbitration in Egypt is the Egyptian Arbitration Act in Civil and Commercial Matters (Arbitration Law) Number (27) of 1994[29] and its amendments of 1997[30] and 2000,[31] which has been enacted based on the UNCITRAL Model Law on International Commercial Arbitration of 1985.[32] This law provides a comprehensive and overarching framework for the arbitration process and procedures in Egypt, where it regulates arbitration as an alternative dispute resolution mechanism. The current arbitration law lays down the procedural rules that govern the arbitration process in 7 main chapters that are divided into 58 articles. Chapter 1 provides general provisions where it applies upon domestic, public and private arbitration, or international arbitration where the Egyptian laws are the substantive governing laws as *lex arbitri*. Moreover, Article 2 clarifies the nature of arbitral commercial disputes arising out of contractual or non-contractual relationships within the scope. Article 3 differentiates between arbitration types and Article 4 provides definitions of some terms. Article 4.1 defines the term arbitration as:

> voluntary arbitration agreed upon by the parties of the dispute according to their free will, whether or not the chosen body to which the arbitral procedures are entrusted by agreement of the parties is a permanent arbitral organization or center.

Further, Article 5 allows the arbitration parties to select the arbitration procedures, and Article 6 provides the parties the possibility to subject their legal relationship to the provisions of standard contract, or international convention or any other document. Moreover, the law specifies the competent courts per Article 9, where the competence to review the arbitral

---

29 Egyptian Arbitration Act in Civil and Commercial Matters Number (27) of 1994, published under the *Egyptian Official Gazette*, Number 16, April 21, 1994.

30 Law Number 9 of 1997 (Amending Some Provisions of the Arbitration Law), published under the *Egyptian Official Gazette*, Number 20, May 15, 1997.

31 Law Number 8 of 2000 (Amending Some Provisions of the Arbitration Law), published under the *Egyptian Official Gazette*, Number 13, April 4, 2000.

32 UNCITRAL Model Law on International Commercial Arbitration, U.N. Doc. A/40/17, Annex I (June 21, 1985), as amended (July 7, 2006).

subject matters referred to by this Law to the Egyptian judiciary, lies with the court having original jurisdiction over the dispute. However, in the case of international commercial arbitration, whether conducted in Egypt or abroad, competence lies with the Appellate Court of Cairo unless the parties jointly agree to refer it to another appellate court in Egypt."

Chapter 2 tackles the arbitration agreement, where Article 10 (1) states:

> the arbitration agreement is an agreement by which the two parties agree to submit to arbitration in order to resolve all or certain disputes which have arisen or which may arise between them in connection with a defined legal relationship, whether contractual or not.

Article 12 stipulates that the arbitration agreement must be in writing. Article 11 indicates that the legal capacity to arbitrate should be concluded merely by natural or legal persons having the capacity to dispose of their rights. Moreover, the underlined article stipulates subject matters which are non-arbitrable such as matters that cannot be subject to compromise or cannot be solved by conciliation. Further, Article 13 clarifies the matter of the substantive claim before the court by one of the arbitration agreement parties concerning a disputed matter that is subject to an arbitration agreement. Article 14 allows the arbitral tribunal to issue interim or conservatory decisions.

Chapter 3 regulates the composition of arbitral tribunals as per a joint agreement between the parties of one arbitrator or more.[33] The acceptance of an arbitrator[34] appointment should be in writing, in addition, an arbitrator has the duty to disclose any circumstances or facts in which are likely to cast doubts on his or her independence or impartiality.[35] Furthermore, grounds for arbitrators' arbitral procedures challenge[36] the role of the competent court in appointing the arbitral tribunal,[37] the termination of the arbitral tribunal mandate,[38] competence of the arbitral tribunal,[39] the principle of separability of the arbitration clause,[40] and the power of an arbitral tribunal to order interim or conservatory measures.[41] Chapter 4

33 Art. 15 of the Egyptian Arbitration Law.
34 Art. 16 (1,2) of the Egyptian Arbitration Law.
35 Art. 16 (3) of the Egyptian Arbitration Law.
36 Arts. 18 and 19 of the Egyptian Arbitration Law.
37 Arts. 17 and 20 of the Egyptian Arbitration Law.
38 Art. 21 of the Egyptian Arbitration Law.
39 Art. 22 of the Egyptian Arbitration Law.
40 Art. 23 of the Egyptian Arbitration Law.
41 Art. 24 of the Egyptian Arbitration Law.

details the arbitration procedures under articles 25 to 38 that are based on the UNCITRAL Model Arbitration Rules, such as the parties' capacity to determine the governing procedural rules,[42] equal treatment of the parties in arbitration,[43] the commencement of arbitration,[44] the seat of arbitration, the arbitration language, and hearing of witnesses.[45] Chapter 5 regulates the arbitral award and the closure of the arbitration procedures in Articles 39 to 51. Lastly, Chapter 6 regulates the annulment of arbitration awards in Articles 52 to 54. Chapter 7 regulates the recognition and enforcement of arbitral awards in Articles 55 to 58.

Insolvency

The Egyptian Commercial Law Number 17 of 1999[46] has previously regulated bankruptcy procedures and preventive reconciliation under Chapter 5. This law has been abrogated and replaced by the Bankruptcy Law Number 11 2018.[47] The new legislation has dealt with bankruptcy procedures and preventive reconciliation besides restructuring of companies.

United Arab Emirates (UAE)

Arbitration

Arbitration has become a wide-spread method of dispute resolution in the UAE, and in 2018, UAE has introduced the first standalone law on arbitration which is the Federal Arbitration Law Number (6) of 2018[48] which has been enacted based on the UNCITRAL Model Law on International Commercial Arbitration of 1985. This law repealed the previous and non-comprehensive chapter on arbitration in the Civil Procedures Law under Articles 203 to 218 of the UAE Federal Law Number (11) of 1992. The UAE arbitration law provides an overarching framework for the

42 Art. 25 of the Egyptian Arbitration Law.
43 Art. 26 of the Egyptian Arbitration Law.
44 Art. 27 of the Egyptian Arbitration Law.
45 Arts. 28, 29, and 33 of the Egyptian Arbitration Law.
46 Egyptian Commercial Code Number 17/1999, Egyptian Official Gazette, Issue Number (119), May 17, 1999.
47 Egyptian Insolvency Law Number 11/2018, Egyptian Official Gazette, Issue Number 7 (d), Feb. 17, 2018.
48 UAE Arbitration Law Number (6) of 2018, published under the UAE Official Gazette, Number 630, May 15, 2018.

arbitration process and procedures to facilitate the recognition and enforcement of foreign arbitral awards. The current legislation enacted 61 Articles regulated in main 6 chapters. Chapter 1 provides definitions and scope of application, where arbitration is defined as "a regulated procedure by law in which a dispute between one or more parties is submitted, by agreement of the parties, to an arbitral tribunal which makes a binding decision on the dispute."[49] As well, the arbitration agreement is an agreement between parties to submit to arbitration, made prior or after a dispute has arisen. The law has specified the competent court, which is the federal or local court of appeals agreed upon by the parties or in the jurisdiction where the arbitral procedures have taken place. Under Article 2, the law regulates the scope of application of the Arbitration Law upon all arbitrations conducted in the UAE unless the parties agree on the application of a different arbitration law, provided that such law does not contravene with the public order of the UAE. Furthermore, the law shall apply to any commercial arbitration conducted abroad where the parties have agreed to submit the arbitration to this law.[50] Moreover; the law clarifies the international character of arbitration, where the law applies to both domestic and international arbitral proceedings. Article 3 adopts an extraterritorial approach, where arbitration is deemed an international event if it is conducted within the UAE conditioned as per some requirements. Chapter 2 regulates the arbitration agreement, the legal capacity to arbitrate (Article 4), and non-arbitrability of subject matters due to its incapability of settlement by conciliation (Article 4.2). Further, the law regulates the arbitration forms (Article 5), the doctrine of severability (Article 6), and Article 7 requires the arbitration agreement to be in writing. Article 8 clarifies the matter of the substantive claim before the court by one of the arbitration agreement parties, where the court shall dismiss any action that falls within the scope of an arbitration agreement between the parties. Chapter 3 describes the composition of an arbitral tribunal (Article 9), appointment and the general condition of arbitrators (Articles 10 and 11), grounds for challenging arbitrators and the challenge procedure (Articles 14 and 15), the termination of the arbitral tribunal mandate and appointment of substitute arbitrator (Articles 16 and 17), the court jurisdiction to consider arbitral measures (Article 18), competence of arbitral tribunal (Articles 19 and 20), interim or conservatory measures (Article 21). Chapter 4 details the arbitration procedures in Articles 22 to 36. Chapter 5

49 Art. 1 of the UAE Arbitration Law.
50 Art. 2 of the UAE Arbitration Law.

regulates the arbitral award, the annulment and recognition and enforcement of arbitral awards (Articles 37–57). Chapter 6 includes final provisions (Articles 58–60).

Insolvency

The UAE has issued a law to regulate insolvency disputes, the federal decree Number (9) for 2016 has provided and regulated mechanisms seeking to avoid bankruptcy cases and the liquidation of debtors' assets, including consensual out-of-court financial restructuring, composition procedures, financial restructuring and the potential to secure new loans under terms set by the law.[51] This law is applicable on any company established under the Federal commercial company law Number (2) 2015. The companies include companies in which were not established under the commercial law, semi or fully owned companies by the federal or the local government with legislatives for establishment that fall under this law, companies and institutions established in free zones and which do not have provisions to regulate composition procedures or restructuring bankruptcy according to the Federal law Number (8) of 2004 concerning financial free zones, any trade or civil licensed companies.[52] However, the law Number (18) 1993 is applicable on merchants. This law has dealt with individual insolvency cases under chapter 5 of the law.

Arbitrability of Insolvency Related Issues

Palestine

Insolvency as a subject matter in Palestine has been deemed non-arbitrable,[53] due to its characterization as a violation of public policy. This has been the position of the Palestinian legislator and judicial authorities since the issuance of *Al-Majalla* until the issuance of the Palestinian Arbitration Law Number (3) of 2000.

51 For further details, *see* https://www.mof.gov.ae/en/lawsandpolitics/financial-banking-sector/bankruptcy/pages/federalbankruptcy.aspx.

52 *Ibid.*

53 Yousef Shendi, Domestic and International Arbitration under the Palestinian Arbitration Act Number (3) of 2000: A Comparative Study, Birzeit University, Palestine, 2014.

Arbitrability of the Subject Matter

The arbitrability of insolvency has not been regulated directly within the Palestinian Arbitration Law, or the Commercial Law Number (12) of 1966 or in case law. Moreover, the Palestinian Arbitration law Number (3) of 2000 has specified clearly under Article 4 the non-arbitrable subject matters where it states, "the provisions of this law shall not apply to the following matters: 1. Issues related to public order in Palestine. 2. Issues that cannot be solved by conciliation by law. 3. Disputes related to personal status." Moreover, Article 2 of the Ministerial Council Decision Number (39) of 2004 regarding the regulations' implementation of Arbitration Law Number (3) of 2003 has clarified the matters that are non-arbitrable such as penalties and disputes related to nationality and personal status matters such as divorce, inheritance. However, this article provides that financial claims arising out of personal status disputes can be arbitrable upon the consent of parties.

Article 43 of the arbitration law provides grounds of annulment of arbitral awards in cases of violation of public policies in Palestine, where parties are granted the right to appeal the final arbitral award before the competent court. As well, Article 48 of the arbitration law refers to cases where the competent court upon its own consideration can refuse to enforce a foreign arbitral award if it violates the public order in Palestine.[54] Furthermore, the Palestinian Execution Law Number 23 of 2005[55] in Articles 36 and 37 provides grounds for enforcement of foreign arbitral awards in Palestine, in case they do not contradict with the Palestinian laws or the supreme national interest.[56] Article 37 stipulates the conditions of execution of foreign judgments in Palestine where they should not include any contraventions of the public order and morals in Palestine.[57] Moreover, Article 38 refers to the enforcement of arbitral awards in Palestine in the condition that the arbitral award has been awarded in arbitrable matters according to the Palestinian laws.

---

54 Mohammad Adeb Abu Shehab, An Analysis of the Enforcement of Foreign Arbitration Awards in Palestine: Realities, Drawbacks, and Prospects, in the Arab Law Quarterly 36, p. 5, 2020.

55 Palestinian Execution Law Number 23 of 2005, published under the Palestinian Official Gazette, Number 63, April 27, 2006.

56 Art. 36(1) of the Palestinian Execution Law Number 23 of 2005. Ramallah Court of Appeal, Number 891/2018, date Nov. 29, 2018. The Palestinian Court of Cassation held in Ramallah, Number 302/2016, date Dec. 21, 2016.

57 Art. 37(2) of the Palestinian Execution Law Number 23 of 2005.

Therefore, it is clear that Palestinian legislator has followed the international trend to limit the scope of arbitrability on the basis of public policy considerations.[58] Overall, matters and issues under provisions or statute that are of public policy nature cannot be arbitrable within the Jurisdiction of Palestine.

Arbitration Agreement Validity

The Palestinian Arbitration Law has been silent regarding the validity of arbitration agreement in insolvency disputes and therefore the arbitrability of insolvency matters have not been considered in the arbitration law. The Commercial Law Number 12 of 1966 has also stayed silent on this regard. However, the arbitration law states that an arbitration agreement will be deemed valid if it is in writing[59] and entered into by natural or legal persons who enjoy legal capacity to hold rights regardless of the nature of the legal relation subject to the conflict,[60] without jeopardizing the provisions of Article 4 of this law. Therefore, insolvency related matters are considered as non-arbitrable in the Palestinian jurisdiction as they involve sensitive public policy matters that cannot be settled by arbitration, and such matters fall under the exclusive jurisdiction of national courts.

Effects of Insolvency on Arbitration Procedures

In the Palestinian jurisdiction, the insolvency regime applies following a filing for insolvency either by the insolvent[61] or by the creditors[62] and after a declaration by a domestic court. The court declaring the insolvency might impose conservatory measures to safeguard the insolvent's assets that affect its creditors.[63] Therefore, according to the Palestinian commercial law, the insolvent loses the competence to manage his assets including selling or transfer any of his property, or to be entitled to make any payment or receipt,[64] and a court-appointed manager chosen by the court must

58 The Palestinian Court of Cassation held in Ramallah, Number 1177/2017, date 28/1/2018. Ramallah Court of Appeal, Number 238/2017, May 3, 2017.
59 Art. 5(2) of the Palestinian Arbitration Law.
60 Art. 2 of the Palestinian Arbitration Law.
61 Art. 318 of the Trade Law (Number 12 of 1966). Ramallah Court of Appeal, Number 928/2017, date Dec. 31, 2017.
62 Art. 319 of the Trade Law (Number 12 of 1966).
63 Art. 320 of the Trade Law (Number 12 of 1966).
64 Art. 327(2) of the Trade Law (Number 12 of 1966).

manage the insolvency assets.[65] Thus, the party's insolvency will affect its legal rights and its existing and future legal relationships including all arbitral procedures.

Effects of an Insolvency on the Parties' Capacity to Arbitrate

As it has been mentioned before, the Palestinian Arbitration Law under Article 2 defines the legal capacity to arbitrate where the natural and legal persons who enjoy legal capacity can enter into arbitration agreement. Therefore, it is clear that the arbitration law allows any person capable of entering into contracts to opt for arbitration as per their contractual relationships. However, when an insolvency is declared by the competent court the parties lose their ability to arbitrate their disputes.

Effects of an Insolvency on the Recognition and Enforcement of Arbitral Awards

The Palestinian arbitration law does not regulate the effects of insolvency on the recognition and enforcement of arbitral awards, however, it should be stated that the arbitration law under Article 43 provides grounds for the annulment of arbitral awards by the competent court in case of violation of public order. Article 43 stipulates that:

> the arbitration parties shall have the right to appeal against the arbitration award before the competent court for any of the following reasons: in case of violation of the public order in Palestine.

Therefore, arbitral awards of insolvency disputes are deemed void and in violation of the public order in Palestine.

Moreover, the competent courts may refuse to enforce foreign arbitral awards in case of violation of the public order in Palestine; this has been clearly stipulated under Article 48 of the Palestinian arbitration law. Furthermore, Article 37 of the Palestinian Execution Law Number (23) of 2005 provides general conditions where arbitral awards can be enforced in Palestine where it should not violate the public order in Palestine.

---

65 Arts.327(1) and 338 of the Trade Law (Number 12 of 1966).

Egypt

The non-arbitrability of public policy matters in Egypt has heavily manifested itself in the status quo non-arbitrability of insolvency. Due to this issue, an amendment of the commercial code Number 17/1999 manifested in the tailoring of Article 644[66] took place. It is worth mentioning that the underlined article was further reinforced with the issuance of the Insolvency Law Number 11/2018[67] under Article 162. Article 162 of the Insolvency Law has deemed insolvency as a subject matter arbitrable conditioned upon the approval of the competent authority and conduct of judicial hearing. However, the pre-mentioned amendment provides a mere technicality for the commencement of arbitral procedure on a non-arbitrable subject matter as an exception and not as a general rule. Thus, insolvency is still characterized in the Egyptian jurisdiction as non-arbitrable. This has led to a low percentage of insolvency disputes arbitrations. The Doing Business Report of 2020 indicates that the average time for the resolution of an insolvency dispute in Egypt is approximately 2.5 years.[68]

Arbitrability of the Subject Matter

In 1994, Egypt legislated its first arbitration law where it incorporates the UNCITRAL Model law provisions, with some differences represented in the scope and domain of arbitrable subject matters.[69] Businesses in Egypt had long suffered from the de facto consequences[70] of the judicial broad

66 Egyptian Commercial Code Number 17/1999, Art. 644: "If the dispute is one of an unspecified value or its value exceeds five thousand pounds, then the commencement or acceptance of arbitration shall not be effective until after the bankruptcy judge ratifies its terms, and the bankrupt is called to appear at the certification and the bankruptcy judge hears his statements in case of his attendance, which his objection shall have no effect. The bankruptcy judge's decision may be appealed before the court if it was issued rejecting the ratification of the composition or arbitration terms."

67 Egyptian Law Number 11/2018 regarding the regulation of restructuring and bankruptcy settlement.

68 World Bank, Doing Business Report (2020).

69 Administrative contracts were inarbitrable as part of the public policy of the country. Egypt: A New Law on Arbitration, 10 Arab Law Quarterly 31-33 (1995).

70 Ibrahim Shehata, The Ministerial Approval Requirement for Arbitration Agreements in Egypt: Revisiting the Public Policy Debate, Journal of International Arbitration, https://shehatalaw.com/wp-content/uploads/2020/06/Shehata-and-Partners-The-Ministerial-Approval-Requirement-for-Arbitration-Agreements-in-Egypt-Revisiting-the-Public-Policy-Debate.pdf.

interpretation of Article 58 of the Arbitration Law Number 27/1994,[71] where it deems all subject matters in violation of public policy as non-arbitrable, including insolvency disputes.

Due to this issue, the Egyptian legislator had to tailor Article 644 of the Commercial Code Number 17/1999, manifesting later with the issuance of the Insolvency Law Number 11/2018 under Article 162, where it deems insolvency as a subject matter arbitrable conditioned upon the approval of the competent minister and upholding of judicial hearing. This complicated adjudication system of referring insolvency disputes to arbitral tribunals has become a persistent issue upon the high increase rates of businesses' insolvencies in Egypt, especially during COVID-19 recession.[72]

This is the status quo of insolvency arbitrability in Egypt.[73] However, before the issuance of Article 644 of the Commercial Code Number 17/1999, and Article 162 of the Insolvency Law,[74] where it states:

> The insolvency Judge may authorize the bankruptcy trustee with conciliation or arbitration concerning any dispute relating to bankruptcy after consulting with the insolvent and his trustee. If the dispute cannot be quantified, or its sum value exceeds EGP 20,000, then conciliation or acceptance of arbitration cannot come into force without the approval of the insolvency Judge.[75]

Insolvency as an absolute rule was inarbitrable.

Arbitration Agreement Validity

To determine the validity of an arbitration agreement or clause framing insolvency as a subject matter falls into three scenarios or types within the Egyptian jurisdiction: an arbitration agreement or clause entered by an

---

71 The Egyptian Arbitration Law Number 27/1994, Art. 58: "The application to obtain leave for enforcement of the arbitral award according to this Law shall not be granted except after having ascertained the following: a) That it does not contradict a judgment previously rendered by the Egyptian Courts on the subject matter in dispute; b) That it does not violate the public policy in the Arab Republic of Egypt; and c) That it was properly notified to the party against whom it was rendered."

72 R., M. Elsaman, "A Legal Perspective on Covid-19 in Egypt: The Impact on Civil and Administrative Contracts," Transnational Dispute Management Journal, June 30, 2020.

73 Insolvency Law Number 11/2018.

74 *Ibid*, Art. 162.

75 International Bar Association Arbitration Committee, IBA Toolkit on Insolvency and Arbitration Ibanet.org (2021), https://www.ibanet.org/MediaHandler?id=087B4D4A-B82E-4FAC-817F-64EE50091D66.

insolvent post the declaration of its insolvency, this type is deemed invalid, due to the loss of eligibility to manage his assets as a rule.[76] Second, an arbitration agreement or clause entered by an insolvent pre the deceleration and mistrust period, this type is deemed valid based on Article 588 where it conditioned the ineligibility of an insolvent to manage his own assets or a third-party assets on the mere declaration of his insolvency, and not the insolvency itself.[77] Lastly, arbitration agreements conducted pre-declaration of insolvency but during the mistrust period, this type is dependent upon the discretion of the bankruptcy secretary in Egypt.

Regardless of arbitral agreements validity, the legal effects of those agreements and clauses are mostly affected by the declaration of insolvency. Therefore, if an arbitration clause is enacted within a contract, which was conducted during the period of mistrust, the arbitration clause or the agreement's validity is most likely to be affected if not deemed invalid under the jurisdiction of Egyptian courts. This validity of an arbitration clause or agreement conducted prior to the insolvency declaration but during the mistrust period is determined by the competent authority in Egypt; the insolvent secretary. Therefore, if an arbitration agreement were conducted between two parties prior the issuance of the Insolvency Law Number 11/2018,[78] and prior to the issuance of the Commercial Code Number 17/1999 framing the adjudication of an insolvency dispute before an arbitral tribunal; it would have been deemed invalid under regardless of the insolvency declaration, due to its absolute non-arbitrability and violation of public policy.

Effect of Insolvency on Arbitration Procedures

Arbitration procedures in jurisdictions where insolvency as a subject matter is arbitrable whether as a general rule or exception are affected by the regulation of insolvency as a subject matter under insolvency, commercial, or even civil legislations. In Egypt, an insolvent whose insolvency has been officially declared as per the Commercial law Number 17/1999 loses the competence to manage his assets, including participating in an adjudication procedure where his assets are the ground of execution. Therefore, his eligibility to enter arbitral agreements regarding a dispute deriving from his insolvency or in relation to his assets, or the mere act of enforcing

76 Art. 588 (2), the Commercial Law Number 17/1999.
77 *Ibid.*
78 Insolvency Law Number 11/2018 and amendment of the Commercial Code Number 17/1999.

an arbitral award on his assets has been deemed invalid, and in violation with Article 588 (a) of the Commercial Law Number 17/1999.[79]

The filing of a dispute is the first affected procedure due to insolvency as Article 162 of the Insolvency Law Number 11/2018, where it states that arbitral procedures cannot be commenced if the insolvency dispute values to more than EGP 20,000 or is deemed invaluable before arbitral forums without obtaining ratification from the competent authority, or it shall be deemed void and invalid. This ratification or grant of arbitration approval must occur through a court hearing before the Bankruptcy judge according to Article 644 of the Commercial Code Number 17/1999, and (162) of the Insolvency Law Number 11/2018, and any objections from an insolvent during those hearings hold no legal value.[80] Arbitration procedures might also be affected in case of issuance of an insolvency declaration through a judicial forum in accordance with Articles 560 and 561 of the Commercial Law Number 17/1999 where all commenced arbitral proceedings shall be suspended.

Effects of an Insolvency on the Parties' Capacity to Arbitrate

Before the issuance of the Insolvency Law Number 11/2018 and amendment of Article 644 of the Commercial Law Number 17/1999, when an insolvency has been declared both parties by default lost their capacity to arbitrate their disputes.

This, however, has changed per Insolvency Law Number 11/2018 under Article 162 and the amendment of the Article 644 of the Commercial Code Number 17/1999 as parties to an insolvency dispute can opt for arbitration if the stipulated conditions are fulfilled. Article 162 of the Insolvency Law Number 11/2018 states that if the dispute values to more than EGP 20,000 or its sum value is not determined, then parties cannot opt for arbitration unless they have submitted their dispute before the competent authorities and the insolvent party has appeared before the Bankruptcy Judge.

It is worth mentioning, that the insolvent loses his capacity to commence or proceed any arbitral procedures, when the deceleration of insolvency has been issued in accordance with Article 162 of the Insolvency

79 Art. 588 (a), Commercial Law Number 17/1999.
80 Art. 644, Art. 162, Commercial Law Number 17/1999.

Law Number 11/2018, and Article 573 (1)[81] of the Commercial Law Number 17/1999, this competence gets transferred to the insolvency secretary who has been appointed by the judge.

The arbitral proceedings must be suspended when the parties declare insolvency as per Article 560 of the Commercial Procedures Number 17/1999, which leads to the parties' incapability to arbitrate their disputes, unless they meet the stipulated requirements of Article 162 of the Insolvency Law Number 11//2018, only then they shall acquire their capacity to arbitrate the insolvency dispute once again.

Effects of Insolvency on the Recognition and Enforcement of Arbitral Awards

Before the amendment of the Insolvency Law Number 11/2018 and amendment of the Commercial Code Number 17/1999, insolvency as a subject matter was deemed non-arbitrable due to its violation of Public Policy. Thus, Article 53 of the Egyptian Arbitration Law Number 9/1997 explicitly stipulates that an arbitral award adjudicating a subject matter which is in violation of public policy shall be admissible as a ground for annulment; this is an adaptation of Article 5 of the New York Convention.[82]

Moreover, Article 53 (2) of the Egyptian Arbitration Law Number 9/1997[83] explicitly stipulates that an arbitral award shall not be enforced in the jurisdiction of Egypt unless the competent judicial authorities have verified that the arbitral award has not adjudicated a non-arbitrable subject matter. Thus, during the pre-insolvency Law Number 11/2018 era an arbitral award in which has adjudicated an insolvency dispute shall be deemed non-enforceable by the competent authorities. Consequently, if an arbitral award adjudicating insolvency as a subject matter was issued during the time frame of the Commercial Code Number 17/1999 and Insolvency Law Number 11/2018, then it would be deemed valid in case of its satisfaction of the conditions as per Article 162 of the Insolvency Law and Article 644 of the Commercial Code Number 17/1999.

---

81 Egyptian Commercial Code Number 17/1999, Art. 573(1): "The bankruptcy trustee manages and preserves the bankruptcy funds and acts on behalf of the bankrupt in all cases and all actions required by this agency."

82 Convention on the Recognition and Enforcement of Foreign Arbitral Awards Done at New York, June 10, 1958; entered into force, June 7, 1959 United Nations, Treaty Series, vol. 330, p. 38, Number 4739 (1959).

83 Egyptian Arbitration Law Number 9/1997, Art. 53(2).

Article 560 of the Commercial Code Number 17/1999 regulates situations where an insolvency declaration is issued post or at the time of the issuance of a final arbitral award, or an interim arbitral decision. The underlined article states that an arbitral award shall be suspended in case an insolvency declaration is issued. However, this rule is merely applicable to situations where the insolvent opposes the arbitral procedures before the declaration of his insolvency from a national judicial forum and does not apply in situations where the insolvent has by consent adjudicated his disputes through arbitration and then a judicial verdict was issued regarding or in relation to the arbitral procedures scope without his challenge, in the latter case, the arbitral award shall be enforced even if a judicial decision was issued contrary to the arbitral award, and regardless of his latter declaration of his insolvency by a national judicial forum. This rule was set by the High Supreme Court of Egypt in Case Number 8/22.[84]

United Arab Emirates

Arbitrability in the United Arab Emirates (UAE) is defined similarly to most MENA region countries, as subject matters related to public policy are considered non-arbitrable. Public Policy has been defined by the Federal Law of Civil Transactions Number 5 of 1985[85] and its 2020 amendment[86] under Article 3 as:

> Public policy shall be deemed to include matters relating to personal status such as marriage, inheritance, and lineage, and matters relating to systems of government, freedom of trade, circulation of wealth, rules of individual ownership and the other rules and foundations upon which society is based, in such a manner as to not conflict with the definitive provisions and fundamental principles of Islamic Shari'a.

This has been read to include insolvency.

---

84 The Egyptian High Supreme Court, Case Number 8 /22. In this precedent, it was ruled by the supreme court of Egypt that in case an arbitral award issued by the consent of parties—both the insolvent and opposing party—contradictory to a judicial verdict or judgment regarding the same scope of dispute, the prior shall possess the entitlement of enforcement and not the latter. Egyptian High Supreme Court, Judicial year of 22, Hearing of Aug. 4, 2001.

85 Civil Transactions Law of the United Arab Emirates State Number 5/1985, UAE Gazette, Dec. 15, 1985.

86 Federal Decree-Law Number 30, *UAE Gazette*, Sep. 27, 2020.

Arbitrability of the Subject Matter

The Federal Arbitration Law of UAE Number 6/2018 has abstained from providing any direct framework for insolvency as a subject matter. However, Articles 2(1) and 37(2) of the Federal Arbitration Law Number 6/2018 states that if the subject matter of an arbitration is in violation of the public policy, then the arbitral clause or agreement shall be invalid. In addition, as per the Insolvency Law Number 3/1936 and its federal amendment Number 9 (2016),[87] insolvency has been deemed a public policy subject matter in the UAE.

However, the position of UAE Arbitration Law Number 6/2018 under Article 37(2) is not absolute. Article 747 of the Federal Commercial Law Number 18/1993[88] provided a limited ground for the arbitrability of insolvency in the UAE. It stipulates that the legal trustee of an insolvent is eligible to commence arbitration on behalf of the Insolvent, if the authorities' approval has been obtained.[89] This legal position has been further reinforced as per Article 53(2) of the Federal Insolvency Law Number 3/1936,[90] where it further underlines Article 747 of the Commercial Law Number 18/1993 regarding the arbitrability of insolvency by the legal trustee of the insolvent in the UAE.

The arbitrability of insolvency has been complicated as per the stipulated conditions of the arbitrability of insolvency under Articles 747 and 53 of the Insolvency and Commercial Federal Codes from the obligation to obtain the bankruptcy judge's approval to the obligation of conducting a judicial hearing for the insolvent. This process has been further complicated with the implementation of Article 203 of the Civil Procedures Law (Federal Law Number 11 of 1992). Article 203 of the Civil Procedures Law stipulates that an arbitral tribunal cannot have the jurisdiction to determine the merits of a dispute unless all parties of the dispute sign a written agreement explicitly specifying that parties of the dispute grant the tribunal, the right to commence an arbitration, even if an arbitral agreement or clause already exists. This article can be used by insolvent parties to an arbitral agreement to prevent the commencement or continuation of the arbitration proceedings.

---

87 Federal Decree-Law Number 9/2016, *UAE Gazette*, Sep. 20, 2016.
88 UAE Commercial Law Number 18/1993, *UAE Gazette*, Sep. 7, 1993.
89 Art. 747, UAE Commercial Law Number 18/1993.
90 Art. 53, the Insolvency Law Number 3/1936.

Arbitration Agreement Validity

The Federal UAE Arbitration Law Number 6/2018 has not stipulated the validity of the Arbitration clauses or agreements neither in cases where it regulates subject matters breaching public policy in the UAE nor in cases where it explicitly regulates insolvency disputes. Alike, the Commercial Code has also failed to provide any regulatory articles for the validity of arbitral agreements and clauses in cases of regulating and framing insolvency disputes. However, under Article 2(3) of the Commercial Law Number 18/1993, all agreements shall be deemed invalid and void in case they violate public policy. The Federal Commercial Code Number 18/1993 of the UAE has no mention of the validity of arbitration agreement regulating insolvencies.

The Federal Civil Code Law Number 5/1985 has stipulated that an arbitration agreement or clause regulating or framing a specific subject matter is valid and binding in principle. However, it is not absolute, for the parties would have to sign a written agreement of their consent to refer their dispute to arbitration. More importantly, Article 203 of the Federal Procedural Law explicitly stipulates that even if an arbitral agreement or clause exists, the arbitrability of the disputed subject matter shall still be considered by judicial authorities. So, in case an arbitral clause or agreement has regulated insolvency as a subject matter, the court or tribunal would possess the discretion and right to assess the satisfaction of insolvency arbitrability requirements stipulated as per Article 747 of the Federal Commercial Law Number 18/1993. Moreover, a written signed agreement for dispute referral shall be needed for the commencement of arbitral procedures. This has further complicated the adjudication procedure of insolvency via arbitral platforms and added further risk factors to the opposing party. This can be manifested in the simple refusal and abstaining of the insolvent to sign the written agreement post his insolvency to avoid arbitration, or the simple prolongation of arbitral procedures, by having to go through formal judicial approvals and hearing by the Bankruptcy judge as per Article 747 of the Commercial Code Number 18/1993.

Effect of Insolvency on Arbitration Procedures

The Federal Arbitration Law Number 6/2018 has not explicitly regulated the validity and implications of adjudicating insolvency on arbitral procedures, however it did regulate the status of arbitral procedures in cases where the contracts and frameworks of arbitral clauses have been deemed invalid or void. Article 6 of the Federal Arbitration Law Number 6/2018 stipulates that in case the contract of the arbitral clause is deemed void or invalid, and arbitral proceedings have already been commenced, the arbitral procedures shall neither be affected nor terminated. Therefore, it is understood that in case of a successful commencement of arbitral procedures regarding an insolvency dispute in the UAE, based on an arbitral clause in which if its contract has been deemed void in later stages, the arbitral procedures shall neither be suspended nor terminated. Moreover, Article 8 explicitly stipulates that in case a challenge regarding the validity and enforceability of the arbitral agreement or clause was filed before a judicial forum, it shall not lead to the suspension or termination of arbitral procedures. This can be applied in cases where the insolvent or a third-party filed a suit before a judicial forum with a request to suspend or terminate the arbitral procedure in regard or due to the validity and status of the arbitral clause or the contractual framework it falls under.

Arbitral procedures are further affected when adjudicating insolvency or bankruptcy disputes in the UAE. This can be shown under Article 747 of the Federal Commercial Code Number 18/1993, where it stipulates that to commence arbitration procedures upon or in relation to an insolvency dispute, several judicial and pre-arbitration procedures shall take place:

(1) in case the sum value of the underlined dispute is less than 10,000 UAE pounds, then the competent authority shall possess the discretion to permit the insolvent's trustee to commence arbitration procedures upon conducting a hearing for the insolvent himself. Thus, it is understood that in this situation arbitration procedures are considered suspended and conditioned upon the conducting of the insolvent's hearing before the competent authority, and the issuance of the insolvency judge decision on the commencement of arbitral procedures; and

(2) in case the value of the dispute merits to more than 10,000 UAE pounds or has an undefined value, then a hearing before the competent authorities is required, in addition to the ratification of the arbitral agreement or clause conditions and scope by the insolvency judge, in order to issue a judicial decision to commence arbitral procedures.

Therefore, arbitral procedures for the adjudication of an insolvency dispute cannot be commenced and shall be deemed suspended until the fulfillment of a judicial hearing, ratification of the arbitral agreement or clause by insolvency judge, and lastly the issuance of a judicial verdict permitting the parties to commence arbitral procedures. This shall in its turn prolong arbitral procedures and cause further complications.

Arbitral procedures of an insolvency dispute in the UAE can be further prolonged with the implementation of Article 203 of the Civil Procedural Law Number 5/1985 as for the established arbitral tribunal to determine its jurisdiction upon any dispute and subject matter including insolvency, it shall be conditioned upon the ratification of a written agreement by both parties where it explicitly indicates parties' consent to arbitrate their dispute. This is severely problematic as it not only affects the binding nature of arbitral agreements and clauses, but also grants the insolvent party who is unwilling to arbitrate a dispute—where an arbitral award is mostly to be enforced upon his assets, to willingly refrain from ratifying and signing the underlined written agreement to avoid arbitration.

Moreover, an insolvent in the UAE is entitled to an insolvent shield or protection under Articles 9 and 10 of the Insolvency Law Number 9/2016. This legal shield led to the protection of the insolvent assets from all legal or de facto actions taken against it, including arbitral procedures. Therefore, if an insolvent had ratified an arbitral agreement or clause, before the occurrence of his or her insolvency, then it shall not be applied in case he or she was granted insolvent protection. Therefore, no arbitral procedures can be commenced.

Moreover, under Article 10(2) of the Insolvency Law Number 9/2016 if an insolvent ratified an arbitral agreement or clause post the granting of the insolvency shield, arbitral procedures may not commence as per the judge discretion, as the insolvent loses his eligibility to enter into any form of agreements, including arbitral agreements.

This in turn leads, and has led, to malicious and bad intent implementation of this right by the insolvent to prevent arbitration procedures upon his assets. To prevent this from happening, the Federal Insolvency Law Number 9/2016 under Article 15(3) has explicitly prohibited the granting of shielding to an insolvent in case he or she intended to prevent arbitral procedures to commence or proceed against him. This leads the bankruptcy judge to apply a higher level of due diligence and investigation before the granting of the underlining shielding to the insolvent. In other words, further complications and prolongation of arbitral procedures.

Effects of an Insolvency on Parties' Capacity to Arbitrate

The occurrence of Insolvency in the jurisdiction of Emirates does indeed affect parties' capacity to opt for arbitration, regardless of the existence of an arbitral agreement or clause. The first legal effect is manifested through the loss of legal entitlement and capacity of the insolvent to enter and ratify any agreements, contracts, or adjudication procedures including arbitration. This legal capacity is transferred to the insolvency trustee. So, the general rule as per Articles 9 and 17 of the Insolvency Law Number 9/2016, after the official declaration of insolvency, the insolvent is not entitled and lacks the capacity to commence or continue arbitral or judicial procedures but may do so only through a trustee. On the other hand, the opposing party, after the declaration of the insolvency, does not lose his right to commence or proceed with judicial or arbitral procedures against the insolvent; however, it shall be directed to the insolvent trustee and not the insolvent himself.

As per Articles 10 and 15 of the Federal Insolvency Decree—Law Number 9/2016 once an insolvent is granted a bankruptcy shield, two imminent legal implications are applied by default: First, the insolvent loses his legal entitlement and capacity neither to initiate or participate in any adjudication procedures, nor ratify or enter into any form of contract or agreement, including arbitral agreements and clauses. Second, the opponent party is suspended from initiating or opting for judicial or arbitral procedures.

In other words, an insolvent upon the granting of bankruptcy shield loses his or her capacity to opt for arbitration, apply or enter into an arbitral agreement, unless the competent authority decides otherwise.[91] However, this general rule has an exception to it, where the judicial competent authority concludes the bad and malicious intent of the insolvent to suspend or terminate judicial or arbitral procedures by seeking insolvency shield, in this situation the competent authority refuses to grant him or her any shielding.

Effects of an Insolvency on the Recognition and Enforcement of Arbitral Awards

The federal Arbitration Law Number 6/2018 does not explicitly regulate the effects of insolvency on the recognition or the enforcement of arbitral awards. However, Article 53(2) (b) has provided a general rule for the annulment of arbitral awards by judicial forums, in case of its violation of public order. Thus, pre the legislation of Article 747 of the Federal Commercial Law Number 18/1993, where insolvency was deemed an integral part of public policy in the UAE, arbitral awards adjudicating insolvency were deemed void and could be annulled before judicial forums on the

91 The Insolvency Law Number 3/1936, Art. 10(2).

basis of its violation of public policy. However, post the legislation of Article 747, in case the parties have fulfilled the stipulated requirements to commence an insolvency arbitral procedure, then the award shall not be deemed void. Thus, Article 53(b)(2) for the annulment of arbitral awards cannot be applied.

The Federal Insolvency Law Number 3/1936 and its amendment Number 9/2016 also do not explicitly mention the effect of insolvency on arbitral award enforcement or recognition. However, upon the issuance of insolvency shield upon the insolvent, judicial procedures including arbitral procedures shall be suspended. Thus, in case the insolvency shield was applied post the issuance of an arbitral award but pre or during the phase of its enforcement, all enforcement procedures shall be suspended. It is notable that Article 10 does not mention the effect of this suspension on the status and validity of the arbitral award explicitly. However, it can be understood from the general customs and practice in the UAE that in case an arbitral award was issued but not enforced prior the issuance of the insolvency shield, it shall remain valid, however non-enforceable until the lifting of the insolvency shielding or seeking an otherwise decision from the court as per the judge discretion in accordance with Article 10(2) of the Insolvency Law Number 9/2016.

Moreover, the Federal Commercial Law Number 8/1993 also does not mention the enforcement or validity of arbitral awards in cases of insolvency. However, it can be understood from Article 747(2), that an arbitral award in which is issued without the fulfillment of the judicial requirements of the underlining article shall be deemed invalid.

Thereof, we should differentiate between arbitral awards issued before and after the declaration of insolvency:

(1) Arbitral awards made prior the deceleration of insolvency are valid and enforceable in general, however in case of issuing an arbitral award without enforcing it before the competent judicial courts in the UAE, and a declaration of insolvency has been made then it shall be deemed valid but non enforceable, until the competent authorities authorize it per Article 10(2) of the Insolvency Law Number 9/2016;

(2) Arbitral Awards made post the declaration of insolvency are deemed valid and enforceable before the judicial forums, conditioned upon the fulfillment of Article 747 of the Commercial Law Number 18 of 1993. Thus, in case an arbitral award was issued without the fulfillment of Article 747 requirements, then an arbitral award shall not be valid or enforceable; and

(3) Arbitral Awards issued post or during the issuance of the insolvency shield. Those awards as a general rule are deemed invalid and non-enforceable as well. Unless the competent court decided otherwise with the representation of the insolvent trustee, per Article 9 and 17 of the Insolvency Law Number 9/2016.

Conclusion

Arbitration and insolvency both occupy special attention in different jurisdictions in terms of dispute resolution where the current pandemic has had a severe effect on businesses, and insolvency has become more prominent on the commercial transactions and landscape.

Through the analysis, the study examined the interplay between insolvency and arbitration in different MENA regions where businesses opt for arbitration as a commercial adjudication mechanism in solving their disputes. It was concluded that businesses in the MENA region have suffered immensely from insolvency disputes accumulation during the COVID-19 recession, and the difficulty of enforcing arbitral awards or the mere commencement of arbitral procedures regarding insolvency disputes.

For instance, businesses suffering from high rates of insolvencies in Palestine as a captive economy seat, have suffered from an accumulation of unadjudicated disputes for several reasons. First, the prolonged state of emergency and lockdowns in Palestine, along with the issuance of presidential decrees which limit the judicial adjudication to an exhaustive list of "essential litigation" where insolvencies disputes do not fall under. Second, the non-arbitrability of insolvency and non-enforcement of insolvency awards in Palestine as stated above.

Moreover, business activities and profits have also dropped sharply in Egypt as a largest FDI recipient in Africa[92] and a Middle-Income MENA region country, leading to high rates of insolvencies, and accumulation of unadjudicated disputes for several reasons. First, the prolonged state of emergency and lockdowns in Egypt, where physical access to arbitral

92 In 2020, due to the COVID-19 induced economic crisis, FDI flows dropped sharply. According to the Central Bank, FDI inflows dropped to USD 3.09 billion in Q4 of 2019/2020, from USD 4.26 billion in Q1. Foreign investment in Egypt - Santandertrade.com. Restricted Access (santandertrade.com).

panels and judicial authorities for the purpose of adjudication was difficult. Second, Egyptian Insolvency Legislations deeming insolvency non-arbitrable conditioned upon the consent of the competent judicial authorities, along with complicated judicial reviews and procedures for the purposes of commencing arbitral procedures and enforcement of arbitral awards.

Lastly, the UAE as an advanced economic MENA region country, with a flourishing international arbitration seat, has also faced insolvencies and fallbacks in its businesses' activities during COVID-19 recession.[93] This has led by default to an accumulation of insolvency disputes. However, the rates of disputes' accumulation have been significantly less than all other MENA region jurisdictions due to its[94] cybernation of both its judicial and arbitral dispute resolution platforms, where all arising disputes were adjudicated with no restriction to a set of "essential litigations."[95] However, businesses in the seat of UAE still have faced unanticipated hurdles when referring their insolvencies disputes to arbitration within the seat of UAE. These hurdles manifested in the mere fact that the federal arbitration laws of UAE and the state arbitration law of UAE, all deems insolvency non-arbitrable, conditioned upon the obtaining of the competent authorities' approval to commence arbitration, adding additional juridical authority and complications to the arbitral procedures of insolvencies.

Thus, it is quite clear that businesses in the MENA region during the novel COVID-19 pandemic have suffered from insolvencies disputes' accumulation, whether businesses operating in MENA advanced economies and flourishing arbitration seats, businesses operating in MENA low-and middle-income seats, or even captive economies' MENA seats.

---

93 Steedman, Wilson P. Thomas. "*COVID-19 Business Issues in the UAE,*" Squire Patton Boggs, April 2020.

94 "The statistical report showed that the ADJD processed 160,482 judicial requests remotely, while 103,899 court hearings were held via videoconferencing technology. The remote court hearings system was fully activated in all Abu Dhabi courts between April 2020 and the end of February 2021, etc." COVID-19: Abu Dhabi Judicial Department remotely completes 160,482 judicial requests | Government – Gulf Newsletter, Abdullah Rasheed, Abu Dhabi Editor, March 6, 2021. COVID-19: Abu Dhabi Judicial Department remotely completes 160,482 judicial requests | Government – Gulf News.

95 "Dubai International Arbitration Centre (DIAC), Abu Dhabi Global Markets Courts (ADGM Courts), Dubai International Financial Centre Courts (DIFC Courts), Dubai—ICC International Centre for ADR (ICC), and all civil and criminal courts of Dubai and Abu Dhabi have worked fully electronically during the Covid-19 recession." Middle East: COVID-19 in the UAE: Courts and Arbitration Centers, Mohamed El-Khatib, Baker McKenzie Dubai, April 2020. https://www.bakermckenzie.com/en/insight/publications/2020/04/covid19-uae-courts-arbitration-centers.

Deriving from our analytical and doctrinal study above, we can refer this issue to several grounds; first, COVID-19 judicial congestion, and second and most importantly, the non-arbitrability of insolvency, and judicial restrictions or limitations upon commencing and opting for arbitration as a dispute resolution mechanism for insolvencies disputes.